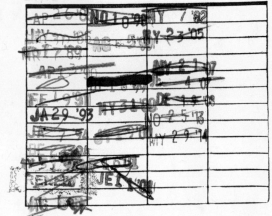

SSSP

Springer Series in Social Psychology

Advisory Editor:
Robert F. Kidd

Springer Series in Social Psychology

Advisory Editor: Robert F. Kidd

Attention and Self-Regulation:
A Control-Theory Approach to Human Behavior
Charles S. Carver/Michael F. Scheier

Gender and Nonverbal Behavior
Clara Mayo/Nancy M. Henley (Editors)

Personality, Roles, and Social Behavior
William Ickes/Eric S. Knowles (Editors)

Toward Transformation in Social Knowledge
Kenneth J. Gergen

The Ethics of Social Research:
Surveys and Experiments
Joan E. Sieber (Editor)

The Ethics of Social Research:
Fieldwork, Regulation, and Publication
Joan E. Sieber (Editor)

Anger and Aggression:
An Essay on Emotion
James R. Averill

The Social Psychology of Creativity
Teresa M. Amabile

Sports Violence
Jeffrey H. Goldstein (Editor)

Nonverbal Behavior: A Functional Perspective
Miles L. Patterson

Basic Group Processes
Paul B. Paulus (Editor)

SSSP

Sports Violence

Edited by
Jeffrey H. Goldstein

Springer-Verlag
New York   Berlin   Heidelberg   Tokyo

U.S.A.

Robert F. Kidd, *Advisory Editor*
Department of Psychology
Boston University
Boston, Massachusetts 02215
U.S.A.

With 6 Figures

Library of Congress Cataloging in Publication Data
Main entry under title:
Sports violence.
  (Springer series in social psychology)
  Bibliography: p.
  Includes indexes
  Contents: Introduction / Jeffrey H. Goldstein—Roman
sports violence / Allen Guttman—Unsporting behavior /
Wray Vamplew—[etc.]
  1. Violence in sports—Addresses, essays, lectures.
2. Aggressiveness (Psychology)—Addresses, essays,
lectures. I. Goldstein, Jeffrey H. II. Series.
GV706.7.S66   1983   796   83-6574

Typeset by Publishers Service, Bozeman, Montana.
Printed and bound by R.R. Donnelley & Sons, Harrisonburg, Virginia.
Printed in the United States of America.
9 8 7 6 5 4 3 2 1

ISBN 0-387-90828-5 Springer-Verlag New York Berlin Heidelberg Tokyo
ISBN 3-540-90828-5 Springer-Verlag Berlin Heidelberg New York Tokyo

Preface

Books about sports, even those written by scholars, are frequently little more than hagiography. They extol the virtue of athletics for participant and spectator alike. Of greater rarity are those that look critically at the political, social, economic, and psychological underpinnings of contemporary sports. Violence in sports is among the relatively neglected issues of serious study. *Sports Violence* is perhaps the first collection of scholarly theory and research to examine in detail aggression within and surrounding sports. As such, it seeks to present the broadest possible range of interpretations and perspectives. The book is, therefore, both interdisciplinary and international in scope.

Two chapters, by Guttmann and Vamplew, are concerned with historical analyses of sports violence. Definitions and perspectives on aggression in general, and sports-related aggression in particular, are the topics of Chapters 4 through 7 by Smith, Bredemeier, Mark, Bryant, and Lehman, and Mummendey and Mummendey. Here, a wide variety of social and psychological theories are brought to bear on the conceptualization of aggression on the playing field and in the stands. Dunning and Lüschen, both sociologists of sport, examine the origins, structure, and functions of violence, of sports, and of their interconnections. Psychological interpretations and research are presented in chapters by Russell and Keefer, Goldstein, and Kasiarz, while Bryant and Zillmann examine the portrayal and effects of aggression in televised sports.

Just as sports violence is not confined to one inevitable perspective, it is not confined to one geographical location. Scholars from Europe, Australia, and North America have contributed to *Sports Violence,* and their discussions are not limited merely to the forms that violence in sports take in contemporary America. Included are accounts of sports aggression in ancient Rome, crowd disorders at British soccer and horse racing, player violence in soccer, and the relationship between Olympics participation and international conflict.

Sports Violence attempts to define, explore, and evaluate what we know about the origins, dynamics, and effects of sports-related aggression. It is intended to serve as a sourcebook for scholars interested in the current state of knowledge about the topic. Throughout the book are summaries and critical evaluations of relevant literature, original research, and suggestions for the direction of future theory and research. The book contains explicit suggestions and many implications for the reduction and control of aggression on and near the playing field. The book will prove useful, as well, to students of aggression and of physical education.

Editing *Sports Violence* has been made all the more enjoyable and easy a task through the support and advice of Bob Kidd and the enthusiastic and professional staff at Springer-Verlag. Mary Hegeler and Bob Keefer ably assisted with the indexing.

J.H.G.
April 1983

Contents

1. **Introduction** **1**
   Jeffrey H. Goldstein

   Definitions 2
   Interpretations 3
   Solutions 4

2. **Roman Sports Violence** **7**
   Allen Guttmann

   Introduction 7
   Sports Violence 9
   Spectator Violence 14
   Conclusion 17

3. **Unsporting Behavior: The Control of Football and Horse-Racing
   Crowds in England, 1875–1914** **21**
   Wray Vamplew

   Types of Crowd Disorder 23
   Crowd-Control Measures 24
   Some Limits of Crowd Control 28

4. **What Is Sports Violence? A Sociolegal Perspective** **33**
   Michael D. Smith

   A Typology of Sports Violence 34
   Conclusion 44

5. **Athletic Aggression: A Moral Concern** 47
Brenda Jo Bredemeier

The Ambiguity of Violence 47
The Valuing of Violence 49
The Psychological Nature of Morality 50
The Psychological Nature of Aggression 55
Athletic Aggression as a Social-Conventional Issue 61
Moral Reasoning and Aggressive Behavior 66
Conclusions 76

6. **Perceived Injustice and Sports Violence** 83
Melvin M. Mark, Fred B. Bryant, and Darrin R. Lehman

Some Examples of Justice-Based Sports Violence 83
Overview 85
Definition of Perceived Injustice 86
Previous Claims About Justice and Sports Violence 87
Other Causes of Sports Violence 89
Perceived Injustices in Sports:
    A Typology and Some Recommendations 90
What Society Can Learn from Sports 100
Are Sports Special? 103
Conclusion 105

7. **Aggressive Behavior of Soccer Players as Social Interaction** .. 111
Amélie Mummendey and Hans Dieter Mummendey

Soccer as a Field for Studying Aggressive Interaction 111
Aggressive Behavior as Social Interaction 113
Aggressive Interaction and Its Evaluation in
    Professional Soccer: Two Case Studies 119
The Referee's Power of Interpretation 123
Conclusions 124

8. **Social Bonding and Violence in Sport:**
A Theoretical-Empirical Analysis 129
Eric Dunning

Introduction 129
Towards a Typology of Human Violence 130
Sports and Violence in Developmental Perspective 131
Violence and the Transformation of Social Bonds 135
Segmental Bonding and the Sociogenesis of
    Affective Violence 138

9. **Sports, Conflict, and Conflict Resolution:**
   Problems of Substance and Methodology **147**
   Günther Lüschen

   Introduction   147
   Factual Accounts and Theoretical Explanations—
       A Short Review   148
   A Structural Interpretation of the Sports Contest   150
   Some Methodological Observations and
       Structural Theory   151
   Conclusion: Instead of a Comprehensive Theory
       Some Praxeological Advances for Sports Policy   152
   Summary   154

10. **Psychological Issues in Sports Aggression** **157**
    Gordon W. Russell

    Introduction   157
    Valves, Vents, and Drains: The Catharsis Hypothesis   159
    Outcome   171
    Conclusions   176

11. **Olympic Games Participation and Warfare** **183**
    Robert Keefer, Jeffrey H. Goldstein, and David Kasiarz

    Introduction   183
    A Test of the Hypotheses   186
    Conclusions   191

12. **Sports Violence and the Media** **195**
    Jennings Bryant and Dolf Zillmann

    The Presence and Nature of Sports Violence   195
    Does Aggression Increase Spectators'
        Enjoyment of Sports?   197
    Media Exploitation of Sports Violence   204
    Where Will It All End?   208

Author Index **213**

Subject Index **221**

Contributors

Brenda Jo Bredemeier, Department of Physical Education, Hearst Gymnasium, University of California, Berkeley, California 94720, U.S.A.

Fred B. Bryant, Department of Psychology, Loyola University, Chicago, Illinois 60611, U.S.A.

Jennings Bryant, Department of Communication, University of Evansville, Evansville, Indiana 47702, U.S.A.

Eric Dunning, Department of Sociology, University of Leicester, Leicester LE1 7RH, England.

Jeffrey H. Goldstein, Department of Psychology, Temple University, Philadelphia, Pennsylvania 19122, U.S.A.

Allen Guttmann, Department of American Studies, Amherst College, Amherst, Massachusetts 01002, U.S.A.

David Kasiarz, Evaluation Research Program, Hahnemann Medical College, Philadelphia, Pennsylvania 19102, U.S.A.

Robert Keefer, Department of Psychology, Temple University, Philadelphia, Pennsylvania 19122, U.S.A.

Darrin R. Lehman, Institute for Social Research, University of Michigan, Ann Arbor, Michigan 48109, U.S.A.

Günther Lüschen, Department of Sociology, University of Illinois, Urbana, Illinois 61801, U.S.A., and Institut Sportwissenschaft, Technische Hochschule, 51 Aachen, Federal Republic of Germany.

Melvin M. Mark, Department of Psychology, Pennsylvania State University, University Park, Pennsylvania 16802, U.S.A.

Amélie Mummendey, Psychologisches Institut der Westfälische Wilhelms-Universität, Schlaunstrasse 2, D-4400 Münster, Federal Republic of Germany.

Hans Dieter Mummendey, Fakultät für Soziologie, Universität Bielefeld, Postfach 8640, 4800 Bielefeld 1, Federal Republic of Germany.

Gordon W. Russell, Department of Psychology, University of Lethbridge, Lethbridge, Alberta T1K 3M4, Canada.

Michael D. Smith, Department of Sociology and Department of Physical Education, York University, Downsview, Ontario M3J 1P3, Canada.

Wray Vamplew, Department of Economic History, Flinders University of South Australia, Bedford Park, South Australia 5042, Australia.

Dolf Zillmann, Institute for Communication Research, Indiana University, Bloomington, Indiana 47405, U.S.A.

Chapter 1

Introduction

Jeffrey H. Goldstein

In recent years sports violence has come to be perceived as a social problem. Commissions have been appointed in Canada and England to investigate violence among hockey players and soccer fans. In the United States, Canada, and West Germany, court cases have been heard concerning the victims or perpetrators of violence in professional sports. Newspapers, magazines, and television programs portray bloodied athletes and riotous fans at hockey, boxing, football, soccer, baseball, and basketball games with what appears to be increasing regularity. But is sports violence actually on the increase? Chapters by Guttmann, Vamplew, and Dunning review instances of violence among athletes and spectators from antiquity to the early 20th century. What they report rivals in magnitude any sports-related violence one might encounter today. Changes in sports rules, developments in the design of equipment, and even the physical characteristics of modern sports arenas evolved in an effort to reduce violence or the consequences of violence. Even though there is greater focus on sports violence in the mass media (see Chapter 12), this attention does not necessarily reflect an increase in the incidence of actual violence. It is possible, and I think reasonable, to assume that the heightened public attention and media focus on sports violence reflect not an increase in the incidence or severity of aggression, but greater public concern with the issue. Contrary to popular belief, there appears to be growing dissatisfaction with sports violence. Some athletes have refused to participate in brawls, management has grown less tolerant of violence because increasingly great sums of money stand to be lost if key players are injured, and there are now fan organizations, such as FANS, that have openly opposed sports violence. Furthermore, following the death of boxer Duk Koo Kim in November, 1982, sports journalists, such as Howard Cosell, have begun to call for stricter controls over violence, and the American Medical Association has urged a ban on boxing.

Among management, athletes, and fans there is an ambivalent attitude toward sports violence. The ambivalence takes the form of justifying the existence of violence in sports, but not taking personal responsibility for it. Coaches and managers tend to blame fans, saying that it is violence that attracts them to the game in the first place. Athletes frequently say that they are opposed to violence, but that it is expected of them by coaches. Fans justify it by attributing aggressiveness to athletes and to situational aspects of the game—you cannot play hockey or football, they say, without violence. The violence is explained away as an inherent part of the game.

In the not too distant past, brutality in sports was merely accepted without comment. Today it is apt to lead to litigation. What once was seen as solely part of a sport is now viewed as behavior that occurs within a larger social framework. When sports were seen as local affairs, before the advent of widespread television broadcasting of sports, violent behavior was likely to be thought of as internal to the game. Once teams lost their local quality, they came to be seen as business franchises, and thus the social norms and regulations that govern business and other forms of social intercourse increasingly came to be applied to behavior in sports.

The fact is that we do not know whether the incidence, prevalence, or severity of sports violence is increasing, decreasing, or remaining constant. In a domain where statistics of every imaginable sort are kept with fervor, no record of violence in sports is maintained. It would certainly be a simple matter for a team or league statistician to note violent incidents, their severity, the individuals involved, when in the course of the game they occur, and so on. Such records would allow us not only to chart the course of sports violence, but to begin to understand it sufficiently to control or prevent it.

Definitions

Any complex act can be imbued with myriad images, interpretations, and meanings. Sports and games, perhaps more than all other areas of social life, are self-contained. Yet behavior within a sport may violate social norms or laws and thus intrude upon the larger society. Hence, sports violence is increasingly a matter of legal or moral concern (see Chapters 4 and 5). Of course, it can also be viewed in terms of general principles of social behavior and integrated into the broader social context (Chapters 6 and 7). Different perspectives on violence may be useful for different purposes, therefore legal, ethical, conflict, equity, and other perspectives may coexist without necessary contradiction. Because these and other viewpoints may be brought to bear on the interpretation of aggression in sports, no single definition of sports violence is either possible or desirable.

Violence among athletes and fans has often been viewed as symbolic of other behaviors. Marsh, Rosser, and Harré (1978) have interpreted "soccer hooliganism" as a ritual display serving purposes of self-presentation and status enhancement. In tracing the origins and nature of violence in sports, Eric Dunning (Chapter 8) argues that as the nature of social bonds has changed in industrial societies, so has the nature of violence in sports changed. Violence in sports has been viewed as a microcosm of the larger society, a social Darwinian position, as symbolic combat, or as a training ground for masculine role behavior (Goldstein, in press). Jennings Bryant and Dolf Zillmann (Chapter 12) note that fans may be attracted to violence in sports because it is a more or less objective indication of the level of motivation and competition of the athletes. This means further that sports violence has value as entertainment.

In short, sports violence may be seen as either reflecting or shaping social norms and values, as either legally punishable "real" violence or as ritual, symbolic play. In any sport where physical contact between players is inevitable or necessary, the line between fair play and unnecessary violence is sure to be equivocal. Is it excessively violent to "rough the kicker" in football? After all, such behavior is frequent enough to be predictable and thus embodied by the rules. These and related issues are discussed in Chapters 4, 5, 6, and 7.

Interpretations

Theoretical analyses of athlete and fan violence focus on three issues: (1) the socio-historical origins of violence, (2) the social and psychological nature of sports violence, and (3) the consequences of sports violence on the subsequent behavior of athletes, fans, and the larger society.

The evolution of modern forms of sport, and of violence within and surrounding sports, are discussed by Guttmann (Chapter 2), Vamplew (Chapter 3), and Dunning (Chapter 8). The nature, if not frequency of sports violence has changed as the social system has changed.

The social meaning of violence within sports is discussed in chapters by Smith (Chapter 4); Bredemeier (Chapter 5); Mark, Bryant, and Lehman (Chapter 6); Mummendey and Mummendey (Chapter 7); Dunning (Chapter 8); and Lüschen (Chapter 9). Here the important theoretical issues include defining excessive violence, the normative and stereotypic nature of much sports violence, and the immediate and long-term social consequences of violence. Rather than viewing violence in sports as an isolated phenomenon requiring its own idiosyncratic explanation, concerted efforts are made in this book to integrate it into the larger social context. Attribution theory, moral development, social learning theory, equity theory, and conflict theory are all brought to bear on the interpretation of sports violence.

Psychological interest in sports violence has focused primarily on the effects of athlete aggression on the aggressiveness of spectators. The issue is the familiar one of vicarious catharsis versus a social learning-stimulation position. This controversy is discussed in chapters by Lüschen (Chapter 9); Russell (Chapter 10); Keefer, Goldstein, and Kasiarz (Chapter 11); and Bryant and Zillmann (Chapter 12). As with psychological research on media violence, empirical evidence in support of a cathartic function of sports violence is lacking. However, the research on this issue is severely restricted with respect to time and place, nearly all of it conducted within the last decade in North America or Western Europe. So the possibility remains that under different as yet unspecifiable conditions, cathartic effects do occur among some fans or athletes. Russell discusses the effects of one such condition, outcome, on spectator aggression. Elsewhere, I have discussed ways in which participation in sports may serve a cartharsis-like function (Goldstein, 1982). Briefly, the process involves both the expenditure of energy and distraction from the cognitive task of "rewriting history" in order to prevent an increase in anger, frustration, or hostility.

Solutions

While the intention of this book is largely to explore the nature of violence in sports, it is inevitable that the empirical and theoretical analyses presented will have implications for the reduction and control of sports-related aggression. No separate chapter on solutions is included here; it would be premature to do so. But in several chapters (Chapters 3, 6, 9, & 11), explicit suggestions are offered for reducing the magnitude of sports violence, and in the remaining chapters, implications for its control are present. As Lüschen notes, one need not know everything about a problem to solve it, and he offers suggestions for the management of sport conflict. Techniques of crowd control, altered perceptions or attitudes that would minimize conflict, and external sanctions that might inhibit fan violence are noted.

Generally, the suggestions for reducing sports violence fall into two categories: external constraints and internal restraints. *External constraints* include changes in the rules or stricter enforcement of the rules concerning violence among athletes and fans; changing the temporal aspects of sporting events such as postgame concerts or several games played in succession; so that the spectators do not all leave at once; changes in equipment to protect athletes better; changes in the design of playing fields, such as the pitch at European soccer fields to minimize fan-player contact and to minimize riots among spectators; increased show of force by police; reduced focus on violence by sports journalists and broadcasters (see Yeager, 1979). *Internal restraints* that would reduce violence consist of changes in the attitudes, values, and perceptions of athletes, management, and fans. Internal restraints are self-imposed inhibitions on aggression and a lowered tolerance for the aggressive behavior of others. Such long-term changes can come about only by emphasizing the nonviolent aspects of body-contact sports, the role of cooperation, aesthetics, and prosocial aspects of competitive athletics.

The chapters in this book have at least one feature in common. They all see violence in and surrounding sports as not unrelated to the historical, social, and psychological context of which sports are a part. While it is possible to take exception to the popular view that sports are a microcosm of society (Goldstein, 1982; in press), nonetheless it is easy to agree with Eitzen (1982, p. 412) that sport "has within it the same maladies as the society in which it resides. If the society is beset with problems of poverty, racism, and other cleavages, then sports contests will not be just a means of escape but also an occasional battleground." If what occurs within a society also occurs within its sports, we should also allow that what occurs within sports will affect what takes place in society (see Chapters 9, 10, 11, & 12).

References

Eitzen, D. S. Sport and deviance. In G. Lüschen & G. H. Sage (Eds.), *Handbook of social science of sport*. Champaign, Ill.: Stipes, 1982.

Goldstein, J. H. Sports violence. *National Forum*, 1982, *62*, 9-11.

Goldstein, J. H. Athletic performance and spectator behavior. In W. L. Umphlett (Ed.), *American sport culture: The humanistic dimensions*. Lewisburg, Pa.: Bucknell University Press, in press.

Marsh, P., Rosser, E., & Harré, R. *The rules of disorder*. London: Routledge & Kegan Paul, 1978.

Yeager, R. C. *Seasons of shame: The new violence in sports*. New York: McGraw-Hill, 1979.

Chapter 2
Roman Sports Violence

Allen Guttmann

Introduction

The idealists of modern sports—Pierre de Coubertin, for instance, or Avery Brundage —have often made conscious use of verbal and nonverbal symbolism derived from the athletic rituals of ancient Greece. The revival of the discus throw and the creation of the marathon are two examples of idealistic historicism; the torch ignited by the sun at the altar of Zeus in Olympia and carried by relay runners to the site of the modern games is another. Coubertin (1894/1966) himself contrasted *"l'athlète d'Olympie"* with his ignoble counterpart, the *"gladiateur de cirque."* Other commentators, disillusioned with the nationalism, commercialism, political instrumentalization, and sheer violence of 20th-century sports, have consistently drawn their analogies not from Delphi and Olympia but rather from Rome and Constantinople. Football players are routinely likened to gladiators and the crowds enthralled by the Indianapolis races or by the Tour de France are said to lust for *panem et circenses.* Critics of modern violence have referred to ancient gore and have concluded in dismay that we too are in a phase of decadent decline or, worse yet, that humankind is biologically programmed to commit mayhem upon itself.

Since most of the references to Roman sports violence are simply references, they are likely to evoke nothing more substantial than a scene from the filmed versions of *Quo Vadis* or *Ben Hur.* It is essential, if one is truly interested in the comparison of Roman with modern American and European sports, to advance somewhat beyond the Hollywood view of the gladiatorial combats and the chariot races of the Roman republic and empire. Before one concludes that modern violence equals or exceeds ancient blood lust, one needs to have a clearer knowledge of what went on in the arena and in the Roman circus. I shall attempt to answer two questions: Just how violent was Roman sports violence? What was the relationship between the intrinsic or internal structure of sports and the level of spectator violence which accompanied them? Ancient evidence suggests that some modern assumptions need revision.

As a preliminary but essential step, the analyst of sports violence, past or present, must define the central concepts. Since others in the present volume will concentrate on the problem of definition, I shall limit myself to the minimum and eschew the scholarly references. Following ordinary linguistic usage, which is imprecise but nonetheless a first approximation, we can say that violence is physical damage done to persons or property. In this sense we can speak of a violent storm or of the violent collision of two football players but not of violent words, which are violent only in a metaphorical sense (just as "sweet talk" is poetically and not physiologically sweet). Within the world of sports, it is arbitrary but convenient to restrict the definition to physical damage done to one's opponent. The injuries that one brings upon oneself, ranging from the tennis player's blistered thumb to the automobile racer's explosive immolation, can be excluded along with worn-out golf balls and tattered archery targets, but the battering inflicted by a boxer and a baseball player's spiking of the second baseman trying to tag him out are both examples of sports violence. (If we insist that damage done to oneself is also sports violence, we must conclude, for instance, that the marathon is a violent sport.) It is immediately obvious that the boxer's punches are an example of legitimate violence while the base-runner's spiking is not. The boxer's punches are legitimate because they are morally separable from those of a street-corner thug; they are within the rules of the game. The base-runner's spikes, however, are not supposed to be used to wound his opponent; such use is foul play and ludically illegitimate. That the players and fans sometimes find spiking acceptable indicates that the official rules are not infallible guides to the actual moral consensus. Despite the difficulty in knowing exactly what is legitimate violence and what is not, it is important that the theoretical differences remain clear. One may deplore the violence of a game of rugby, but it is morally distinguishable from the violence of the runner in a 1500-meter race who jabs his rival in the ribs. The former is a case of legitimate ludic license and the latter of illegitimate excess. In discussing sports violence, it is always necessary to be clear about the nature as well as the degree of the damage done. Within the context of Roman sports, we have the somewhat paradoxical situation whereby a gladiator's lethal sword thrust was legitimate violence while the charioteer who used his whip against an opponent violated the rules of the game and acted illegitimately even if the opponent was only slightly injured. These examples are, of course, from a Roman perspective. Few modern sports fans have argued for the reintroduction of gladiatorial games as legitimate violence.

In differentiating sports violence into its legitimate and illegitimate forms, I have thus far omitted mention of the violence committed by the spectators. Clearly, the "soccer hooliganism" and *Randalieren* of British and German soccer fans are sports-related behavior, but knifing fans of rival teams and throwing beer cans at the umpire are not, strictly speaking, examples of sports violence. We must then distinguish between sports-related violence and sports violence. Since spectator riots and similar phenomena are not *sports* violence, we need not restrict the concept of *sports-related* violence to damage done to an opponent whom one meets within the rules of the game, that is, damage done to property and injuries inflicted upon bystanders are an important part of spectator violence. One of the most difficult questions faced by scholars is the degree to which such sports-related spectator violence has anything at all to do with the sports events that occasion it.

My discussion will concentrate on the legitimate (to the Romans) sports violence of the gladiatorial games and on the illegitimate (from an official point of view) sports-related violence of the gladiatorial and circus spectators. My concentration on Rome's two most popular spectator sports seems justified because Greek athletic contests—running, jumping, throwing, and so forth—had only a limited interest for the Romans, either as participants or as spectators, while popular ball games like *harpastum* seem to have been either noncompetitive pastimes or else contests which attracted few, if any, spectators. The historical sources, at any rate, have far more to say about gladiators and charioteers than about runners, wrestlers, and *harpastum* players.

Since I have, on more than one occasion, argued that sports are, by definition, nonutilitarian physical contests carried out for their own sake, I must concede that the gladiatorial games were true sports in the strictest sense only for those, probably a minority, who volunteered, who were attracted by the risk involved, by the sheer love of mortal combat (Guttmann, 1978). The others, the majority, fought not "playfully" but in earnest, not of their own free will but under coercion. It is also possible that a prisoner of war sent into the arena as part of the gladiatorial games might have welcomed the opportunity to pit himself against a Roman volunteer or even against a fellow prisoner. This possibility seems quite plausible when one considers that the epitaphs of fallen gladiators speak not of injustice or coercion but of the acceptance of one's fate, of prowess, even of glory (Robert, 1971). The problem of motivation is difficult to decide in practice; it is the same problem one encounters today in the form of paid professionalism. Do Jimmy Connors and Martina Navratilova still play for the love of the game? It is likely that motives are and were mixed. Since there is no way empirically to establish the degree to which gladiatorial combats (or modern tennis matches) are autotelic, that is, activities conducted for their own sake, it seems reasonable to admit that theory is clearer than practice and to accept the convention which classifies them as sports.

Sports Violence

Like the ball games of the Mayans and Aztecs, which ended in ritual sacrifice, gladiatorial combats originated as an aspect of Roman religion (and thus, in this respect as well, were not true sports in the strictest sense because they were not, at least in their origins, autotelic). The Greeks of Homer's *Iliad* were content that the funeral games in honor of the fallen Patroklos terminated not in literal but merely in symbolic death, that is, in athletic defeat, but the Romans, who may have adopted this particular custom from the Etruscans, celebrated funeral games in which the dead were honored by additional deaths (Balsdon, 1969; Grant, 1967). The first games, held by Marcus and Decius Brutus in honor of the father in 246 B.C., consisted of three duels (six gladiators) and were held in the cattle market (Friedländer, 1908-1913). One can assume that the number of spectators was fairly small. In the centuries that followed, Livy, Polybius, Suetonius, Tacitus, and other Roman historians recorded an apparently irreversible tendency towards the spectacular in that the number of gladiators continually increased and the facilities available to the spectators grew ever grander. By 183 B.C., there were 60 duels; in 65 B.C., Julius Caesar celebrated his election to the aedileship with combats among 320 pairs, staged in a wooden amphitheater constructed especially for the event. By this time, gladiatorial games functioned as much more than funeral observances and had become a complex fusion of religious, political, and—presumably—ludic elements.

The Senate, worried about the manipulation of the populace by means of these magnificent spectacles, attempted to limit the number of gladiators at any single set of *ludi* to 60 pairs, but the effort was futile and, in imperial times, emperors (except for the stingy Tiberius) seem to have competed among themselves to see who could stage the most grandiose show. Throughout the empire, temporary stadia of wood gave way to monumental stone structures the most famous of which is the "Colosseum" erected by the Flavians (Vespasian and his son Titus) and more accurately called the Flavian amphitheater. This gigantic structure, finished in 80 A.D., seated 50,000. It was dedicated with a festival lasting 100 days (Balsdon, 1969). The emperor Trajan is said to have celebrated his victory over the Dacians with combats among 10,000 gladiators, a spectacle which failed numerically to equal the naval battle staged by Claudius in 52 A.D. with 19,000 combatants.

How many of the gladiators actually died to please the gods and to placate the mob? We have no statistical evidence, but we do know that the lives of the defeated were often spared by the *munerarius* (the private citizen who gave the games), by the emperor, or by imperial officials. The crowd was not always in a "thumbs-down" mood. Evidence for a lower mortality rate than one might think comes from Roman law. When gladiators rented to private persons were killed, the law provided for generous reimbursement of the entrepreneur (*lanista*) who owned the gladiators. In such a case, the *munerarius* was required to pay the *lanista* 50 times the rental cost (Wacke, 1977). Death was probably not the usual outcome when two professionals, slave or volunteer, met in the arena.

That many gladiators were professionals is a certainty. Although their status was officially very low, they unquestionably enjoyed popularity enough for a number of free citizens to volunteer for the *munera* (gladiatorial games). Exactly how many of the gladiators were free men is and will remain uncertain, but an Italian scholar who has studied 82 Latin documents concerned with the gladiators at Pompeii has concluded that many were citizens and some were "*equestre o senatoria*" (Tumolesi, 1980). That the spectators preferred free men to slaves or criminals is suggested by the character Echion in *The Satyricon* of Petronius, who speaks excitedly of an imminent show with new fights "and . . . not a slave in the batch" (1959, p. 42). Michael Grant's (1967) explanation for this preference is simple but convincing: "Free fighters were more sought after than slaves, presumably because they showed greater enthusiasm" (p. 31).

The historian Suetonius (1957) tells us that Augustus "sought to enhance *virtus* and *pietas* by preserving the dignity of senators and knights, whose participation he forbad" (pp. 220-222), but unscrupulous emperors like Caligula and Nero actually ordered senators and knights to take up the sword and risk their lives before the multitude. Quite apart from such despotic compulsion, there seems always to have been a number of aristocrats and plebians too who were ready and eager to risk their lives in combat. The emperor Commodus adored the bellicose sport and scandalized Roman moralists with his boasts of having fought 1,000 gladiatorial duels. There were rumors that his mother, Faustina, had slept not with his putative father, Marcus Aurelius, but rather with the renowned gladiator Martianus. The rumor epitomizes the ambivalence of the Romans in regard to this most violent of sports; the story denigrates Commodus and simultaneously indicates that his royal mother found the gladiator more seductive than her husband, the philosopher-emperor. The poet Juvenal (1958) agrees that athletes—then as now—were idolized by female spectators; Eppia, the senator's wife, is said to have thought gladiators

> look better than any Adonis:
> This is what she preferred to children, country, and sister,
> This to her husband. (p. 67)

And an inscription on a wall in Pompeii says that Celadus the Thracian (i.e., a gladiator who fought as a Thracian) was *"suspirum et decus puellarum,"* which one might freely translate as "the heartthrob of all the girls" (Grant, 1967, p. 96). In the *Palaestra* where Celadus and his fellows lived, the excavators of Pompeii found the bejeweled skeleton of a woman whose weakness for martial virility seems to have led her foolishly to brave the dangers of erupting Vesuvias (Hoenle & Henze, 1981, pp. 17-18).

Commodus and his fellow volunteers were almost certainly a minority, perhaps a small one. Most of their "colleagues" were condemned criminals, prisoners of war, or slaves purchased by the *lanista* from owners eager to profit from a marketable skill or simply anxious to rid themselves of a particularly unruly piece of property. The poet Horace (1959) refers in his *Epistles* to those who get themselves hopelessly in debt

> and so
> End up in the driver's seat of some vegetable cart
> Or in a gladiatorial show. (p. 216)

There was, for persons of this sort, a special technical term. They were the *auctorati*, those who sold themselves; they were legally derogated as *infamus* but were not deprived of citizenship. In respect to motivation, they occupy a middle position between the volunteers and the coerced. Criminals condemned to death (the *damnati ad mortem*) were sent weaponless into the arena, but others guilty of noncapital crimes were trained in private or, later, in the imperial gladiatorial schools and were usually granted their freedom if they survived 3-5 years of combat (which most did not). Prisoners were allowed to fight with the weapons and armor they were accustomed to, which gave rise to the Thracian, Gallic, Samnite, and other ethnic styles among the gladiators (Backhaus, 1972). One result of this stylization was that an Italian volunteer might have fought in the armor and with the weapons traditional among the Gauls and Spaniards.

My concern to identify an element of free will within the violent world of gladiatorial combat and my suggestion that death may have been less frequent than critics sometimes assume are not meant as an apology for what was undeniably a sadistic spectacle. Noting the tendency of the *munera* and the *venationes* (combats among animals or between men and animals) to become not only brutal but also sensationalistic and perverse, the historian Ludwig Friedländer (1908) commented:

> soon bloodthirsty combats and magnificent scenery failed to excite the dulled nerves of the mob, aristocratic or vulgar; only things absolutely exotic, unnatural, nonsensical, tickled their jaded senses. (Vol. 2, p. 43)

The truth of Friedländer's observation can be seen when we consider that modern boxers and wrestlers are divided into weight categories in order to establish roughly equal conditions for the match. The gladiatorial games dispensed with such scruples. As the quotation from Friedländer suggests, lack of concern for equality gave free rein to the sadistic imagination. It was clearly not enough that gladiators fought in different styles and with different equipment, so that a *retiarius* armed with a net and trident fought a *myrmillo* whose sword, shield, and helmet marked him stylistically if not ethnically as a Gaul. In the *Satyricon*, Echion looks forward excitedly to a "girl who fights from a chariot" and the emperor Domitian tickled the senses of the masses when he pitted women against dwarves (Dio Cassius, 1914-1927, Vol. 8, p. 335). It was, wrote Juvenal (1958), difficult *not* to write satire:

> When a limp eunuch gets wives, and women, breasts Amazon-naked,
> Face wild boars at the games . . . . (Vol. 1, p. 18)

And Christians were, as popular mythology still remembers, condemned to fight, either armed or weaponless, against gladiators or against wild animals. When they went to their deaths, the statues of the pagan gods were veiled—as they were when ordinary criminals were torn to bits (Auguet, 1972).

Needless to say, the Christians were the most vocal and finally, the most effective foes of the gladiatorial games (Weismann, 1972). The poet Juvenal wrote satirically about the mob and its need for bread and circuses, but he and most other educated Romans seemed to have taken sports violence for granted. The historian Suetonius was indignant when Caligula, jealous of a handsome spectator, ordered the youth dragged from his seat and matched him against the professional gladiators, but the historian's indignation was not aroused by the atrocity of the games per se, only by Caligula's bit of illegitimate sports-related violence. The philosopher-statesman Cicero praised the *munera* because they allegedly strengthened the spectators' fortitude. The poet Ovid (1957) urges women to "go and look at the games, where the sands are sprinkled with crimson" (pp. 164-165). The motive here is not increased fortitude but rather a chance to display one's physical charm, but the poet assumes that the bloodshed in the arena is no obstacle to amorousness in the stands. The philosopher-dramatist Seneca was among the handful of pagan moralists who expressed the kind of horror which many 20th-century critics feel at sports violence far less bloody than the *munera*. For Seneca (1917), the gladiatorial combats were "*crudelior et inhumanior*" (Vol. 1, pp. 30-31). His comment on the spectators was certainly not the last word on the subject, but it is difficult to imagine a more succinct verdict: "*Mane leonibus et ursis homines, meridie spectatoribus suis obiciuntur*" ("In the morning they throw men to the lions and the bears; at noon, they throw them to the spectators").

Among the Christian moralists, Tertullian (1931) was the most influential. His tract, *De Spectaculis*, set the pattern for patristic invective and protest. His objections were partly to the violence in the amphitheater, but he was also appalled by the frenzy of the spectators:

> Look at the populace coming to the show—mad already! disorderly, blind, excited already about its bets! The praetor is too slow for them; all the time their eyes are on his urn, in it, as if rolling with the lots he shakes up in it. The signal is to be given. They are all in suspense, anxious suspense. One frenzy, one voice. (pp. 271-273)

Salvian (1930), the 5th-century bishop, showed the same outrage:

> there is almost no crime or vice that does not accompany the games. In these the greatest pleasure is to have men die, or, what is worse and more cruel than death, to have them torn to pieces, to have the bellies of wild beasts gorged with human flesh! to have men eaten, to the great joy of the bystanders and the delight of onlookers, so that the victims seem devoured almost as much by the eyes of the audience as by the teeth of beasts. (p. 160)

It was not only the violence and sadism that horrified Christian moralists; they were also shocked by the idolatry of the games. A modern historian (Ville, 1960) has asserted that the games held under Constantine and the other Christian emperors were, despite the presence of pagan priests and images, "unrelated to the cult of the gods or the cult of the dead" (p. 289), but this reluctance to take pagan ritual seriously may be the bias of modern secularism. It is certain that Tertullian and probable that the post-Constantine church fathers were scandalized by the procession of priests carrying images of the Roman gods. Following Tertullian closely, Novatian (1931) expressed Christian horror when he cried out, "*Idolatria . . . ludorum omnium mater est*" ("Idolatry is the mother of all these games"). It was largely the result of Christian opposition that the emperor Honorius finally closed the gladiatorial schools in 399 A.D. In the following century, the combats—which had become popular in the Greek as well as in the Latin half of the late Roman empire—gradually died out. The *Venationes* lasted longer than the combats of men against men, but they assumed a milder, less violent form: "Gone were the heavy armour and shields of the . . . *Venator*, to be replaced by a variety of devices designed to protect the combatants, both human and animal . . . These scenes carved on consular diptyches suggest the tricks and turns of a modern circus act rather than the deadly combat of the Colosseum" (Schrodt, 1981, 51).

In the tracts by Tertullian, Novatian, and other church fathers, protests against violence are mixed together with horror at idolatry because, as indicated earlier, gladiatorial violence was, in Roman eyes, not only legitimate but also sacred. After a slave dressed as the god Mercury jabbed a fallen gladiator with hot irons to make certain that death was not feigned, another slave in the garb of Dis Pater dragged the corpse away, after which the dead man's blood was offered to Jupiter Latiaris by the priest who served him. That the gladiators entering the arena saluted the emperor and declared themselves ready to die was but another indication that the games continued to benefit from a religious legitimation; after all, the emperor was an officially recognized divinity. From a Christian perspective, the assertion that the emperor was divine was, of course, the ultimate blasphemy and the worst of idolatries, but Tertullian's rage did not lessen the fact that the Romans certainly felt no conflict between piety and bloodshed. Twentieth-century platitudes about the unity of all religions are based upon well-meant ignorance. Roman assumptions about the ludic *and* religious legitimacy of the gladiatorial violence may make it easier for us to understand contemporary American and European authors for whom sports have become a secular religion.

Spectator Violence

Turning from sports violence to sports-related spectator violence, we discover that the fans of the circus were much more violence-prone than those of the arena. The gladiatorial spectators did occasionally riot. The historian Tacitus (1959) reports that tumults broke out in Pompeii during the *munera* and the city was for a decade deprived of the right to stage the games. In comparison to later outbursts of spectator violence among the enthusiasts for chariot racing, however, the disturbances at Pompeii were minor. One reason may be that the chariot races were even more popular than the *munera*, a fact indicated architecturally by the size of the *circus maximus* in Rome, which is said to have held a quarter of a million spectators, five times as many as the Flavian amphitheater (Kindermann, 1979; Verspohl, 1976). We have additional quantified evidence on relative popularity in the form of the religious calendar. In the middle of the 4th century, the 175 days of *ludi* were divided into 10 days of gladiatorial games, 64 days of chariot races, and 101 days of theater. One must remember, however, that an economic factor probably played an important role in this breakdown; mime, pantomime, and other forms of drama forming the *ludi scaenici* were less expensive to stage than the *munera* and the *ludi circenses*. Commenting on the relative rarity of gladiatorial games in Greece itself (during Roman rule), a French historian concludes sadly that the economic factor was more important than moral considerations (Robert, 1971).

Since my present focus is not on Roman sports per se but rather on sports violence and sports-related violence, the chariot-race spectators concern us more than the races themselves. (For details on the chariot races, see Harris, 1972, chapters 10-14.) Nonetheless, it is helpful to remember that the races, like the gladiatorial games, probably had their origins in Roman cult and never completely lost their religious associations. They were contested by charioteers divided into four teams invariably referred to by their colors: the Reds, Whites, Blues, and Greens. The first two teams were eventually absorbed by the second two so that historians commonly speak simply of the Blues and the Greens. Since the chariots were usually *quadrigae*, that is, drawn by four horses, turns about the *spina* ("thorn") which ran down the middle of the course required considerable equestrian skill. Of the charioteers, many were slaves who purchased their freedom with their prize money. Those who were free men were officially of low status, like the gladiators, but were actually lionized by the sports-mad public. Porphyrius, who flourished early in the 6th century, was commemorated by monuments in Constantinople's hippodrome and by at least 32 epigrams in the *Greek Anthology* (Cameron, 1973). That ancient partisanship was at least as emotional as modern is shown by the example of a certain Felix Rufus, who committed suicide on the funeral pyre of his favorite charioteer (Balsdon, 1969).

It is perhaps noteworthy that some of the best studies of Roman sports, which have in general received far less scholarly attention than Greek athletics, have been devoted not to the active but to the passive participants, that is, to the spectators. One reason for this unusual focus is that the passive participants were, judged by modern standards, unusually active, not in sports but in politics. That the average Roman spectator was neither a gladiator nor a charioteer is clear (and in this respect the Romans probably differed from the ancient Greeks and certainly differed from the modern Europeans and Americans who, contrary to popular opinion, are very likely to be active athletic participants in their favorite spectator sports).

The athletically inactive Roman citizen was politically involved but scarcely in the forms presently institutionalized within modern political democracies. Neither Rome nor Constantinople, nor any other city of the Roman Empire, had political parties of the sort familiar to modern Europeans and Americans. In the absence of such parties, Roman sports became a mechanism for the expression and also for the manipulation of popular opinion (Hardy, 1977). They were a "safety-valve for dissatisfaction and a substitution for democratic assemblies" (Bollinger, 1969). The ancient historian Josephus seems to have believed erroneously that the passion for chariot races was actually motivated by a desire to petition the emperor, so that the political function was more important than the ludic one.

Sports spectators, like theater spectators, greeted emperors with shouts of acclamation or with cries of anger. Since a series of laws dating back to republican times reserved different sections of the theater, the circus, and the arena to different social classes, the emperor was likely to be confronted by insults from one *cuneus* (wedge) and shouts of approval from another. He had before him a vivid image of public opinion, a kind of animated Gallup Poll. Since the theater offered a verbal spectacle, it was easy for the crowd to express agreement or disagreement with specific sentiments. When the actor Laberius remarked from the stage, "*Necesse est multos timeat quem multi timent*" ("It is necessary that he whom many fear, fear many"), the entire audience is said to have understood the allusion and to have turned to look at Julius Caesar (Bollinger, 1969). (The actor went unpunished, but Caligula responded to similar impudence by having the offender burned to death.)

Despite the inherently nonverbal performances of the circus, tumultuous protest was frequent. In 196 A.D., the historian Dio Cassius reported a day of racing during which there was an eerie silence after the sixth race, then clapping in unison and cries for peace. Dio attributed to the gods the amazing coordination of this antiwar protest, but modern historians are inclined to ascribe the timing to claques which were highly developed as the cheerleaders of Roman antiquity (Bollinger, 1969, 32-33). In an age that lacked modern means of mass communication, the *ludi* were often used by the rulers as well as by the ruled. Byzantine emperors and their consorts sat, surrounded by officials, in the imperial box, visible symbols of power and glory. As Alan Cameron (1976) has noted, heirs to the throne were presented at the circus; on a more mundane level, criminals were often punished there and cowardly soldiers publicly humiliated.

The protests of sports spectators were not always limited to shouts of disapproval. The public was often violent and to a degree still unknown in the modern world. Although chariot races were nonviolent in the sense that the drivers were prohibited by the rules from doing each other physical damage, they occasioned an incredible amount of sports-related spectator violence. In 190 A.D., the races at the *circus maximus* were interrupted by a maiden who rushed forward, accompanied by a group of children, to accuse the official Cleander of hoarding grain. The crown took to the streets, threatened the emperor's villa, and succeeded in "persuading" Commodus to fire Cleander (Whittaker, 1964). Rioters set Constantinople's wooden hippodrome on fire in 491, 498, 507, and 532, after which Justinian invested in a marble stadium (Guilland, 1948). In the 5th and 6th centuries, spectator violence in the Byzantine Empire increased to the point where troops were repeatedly called upon to restore order. After a victory by Porphyrius in 507 in the circus at Antioch, the jubilant Greens ran amok and, in the course of the riot, burned the local synagogue, a quite typical instance of anti-Semitism (Cameron, 1976). The worst of these many riots took place in Constantinople in 532 when supporters of both the Blues and the Greens joined forces on the ides of January. Prisoners about to be executed were rescued by the mob which ignored Justinian's attempt to appease them with the promise of additional games. By the 15th, the emperor acceded to demands that he dismiss John of Cappodicia and other unpopular officials. By the 18th of January, the mob proclaimed a new emperor, Hypatius, nephew of Anastasius, and a number of senators paid homage to the new ruler. Fortunately for Justinian, his most skillful general, Belisarius, arrived in time to save the day—at the cost of an estimated 30,000 lives (Cameron, 1976). In comparison with this bloodbath, the worst outbreaks of Latin American soccer fans seem relatively innocuous. We can assume that the sports-related violence of the circus factions was perceived by the rioters as legitimate protest while the Byzantine officialdom undoubtedly saw illegitimate excess.

In his masterful book, *Circus Factions*, Alan Cameron has shown that the unruly charioteer fans of Rome and Constantinople were neither organized into political parties nor representatives of theological positions. (Previous historians had held both views.) Whether the hardcore adherents of the Blues and Greens were "simply supporters' clubs" and wholly nonpolitical can, however, be debated, despite Cameron's evidence, because there is a distinction to be drawn between political behavior and political behavior institutionalized into parties. Cameron concludes that the "circus factions deserve no prominent mention in any history of popular expression" (p. 311). In his view, politics merely provided "a convenient facade for the colors to fight each other openly and with impunity" (p. 84). Although Cameron's authority is generally acknowledged, his insistence that the violence committed by supporters of the Blues and Greens was entirely nonpolitical is less persuasive than Traugott Bollinger's (1969) argument that the spectacles were often "gatherings of a political character" (p. 24). Cameron concedes in an adjectival clause that there may have been "differences in behavior and even social class" among the faction members, but he holds that "partisans of both colors really moved in much the same world: young men with time on their hands—the jeunesse dorée rather than a representative cross section of the whole population" (1976, 101). All modern evidence of an analogous nature indicates that Cameron is right to doubt that the factions were a representative cross section, but, if there *were* differences in social class, then differences in behavior were inevitable and it is quite impossible to believe that such class-based differences were wholly unpolitical. Within the context of modern sports, the baseball fans of Chicago divide into partisans of the White Sox and followers of the Cubs; in Glasgow, soccer enthusiasts back either the Rangers or the Celtics; in Bordeaux, there are four rugby clubs appealing to four different social groups; in Munich, one can cheer for 1. F. C. Bayern or 1860 München. In these and other instances, various crass and subtle behavioral differences—including political differences—are detectable. That Cameron, despite his erudition, cannot detect similar patterns in ancient Rome or Constantinople is probably due to antiquity's lack of interest in such matters and to the subsequent scarcity of documentary evidence. There was no Byzantine social scientist to seek whatever statistically significant correlations there may have been between faction membership and political behavior. Cameron's conjecture that both factions were comprised of the jeunesse dorée may be valid, but, if it is, then the sports-related violence of Constantinople differed markedly from that of modern New York, Manchester, Hamburg, and Lyons, where violence is associated with alienation among the deprived rather than among the privileged.

Conclusion

Whether or not one accepts Cameron's conclusions about the nonpolitical behavior of the Blues and the Greens, he stands out among historians because of his efforts to move beyond description to analysis and evaluation. Not even the best of the presently available studies can provide definitive answers to our sociological and social-psychological questions, but we can safely conclude that Roman sports were certainly more violent than those of modern Europe and North America. And they probably surpassed the violence of Latin American sports as well. This conclusion holds for both the legitimate violence within sports (gladiatorial games vs. boxing or American football) and for the illegitimate sports-related violence of the spectators (the Nike riots with 30,000 dead vs. the 300 killed in Lima in 1964 when Peruvian soccer fans protested a disallowed goal). In Roman sports we have seen that the relatively nonviolent chariot races led to incomparably more spectator violence than the frequently mortal combats of the gladiators. We can surely conclude that the internal structure of the sport does not *determine* the level of spectator violence. Since modern social-psychological research has shown fairly conclusively that those who watch a violent sport experience an increase in aggressiveness, that is, in the propensity to act violently (Guttmann, 1981), we can be fairly sure that the internal structure, that is, the level of intrinsic violence, does matter, but other factors, such as the degree of social disorganization within a society, are more important than the nature of the sport. It follows, therefore, that "soccer hooliganism" and similar forms of sports-related spectator violence are less likely to be diminished by a

18   Allen Guttmann

reduction in the number of fouls committed on the field than by a resolution of the
basic social problems responsible for the disposition to violence. Full employment
and the end of racial discrimination will do more to eliminate sports-related violence
than the abolition of prizefights or the return of fair play to the football field.

References

Auguet, R. *Cruelty and civilization*. London: Allen & Unwin, 1972.
Backhaus, W. Öffentliche spiele, sport und gesellschaft in der römischen antike. In
    H. Ueberhorst (Ed.), *Geschichte der leibesübungen* (6 vols.). Berlin: Bartels &
    Wernitz, 1972.
Balsdon, J. P. V. D. *Life and leisure in ancient Rome*. London: Bodley Head, 1969.
Bollinger, T. *Theatralis licentia*. Winterthur: Hans Schellenberg, 1969.
Cameron, A. *Porphyrius the charioteer*. Oxford: Clarendon Press, 1973.
Cameron, A. *Circus factions: Blues and Greens at Rome and Byzantium*. Oxford:
    Clarendon Press, 1976.
Coubertin, P. de. Circular letter, 15 January 1894. In L. Diem (Ed.), *L'Idee olym-
    pique*. Cologne: Carl Diem-Institut, 1966.
Dio Cassius. [*Roman history*] (9 vols.) (E. Cary & H. B. Foster, Trans.). New York:
    Macmillan, 1914-1927.
Friedländer, L. [*Roman life and manners under the early empire*] (4 vols.) (J. H.
    Freese & L. A. Magnus, Trans.). London: Routledge, 1908-1913.
Grant, M. *Gladiators*. London: Weidenfeld & Nicolson, 1967.
Guilland, R. The hippodrome at Constantinople. *Speculum*, 1948, *23*, 678-680.
Guttmann, A. *From ritual to record: The nature of modern sports*. New York:
    Columbia University Press, 1978.
Guttmann, A. Zum verhalten der zuschauer im sport. *Sportwissenschaft*, 1981, *11*,
    66-68.
Hardy, S. Politicians, promoters, and the rise of sport: The case of ancient Greece
    and Rome. *Canadian Journal for the History of Sport and Physical Education*,
    1977, *8*, 1-15.
Harris, H. A. *Sport in Greece and Rome*. Ithaca, New York: Cornell University
    Press, 1972.
Hoenle, A., & Henze, A. *Roemische amphitheater und stadien*. Zurich: Atlantis,
    1981.
Horace. [*Epistles*] (S. P. Boyie, Trans.) Chicago: University of Chicago Press, 1959.
Juvenal. [*Satires*] (R. Humphries, Trans.) Bloomington: Indiana University Press,
    1958.
Kindermann, H. *Das theaterpublikum der antike*. Salzburg: Otto Müller, 1979.
Novatian. [*De spectaculis*] (T. R. Glover, Trans.) London: Heinemann, 1931.
Ovid. [*Ars amatoria*] (R. Humphries, Trans.) Bloomington: Indiana University
    Press, 1957.
Petronius. [*Satyricon*] (W. Arrowsmith, Trans.) Ann Arbor: University of Michigan
    Press, 1959.
Robert, L. *Les gladiateurs dans l'orient Grec* (2nd ed.). Amsterdam: Adolf M. Hak-
    kert, 1971.

Salvian. [*On the government of god*] (E. M. Sanford, Trans.). New York: Columbia University Press, 1930.

Schrodt, B. Sports of the Byzantine empire. *Journal of Sport History*, 1981, *8*, 40-59.

Seneca. [*Ad lucilium epistulae morales*] (3 vols.) (R. M. Gummere, Trans.). London: Heinemann, 1917.

Suetonius. [*The twelve Caesars*] (R. Graves, Trans.). Harmondsworth: Penguin, 1957.

Tacitus. [*Annals of imperial Rome*] (M. Grant, Trans.). Harmondsworth: Penguin, 1959.

Tertullian. [*De spectaculis*] (T. R. Glover, Trans.). London: Heinemann, 1931.

Tumolesi, P. S. *Gladiatorum pari*. Rome: Edizioni di Storia e Letterature, 1980.

Verspohl, F. J. *Stadionbauten von der antike bis zur gegenwart*. Giessen: Anabas, 1976.

Ville, G. Les jeux des gladiateurs dans l'empire chrétien. *Mélanges d'Archéologie et d'Histoire de l'Ecole Francaise de Rome*, 1960, *72*, 289.

Wacke, A. Unfälle bei sport und spiel nach römischem und geltendem recht. *Stadion*, 1977, *3*, 4-43.

Weismann, W. *Kirche und schauspiele*. Wurzburg: Augustinus-Verlag, 1972.

Whittaker, C. R. The revolt of Papirius Dionysius A.D. 190. *Historia*, 1964, *12*, 348-369.

Chapter 3

Unsporting Behavior: The Control of Football and Horse-Racing Crowds in England, 1875-1914

Wray Vamplew

Almost any event in Victorian England which brought together a large gathering of people could result in crowd disorder. Violence frequently broke out at all sorts of mass meetings "from Salvation Army processions to demonstrations of the unemployed, industrial disputes, . . . eviction scenes, Orange celebrations, public hangings" (Richter, 1971; see also Bailey, 1977; Cunningham, 1971; Price, 1972). Sports crowds were no exception.[1] Disorder was common at horse-racing events in mid-Victorian England. At several metropolitan meetings the disturbance was so bad that in 1879 Parliamentary legislation was used to suppress them (Spencer, 1900). Other meetings also had their troubles, particularly when backers felt that they had not had a fair run for their money or when bookmakers welshed on winning bets (Curzon, 1892; Fairfax-Blakeborough, 1927). Writing in 1870, J. H. Peart, right-hand man of the famous trainer John Scott, unfavorably contrasted the English situation with that of Chantilly in France where "the arrangements on the racecourses are far beyond what they have in England. The roughs are kept in their proper place, and there was no hustle or confusion, and no fear of being robbed of your wallet." Football (soccer) too had its crowd problems. The minute books of the Football Association and the Football League Management Committee clearly support the conclusion of one football historian whose study of contemporary comments revealed that "riots, unruly behaviour, violence, assault and vandalism appear to have been a well-

---

[1] This contribution concentrates on soccer and horse racing, the two major crowd-drawing sports in late 19th century England. At this time it was "no rare thing in the North and Midlands for twenty to thirty thousand people to pay money to witness a League match or important cup-tie" (Shearman, 1895, p. 166) and, in racing, crowds of 10,000-15,000 were not unusual with double this at leading fixtures and perhaps 70,000-80,000 at a major Bank Holiday meeting (Richardson, 1901, p. 213). Despite difficulties in identifying crowd composition it is generally accepted that working men provided the bulk of spectators both in soccer and horse racing (Mason, 1980; Tischler, 1981; Vamplew, 1976, pp. 131-137).

established, but not necessarily dominant pattern of crowd behaviour at football matches at least from the 1870s" (Hutchinson, 1974).[2]

Yet over time the disorder at both sports apparently declined. By the turn of the century one knowledgable commentator could claim that "ruffianism [was] practically unknown" at the enclosed racecourses and, in soccer, media mention of field invasions was less frequent and a comparison of 1910-1912 with 1895-1897 shows that significantly fewer clubs were being cautioned by the Football Association because of spectator misbehavior (Hutchinson, 1974; Ord, 1903). The reason for the improvement is not hard to find, for the decline in disorder in both sports correlates well with the rise of commercialism.

Commercialized sport for the masses was essentially a product of the late 19th century when entrepreneurs responded to the dual stimuli of rising working-class incomes and increased leisure time. Until 1875 anyone could watch a race meeting free of charge, but in that year Sandown Park was established as an enclosed course which demanded an entry fee from all spectators. It was an immediate financial and racing success and spawned a host of imitators so that by 1900 racing was taking place at enclosed courses all over England. Commercialism within soccer was boosted by the recognition of professionalism in 1885 and, 3 years later, by the inauguration of the Football League, a competition designed to provide regular weekly matches between the leading English teams. In both sports, clubs and members' committees gave way to companies and boards of directors (Tischler, 1981; Vamplew, 1976).

Inevitably these developments required heavy investment. In racing the issued share capital of Sandown Park was £26,000, of Haydock Park £28,000, and of Newbury, a major development in the early 20th century, £80,000. In football, Manchester United spent nearly £36,000 on its new stands in 1909, Blackburn Rovers expended £33,000 on its Ewood Park ground in the decade from 1905, and Everton laid out £41,000 at Goodison in the 3 years to 1909 (Francis, 1925; Keates, 1929). Sports promoters thus had a lot to lose if disorderly crowds got out of hand and destroyed valuable property. Additionally, there was the threat to gate receipts if spectator violence dissuaded people from attending or if it led the sports authorities to close the ground or revoke the license of the racecourse.

Course executives and club directors took steps to protect their financial interests by devising methods of crowd control. It is probable that structural strains and social tensions were at the root of the sports crowd disorders. Such a hypothesis certainly has relevance to any explanation of the involvement of the working-class in sports crowd disorder. To many working men sport performed a compensatory function, providing relief from the monotony of work and allowing them openly to challenge authority by shouting at the referee or official. Football fans could rarely triumph over social and economic institutions, but their team could defeat its opponents. Additionally the racegoer could seek to control his fate by using his skill to select winning horses. The intense role of sport in such people's lives meant that their reaction to sports events became highly emotional (Carroll, 1980; Ingham *et al.*, 1978; Marsh, Rosser, & Harré 1978; Smith, 1975; Trivizas, 1980; Vamplew,

---

[2] Clearly Taylor (1971a, pp. 353, 373; 1971b) is in error in claiming that pitch invasion was not common practice until after World War II.

1979, 1980). However, even if the sports promoters had appreciated this, there is little that they could have done to rectify the situation. Hence they concentrated on a variety of measures designed either to reduce the triggers to disorder or to contain any disturbances which did break out. This was not problem-free as the motivations of sports-crowd rioters can differ considerably and hence require different control measures.

Types of Crowd Disorder

A recent work by social psychologists has classified sports crowd disorders into five major categories, depending on the apparent motivation of those involved, all of which can be found at the sports events being examined here (Mann & Pearce, 1978; see also Mann, 1979). (Unfortunately, limitation of time and other resources has not allowed any quantified measure of relative occurrence of different types of riot to be made.) *Frustration* disorders occur when spectator's expectations of access to the game and the way it will be played or adjudicated are thwarted. A prime example of this occurred at Everton in 1895, when the referee allowed a match to start but then declared the pitch unplayable after only 30 minutes of play. A mob threw stones through every window available, woodwork was smashed and then used as weapons, and threats were made to burn down the stands. Eventually two contingents of police answered the call for assistance, drew their batons, attacked the rioters, and cleared the ground (Keates, 1929). Perceived injustice can also become a source of frustration as when fans believe that an incompetent or biased official has cost their team victory: in the early years of the Football League referees frequently had to run the gauntlet of disgruntled spectators. Similarly, jockeys who did not try their best, or bookmakers who refused to pay out winning punters, triggered many riots at mid-Victorian race meetings.

Outlawry disorders occur when groups of violence-prone spectators use sports events to act out their antisocial activities by attacking officials, fighting with rival fans, and destroying property. Such crowd violence is seen as the work of a delinquent or criminal element. It is difficult to pinpoint historical examples particularly as this type of rioter no doubt would join in most other disturbances. A possible indication of their existence comes from a critic of those professional sports organized for betting purposes, who claimed that such sports attracted "a varying but always large blackguard element," "a mob of loafers," and "a base rabble," and that "disorder and attacks on the police are not things of rare occurrence among the rougher spectators." Another critic of horse-racing crowds blamed the railways for "facilitating the movement of bands of indolent roughs." A further lead is the comment on soccer crowds that "it all depends upon the measure of civilization in your locality whether there is or is not a good deal of fighting after the match" (Edwards, 1892). Unfortunately, all these comments suffer from being labels applied by outside observers who can only indirectly perceive the motivations of the groups involved.

The third category of disorder is that of *remonstrance*. This occurs when a section of the crowd uses the sports event as an arena for the expression of political grievances. In the early 20th-century, sports events were used as a means of political protest by the suffragettes. Sport was a bastion of male chauvinism and exclusiveness, thus, when the suffragettes turned to militant protest, sport was an obvious target. Throughout 1913, racecourses, bowling greens, soccer and cricket pitches, and golf courses had their turf torn up and their buildings set on fire. And it was at a sports event, the 1913 Derby, that the suffragettes found their martyr when Emily Davison threw herself under the King's horse and was killed, though this may have been a quest for publicity rather than feminist action directed at the attitudes of the racing authorities (Dobbs, 1973; Vamplew, 1980).

Confrontation disorder breaks out when spectators from rival religious, geographic, ethnic, or national groups come into conflict. Given the appropriate circumstances, smoldering resentment can easily spark into open hostility. Local "derby" games where regional supremacy is at stake are an ideal setting for confrontation riots. In 1880, a time at which Darwen and neighboring Blackburn Rovers were fierce rivals, an incident involving Marshall of the home side and Suter of Blackburn inflamed the 10,000 spectators. Their views as to who was at fault divided according to their allegiance, and the subsequent riot forced the abandonment of the match (Francis, 1925).

Finally, in an *expressive* riot the intense emotional arousal which accompanies victory or defeat, particularly if it is exciting or unexpected, triggers uninhibited behavior. When Blackburn Olympic, essentially a working-class team, beat the Old Etonians in the 1883 Cup Final to take the trophy to the north for the first time, their supporters reputedly went mad with excitement, particularly as the result had been snatched during extra time (Green, 1949).

What is apparent from the above categorization is that no single control measure could cope with all the triggers to disorder and that action which might be suitable for one situation could be inappropriate in another. To some extent, the sports promoters learned this lesson by trial and error and rules for crowd control took time to evolve, but by the end of the 19th century five major methods had been devised: improvements in the conduct of the sport, improvements in the organization of the sports event, segregation within the crowd, control of ancillary activities, and the use of control agents.

Crowd-Control Measures

In most cases, efforts to improve the conduct of the sport came from the national controlling bodies, and not always with the major aim of improving crowd behavior. Nevertheless, with less overt malpractice to anger the crowd, the spectators' propensity to riot clearly would be reduced. In racing, the Jockey Club took steps to clean up the sport by introducing revocable licenses for trainers, jockeys, officials, and even racecourses (Vamplew, 1980). In football, referees were given the power to send players off the field for serious misconduct and by the 1890s any such transgressor could expect to be a spectator for at least a month. The measures taken probably had some effect in racing where most corruption was premeditated and thus susceptible to a deterrent. Yet this was somewhat diluted by frequently reinstating those who had been warned off (Black, 1891). Racing still remained susceptible to corruption because of gambling, but the image of the sport at the turn of the century was certainly less tarnished than at earlier points in time. There was some debate in turf circles as to the degree of misconduct, but most racing men agreed with Alfred Watson (1896), a leading writer on turf affairs, that

> a few rogues are still to the fore, sometimes in prominent places, and not a few others have conveniently elastic consciences, together with excessively liberal ideas of what is permissible, but I do believe that there is far less rascality on the turf than there used to be. (p. 686)

In soccer too, planned corruption was stamped upon by the authorities. When referees' reports revealed suspicious circumstances, the Football Association or the Football League always investigated them and where misconduct was believed to have taken place retribution was severe: Billy Meredith, an international player from Manchester City, for instance, was banned for 3 years for offering a bribe to an Aston Villa opponent and a similar offense led to Colonel T. Gibson Poole, Chairman of Middlesborough, being expelled from the Football Association and hence from most organized soccer (Dobbs, 1973; Football Association, 1911). Whether the scandals which came to light were the tip of an iceberg is a matter for conjecture, but even a stern critic of professional football acknowledged that the game seemed "irreproachably straight" (Edwards, 1892, p. 623). Admittedly this was in the 1890s, but a search of the later literature revealed no general belief that football was a corrupt sport.

Improved organization of the sports events did much to reduce the chances of frustration riots. A simple but effective improvement was to have races and matches start on time. Traditionally, race meetings had commenced in the morning, and the times of the afternoon races depended upon the quality of the luncheon partaken by the race committee. Even then, the method of starting races with a shout of "no" or "go" was apt to lead to false starts. The enclosed courses ran to a much stricter timetable, thanks to the employment of professional starters and, from the late 1890s, the use of the starting gate. In soccer in the 1870s and 1880s, matches frequently had to be abandoned because darkness fell, but, with the coming of professionalism and the development of leagues, a balance was struck between starting late enough to allow fans to get to the matches after work and early enough to allow the games to finish before dark.

Another organizational problem which could anger the crowd was the fielding of weak teams, either because first-team players were being rested prior to an important game, or because teams turned up short-handed. That teams should be at full strength was one of the original rules of the Football League and clubs that broke this rule were fined, sometimes as much as £250, which was the equivalent of a gate of 10,000. When it was a matter of not having enough players, initially it was the player who failed to arrive who was fined, but by 1904 the emphasis shifted to disciplining the clubs for not having sufficient reserves available. As with kick-off times, these policies seem to have been generally successful and by 1914 abuses of the rule were rare.

Segregation of the crowd, another method of crowd control, was first of all a matter of managing the physical environment by fencing off parts of the courses

and grounds, and then it was a question of controlling entry to the various enclosures, stands, and terraces. This was achieved in several ways. One was differential
pricing. By the late 1880s the more important soccer clubs had settled on a 6d.
admission to the ground and an extra 6d. for the stand. With the investment in
improved facilities from the 1890s stand prices were increased, though generally the
6d. ground admission charge was retained. For example, when Manchester United
opened its Old Trafford stadium in 1910, it was still only 6d. to enter the ground
but 1s., 1s. 6d., and 2s. for various sections of the covered stand and 5s. for a
reserved seat in the center stand (Young, 1969). The same practice held also in
racing. At York, for example, in the 1890s, it cost 10s. (5s. for ladies) to enter the
grandstand, 5s. for the paddock, and 2s. 6d. for the second-class enclosures. Another
method of segregation adopted in racing was the reservation of particular areas for
club members, entry to which was controlled by strict social vetting and high sub-
scription costs. In soccer, however, club membership seems to have been more open
socially, and, apart from committee members and their friends, viewing privileges
were restricted to first claim on season tickets.

Both differential pricing and the formation of clubs were primarily economic
policies, designed to increase returns by supplying different markets at different
prices, but they did have the indirect effect of making it easier to contain any disorder to the areas in which it broke out, thus making the disturbance less offensive
to those elsewhere and also possibly making it easier to put down the trouble (Lord
Cadogan on the Turf, 1885). Unfortunately it is also possible that in certain circumstances segregation may have encouraged disorder as crowd density, a significant
influence on spectator behavior, may have been intensified in certain areas. Moreover, if segregation led to the grouping together of similarly motivated spectators,
then, as communication is easier when persons have preexisting group ties, the
dynamics of crowd disorder could spread faster (Smith, 1975). The best policy
regarding segregation was the absolute exclusion of undesirable spectators. Traditionally, at race meetings segregation had been a matter of keeping the riff raff out
of the stands and other exclusive areas. With the development of the enclosed meeting, however, the lower elements of the racing world were not even allowed on the
course. In soccer, too, the authorities insisted that clubs exclude known trouble-
makers. Policies of exclusion at all gate-money sports became easier with the adop-
tion of the turnstile in the late 19th century.

Most sports promoters also took action to control the ancillary activities associated with their sport, in particular drinking and gambling. Less gambling, or at least
more stringently controlled gambling, could lead to fewer precipitating factors, and
less alcohol might prevent some sections of the crowd from becoming uninhibited
and possibly also guard against false perception of events.

No doubt gambling losses and alcohol had contributed to many a crowd fracas at
preenclosed race meetings, but before spectators began to pay at the gate, rentals
from the gaming and drinking booths were vital to the prize funds. It is significant
that complaints about the behavior of the race crowd at Darlington in the 1840s
stressed "the great rioting and drunkenness *in the booths* on the racecourse" (William
Clayton to John Bowes, in Bowes, 1846). With the emergence of the gate-money
course, the number of beer tents was reduced and gambling was restricted to betting

on the races, and the cardsharps, thimblemen, and even/odd table operators were no longer welcomed. In fact, the racecourse executives chose to enforce laws which they had previously disregarded. Legislation of 1853 had made it illegal to monopolize a place for betting purposes and this was interpreted as outlawing gaming booths, and the Vagrancy Act Amendment Act of 1873, which made it illegal to use betting machines, was taken as ruling out roulette and even/odd tables. However, racing faced a special problem in controlling its ancillary activities in that traditionally races had been associated with local holidays and people had come to race meetings in expectation of a carnival. The race promoters were faced with having to persuade the race crowd to accept a dampening of the traditional holiday atmosphere. Their solution was to change the nature of the racing along with that of the race meeting. Long-distance, staying events were increasingly replaced by sprints, handicaps, and races for two-year-olds, all of which had a degree of unpredictability sufficient to make for exciting racing and betting.

Racing had a symbiotic relationship with gambling and could not afford to do without it. Gambling had no such importance for soccer, but as the law stood in the late 19th century, gambling was believed to be legal at any sports events in which gate-money had been charged, providing that the betting was on the event being staged (Vamplew, 1979). It thus seemed that the ground proprietors could do little to prevent gambling. Indeed, it was felt that the police could not eject bookmakers from the ground even if the promoters requested them to do so. Fortunately for the promoters, new interpretations of the law towards the turn of the century made it difficult for the bookmaker to set up business inside the grounds. The 1853 legislation regarding the monopolization of a place for betting purposes was deemed as preventing the bookmaker from standing on a box, under an umbrella, or using any colors or placards to draw attention to himself. In soccer, enforcement of such an interpretation was seen as necessary because of crowd misconduct associated with betting. In the 1890s referees were being assaulted by losing gamblers, but then firm action by the clubs and football authorities, assisted by the police, appears to have reduced drastically the volume of betting taking place at the grounds. In the immediate prewar years, however, coupon betting developed and there was little the football promoters could do about it. Thus, it is possible that spectators had bet on the matches which they were watching and this could have had an adverse effect on their behavior (Mason, 1980; Needham, 1900; Smith, 1897; Tischler, 1981).

It is difficult to determine how much drinking went on at soccer matches. Certainly in the early 20th century, it was claimed that "really there is comparatively little drinking done at football matches" (McGregor, 1907), but, as the claimant was the founder of the Football League and anxious to promote a respectable image for soccer, his views have to be treated with caution. It certainly seems that drinking was an accepted part of sports spectatorship and thus, even though limited and controlled, a possible contributing factor to crowd disturbance.

Keeping the crowd segregated, ejecting troublesome spectators, enforcing ground regulations, and preventing field invasion or encroachments required the use of control agents, namely gatemen and stewards supplied by the club, and police hired from the local force. Gatemen at the enclosed race meetings improved in caliber once they became subject to Jockey Club license, and the best of them would be employed at many meetings and thus, by travelling the racing circuits, would be able to familiarize themselves with defaulting bookmakers and itinerant trouble-makers. Gatemen at football possibly found identification of potential bother-causers easier because of the more regular nature of their events. Stewards and police had the primary function of enforcing compliance with regulations and acting as a deter-rent to troublemakers, but should a disturbance occur they could be employed to contain and put down the disorder. The Football Association and the Football League encouraged, and occasionally ordered, clubs to prosecute spectators who were guilty of causing disturbances and they expected clubs to provide sufficient police protection to keep the crowd in order.

Some Limits of Crowd Control

Crowd disorder could not be totally eliminated. Not all the triggers to disturbance could be removed. Little could be done, for example, about heat-of-the-moment violence on the field of play. Nor were the perceptions of the partisan spectator or racegoer likely to be influenced by legislation or entreaties from the clubs, particu-larly when drinking and gambling remained an accompaniment of both soccer and horse racing. Even though the Football Association acknowledged that the directors of Sheffield Wednesday F. C. had done all they could to ensure proper conduct at the match, local supporters had still assaulted the visiting Preston team on their route from the ground to their hotel.[3] It is also possible that some of the measures intended to solve the disorder may actually have worsened the problem. Improved organization and less misconduct helped swell attendance figures, but increased crowd size and density could aggravate spectator disorder. Segregation of the crowd could also have increased crowd density in some parts of the ground.

Nevertheless, it would appear that a combination of repressive and reformative measures by sports promoters and authorities attained some degree of success in improving crowd behavior. Actions taken to improve the conduct and organization of football and racing did much to reduce the triggers to frustration, confrontation, and expressive disorders; segregation of various sections of the crowd and the abso-lute exclusion of troublesome spectators reduced the danger of confrontation and outlawry disorders; and the stricter controls on gambling and drinking, coupled with the deterrent effect of control agents, lessened the possibility of all kinds of disturbance, except perhaps for remonstrance disorders. If trouble did break out, then the segregation of the crowd, the restricted availability of alcohol, and the presence of the police generally acted to weaken the contagion dynamics of dis-order and to contain the disturbance.

Whether sports-crowd behavior would have improved anyway is questionable. Mather (1959) has argued that in the second half of the 19th century riot was eliminated from English social life and mob disorder conquered, but this seems too

---

[3] Minutes of Sheffield Wednesday Football Club, 21 February 1906. The Football Association then closed the ground for two weeks so "that spectators might be taught that misbehaviour at the conclusion of a match could not be tolerated."

sweeping. More recently Richter (1971) has shown that election violence by rowdy mobs continued throughout the Victorian and Edwardian eras and has claimed that this political disorder was "only one manifestation of [a] violent society" (p. 29). It may be true that riots in the later 19th and early 20th centuries posed no substantial threat to social order, but this does not necessarily mean that they were less violent (Bailey, 1977). Certainly if the social tension and structural strains thesis has any validity, it might have been anticipated that sports crowd behavior, particularly by working men, would have worsened rather than improved. The working-class was becoming increasingly aware and resentful of its relative social, economic, and political deprivation. This led to it generally becoming more militant. In political life trade unions swung to the left and the Labour Party became established; in the social sphere class consciousness became more pervasive than before; and in the economic arena trade union membership accelerated, strikes, often accompanied by violence, were more frequent, and the degree of labor unrest was unprecedented (Dangerfield, 1963; Hunt, 1981; Lovell, 1977; Meacham, 1972). Racegoers and soccer fans were not immune from such influences. That crowd behavior at commercialized sports events appears to have improved must owe much to the actions taken by the sports promoters, particularly when the crowd behavior at their matches and meetings is contrasted with that of the non-League football clubs, who were the ones primarily censured by the Football Association, and with the situation "outside the enclosures [where] the unfortunate state of our racecourses is too notorious to need comment" (Graves, 1900).

Acknowledgments. I am grateful to the Flinders University of South Australia and the Australian Research Grants Scheme for financial assistance towards the research costs of this paper which is part of an ongoing project on the economic and social history of sport in Britain. I am indebted to the Football Association (Lancaster Gate, London), the Football League (Lytham St. Annes), Sheffield Wednesday F. C., York Racing Committee, and Durham County Record Office for access to their archives. An earlier version of the paper was presented at a seminar of the Center for International Studies at the University of Missouri-St. Louis and was made possible by a Weldon Spring Fellowship from that institution.

References

Bailey, V. Salvation Army riots, the "Skeleton Army" and legal authority in the provincial town. In A. P. Donajgrodzki (Ed.), *Social control in nineteenth century Britain.* London: Croon, 1977.

Black, R. *The jockey club and its founders.* London: 1891.

Bowes, J. *Racing and personal correspondence.* Durham County Record Office, 1846.

Carroll, R. Football hooliganism in England. *International Review of Sport Sociology*, 1980, *15*, 77-92.

Cunningham, H. Jingoism in 1877-78. *Victorian Studies*, 1971, *14*.

Curzon, L. H. *A mirror of the turf.* London: Chapman & Hall, 1892.

Dangerfield, G. *The strange death of liberal England.* New York: Capricorn, 1963.

Dobbs, B. *Edwardians at play.* London: Pelham, 1973.

Edwards, C. The new football mania. *Nineteenth Century*, 1892, *32*, 622.

Fairfax-Blakeborough, J. *The analysis of the turf*. London: 1927.

Football Association. *Report of Commission into complaint against Middlesborough F. C.*, 16 January 1911.

Francis, C. *History of Blackburn Rovers 1875-1925*. Blackburn, 1925.

Graves, H. A philosophy of sport. *Contemporary Review*, 1900, *78*, 888.

Green, G. *The official history of the F. A. Cup*. London: Naldrett, 1949.

Hunt, E. G. *British labour history 1815-1914*. London: Weidenfeld & Nicolson, 1981.

Hutchinson, J. Some aspects of football crowds before 1914. In *The working class and leisure*. Mimeo: University of Sussex, 1974.

Ingham, R. et al. *Football hooliganism*. London: Inter-action, 1978.

Keates, T. *History of Everton F. C. 1878/79-1928/29*. Liverpool: Brakell, 1929.

Lord Cadogan on the turf. *Saturday Review*, 1885, *49*, 79.

Lovell, J. *British trade unions 1875-1933*. London: Macmillan, 1977.

Mann, L. Sports crowd viewed from the perspective of collective behavior. In J. H. Goldstein (Ed.), *Sports, games, and play*. Hillsdale, N. J.: Erlbaum, 1979.

Mann, L., & Pearce, P. Social psychology of the sports spectator. In D. Glencross (Ed.), *Psychology and sport*. Sydney: McGraw-Hill, 1978.

Marsh, P., Rosser, E., & Harré, R. *The rules of disorder*. London: Routledge & Kegan Paul, 1978.

Mason, A. *Association football and English society, 1863-1915*. Brighton: Harvester, 1980.

Mather, F. C. *Public order in the age of the chartists*. Manchester: Manchester Univ. Press, 1959.

McGregor, W. Characteristics of the crowd. In B. O. Corbett et al. (Eds.), *Football*. London: 1907.

Meacham, S. The sense of an impending clash: English working class unrest before the First World War. *American Historical Review*, 1972, *77*, 1343-1364.

Needham, E. *Association football*. London: Skeffington, 1900.

Ord, R. Horseracing in the north of England. *Badminton Magazine*, 1903, *14*, 174.

Price, R. *An imperial war and the British working class*. London: Routledge & Kegan Paul, 1972.

Richardson, C. *The English turf*. London: Methuen, 1901.

Richter, D. The role of mob riot in Victorian elections 1865-1885. *Victorian Studies*, 1971, *15*, 25.

Shearman, M. *Football*. London: Longmans, 1895.

Smith, G. O. Football. *Pall Mall Magazine*, 1897, *13*, 370-371.

Smith, M. D. Sport and collective violence. In D. W. Ball & J. W. Loy (Eds.), *Sport and social order*. Reading, Mass.: Addison-Wesley, 1975.

Spencer, E. *The great game*. London: 1900.

Taylor, I. R. Football mad: A speculative sociology of football hooliganism. In E. Dunning (Ed.), *The sociology of sport*. London: Cass, 1971. (a)

Taylor, I. R. Soccer consciousness and soccer hooliganism. In S. Cohen (Ed.), *Images of deviance*. London: Penguin, 1971. (b)

Tischler, S. *Footballers and businessmen.* New York: Holmes & Meier, 1981.

Trivizas, E. Offences and offenders in football crowd disorders. *British Journal of Criminology,* 1980, *20,* 276-288.

Vamplew, W. *The turf.* London: Allen Lane, 1976.

Vamplew, W. Ungentlemanly conduct: The control of soccer-crowd behaviour in England, 1888-1914. In T. C. Smout (Ed.), *The search for wealth and stability.* London: Macmillan, 1979.

Vamplew, W. Sports crowd disorder in Britain, 1870-1914: Causes and controls. *Journal of Sport History,* 1980, 7, 5-20.

Watson, A. F. T. Racing in 1896. *Badminton Magazine,* 1896, *3,* 686.

Young, P. M. *A history of British football.* London: Sportsman's Book Club, 1969.

Chapter 4

What Is Sports Violence?
A Sociolegal Perspective

Michael D. Smith

No rules or practice of any game whatever can make that lawful which is unlawful by the law of the land; and the law of the land says you shall not do that which is likely to cause the death of another. For instance, no persons can by agreement go out to fight with deadly weapons, doing by agreement what the law says shall not be done, and thus shelter themselves from the consequences of their acts. Therefore, in one way you need not concern yourself with the rules of football. (Hechter, 1977, p. 44)

These were Lord Justice Bramwell's instructions to the jury in an 1878 British court case, *Regina* v. *Bradshaw*. A soccer player was accused of manslaughter after he charged and collided with an opposing player, who subsequently died, in a game played under "association rules." The defendant was acquitted, but the judge's pronouncement has been cited of late in North America by those who wish to make the point that sport should not be exempt from the laws that govern our behavior elsewhere.

Seventeen years later, in 1894, Robert Fitzsimmons engaged in a public boxing exhibition with his sparring mate, Riordan, in Syracuse, New York. Riordan was knocked unconscious by a punch to the head and died 5 hours later. Fitzsimmons was indicted for manslaughter. The judge directed the jury as follows:

if the rules of the game and the practices of the game are reasonable, are consented to by all engaged, are not likely to induce serious injury, or to end life, if then, as a result of the game, an accident happens, it is excusable homicide. (Hechter, p. 443)

Fitzsimmons was acquitted. What is noteworthy about this case is that the "rules" and "practices" of the game were taken into account in determining criminal liability, a precedent directly contrary to that established in *Regina* v. *Bradshaw*. It is the Fitzsimmons ruling that has more or less held ever since.

The fact is, sports violence has never been viewed as "real" violence. The courts, except for isolated flurries of activity, have traditionally been reluctant to touch even the most outrageous incidents of sports-related bloodletting; legal experts still flounder in their attempts to determine what constitutes violence in sport. The great majority of violence-doers and their victims, the players, even though rule-violating assaults often bring their careers to a premature close, have always accepted much of what could be called violence as "part of the game." Large segments of the public, despite the recent emergence of sports violence as a full-blown "social problem," continue to give standing ovations to performers for acts that in other contexts would be instantly condemned as criminal. An examination of sports violence that fails to consider these perspectives "does violence," as it were, to what most people, not to mention criminal justice systems, regard as "violence."

A Typology of Sports Violence

What follows is a provisional attempt to answer the question: What is sports violence? I have classified said violence into four types ranging roughly on a scale of legitimacy, from greater to lesser, as shown in Table 4-1. In so doing, I have tried to take into account the views of the law, the players, and the public. The discussion is confined to acts performed by players during the game, or in its immediate context, and to North America. No particular distinction is made between Canada and the United States. The laws of both countries, as they apply to sports violence, seem fundamentally the same. Canadian legal journals freely cite American cases and vice versa. And of course most North American sports are to some degree international on almost every level of competition.

Brutal Body Contact

This category of sports violence comprises all significant body contact performed within the official rules of a given sport: tackles, blocks, body checks, collisions, legal blows of all kinds. Such contact is inherent in sports such as boxing, wrestling, ice hockey, rugby, lacrosse, football, and to lesser degrees in soccer, basketball, water polo, team handball, and the like. It is taken for granted that when one participates in these activities one automatically accepts the inevitability of contact, also the probability of minor bodily injury, and the possibility of serious injury. In legal terms players are said to "consent" to receive such blows (*volenti no fit*

Table 4-1. A Sports Violence Typology

Relatively legitimate		Relatively illegitimate	
Brutal body contact	Borderline violence	Quasicriminal violence	Criminal violence
Conforms to the official rules of the sport, hence legal in effect under the law of the land; more or less accepted.	Violates the official rules of the sport and the law of the land, but widely accepted.	Violates the official rules of the sport, the law of the land, and to a significant degree informal player norms; more or less not accepted.	Violates the official rules of the sport, the law of the land, and players' informal norms; not accepted.

injuria—to one who is willing no wrong is done). On occasion death results and a court case ensues. If the defense shows that the defendant could not have "foreseen" that his actions would cause death, hence did not behave recklessly or negligently, he is found not guilty. This is not as simple as it sounds, of course. Legal scholar Richard Horrow (1980) takes more than 50 pages to explain the complexities of "consent," "foreseeability," and related arguments in his book on sports violence and criminal law. The point is, any blow administered within the formal rules of a sport is legal in effect under the law of the land.

In my view, legal body contact becomes of interest as violence when it develops (or as some might prefer, degenerates) into "brutality." A rising toll of injuries and deaths, followed by public expressions of alarm, then demands for reform, typically signal this condition. An "intrinsically brutal" sport like boxing always hovers not far from this point; for this reason, boxing is almost everywhere regulated by the state, albeit often inadequately. When body contact assumes an importance out of proportion to that required to play the game—when inflicting pain and punishing opponents are systematized as strategy, and viciousness and ferocity are publicly glorified—a stage of brutality can be said to have been reached. Such practices may strain the formal rules of a particular sport, but they do not necessarily violate them.

Sports brutality is not a new phenomenon. The history of football, to take probably the best example, is in part a chronicle of intermittent waves of brutality, public censure, and reform. In 1893 indignation against alleged viciousness in American college football, smoldering for some time, erupted across the country. A campaign led by the magazines *Saturday Evening Post* and *The Nation* caused several institutions to drop the game, including Harvard, one of the first schools to play it on a regular intercollegiate basis. (Parke Davis [1911, p. 98], then the University of Wisconsin coach and later a historian of the game, wrote that the reports of brutish play were somewhat exaggerated. Among the most hysterical must have been that appearing in a German publication, *Münchener Nachrichten*. This report, quoted by Davis, described the Harvard-Yale game of 1893 as "awful butchery," seven participants reportedly being carried in "dying condition" off the field with broken backs, broken legs, and lost eyes.) A popular vaudeville ditty of the day is revealing (Betts, 1974):

> Just bring along the ambulance,
> And call the Red Cross nurse,
> Then ring the undertaker up,
> And make him bring a hearse;
> Have all the surgeons ready there,
> For they'll have work today,
> Oh, can't you see the football teams
> Are lining up to play. (p. 244)

Antifootball sentiment swept the United States again in 1905. In a report somewhat more measured than the one above, a Chicago newspaper published a compilation for the 1905 season showing 18 players dead, 11 from high schools and 3 from colleges, and 159 more or less serious injuries. President Roosevelt called representatives of Yale, Harvard, and Princeton to the White House and threatened to ban the game unless its brutality were eliminated. Stormed Teddy "Rough Rider" Roosevelt: "Brutality and foul play should receive the same summary punishment given to a man who cheats at cards" (Stagg, 1927, p. 253). Rule changes resulted, including the outlawing of the notorious "V" formation, and the furor abated.

Roughing up and intimidating opponents as a legal tactic, however, seems to have gained new life of late. Football is still in the vanguard. Consider the "hook," a sort of legalized on-field mugging whereby a defensive back in the course of making a tackle flexes his biceps and tries to catch the receiver's head in the joint between the forearm and upper arm. Professional player Jack Tatum (Tatum & Kushner, 1979), who likes to think that his hits "border on felonious assault," fondly recalls a well-executed hook (the tactic was outlawed soon after):

> When I felt I could zero in on Riley's head at the same time the ball arrived in his hands, I moved. . . . Because of the momentum built up by the angles and speed of both Riley and myself, it was the best hit of my career. I heard Riley scream on impact and felt his body go limp. (p. 18)

The casualty rates, the ultimate result of this type of play, are not insignificant. The rate in the National Football League is said to be 100%: at least one serious injury per player per season (Underwood, 1979). About 318,000 football injuries annually require hospital emergency room treatment in the United States (Philo & Stine, 1977). In the Canadian Football League, according to a survey conducted by the *Toronto Star* (November 25, 1981), 462 man-games were lost in the 1981 season owing to injury (down slightly from the year before). Observers seem to agree that the high injury rates at all levels of the game are attributable in significant measure to the way football is taught and played: brutishly.

Borderline Violence

In this category are assaults which, though prohibited by the official rules of a given sport (and the law of the land), occur routinely and are more or less accepted by all concerned. To wit: the hockey fistfight, the late hit in football, the high tackle in soccer, the baseball knock-down pitch, basketball "body language," the sometimes vicious elbowing and bumping that takes place in track and road races. Such practices occasionally produce serious injuries, but these are usually dismissed as unfortunate accidents. Borderline violence is essentially the province of referees, umpires, and other immediate game officials, higher league officials and law enforcement authorities seldom becoming involved. Sanctions never exceed suspension from the game being played, plus perhaps a fine.

Borderline violence is tolerated and justified on a number of grounds, most of which boil down to some version of the "part of the game" argument. Take hockey fisticuffs. A National Hockey League player, one of 60 interviewed in 1976-1977, provides this familiar (non)explanation (see Smith, 1979b):

> I don't think that there's anything wrong with guys getting excited in a game and squaring off and throwing a few punches. That's just part of the game. It always has been. And you know if you tried to eliminate it, you

wouldn't have hockey any more. You look at hockey from the time it was begun, guys get excited and just fight, and it's always been like that.

Naturally, because fistfighting is considered legitimate it is not defined by its practitioners as "violence." Also nobody gets hurt in a punch-up, players insist. (This is not precisely true. Of 217 "minor injuries" suffered by players on a Southern Professional Hockey League team over a 3-year period in the mid-1970s, "most" involved the hand or forearm [fractures, sprains, lacerations, etc.] and were usually incurred during fights [Rovere, Gristina, & Nicastro, 1978].) To the majority of professional players the periodic public fuss over hockey fighting is simply a product of the rantings of publicity-hungry politicians (Smith, 1979b):

> I think it's really blown out of proportion. A lot of these politicians trying to get somewhere are just trying to crack down on fighting to get their name in the paper. Most of the guys that say things like that don't know anything about hockey, and they're trying to talk about violence, and they don't even know what they're talking about. I don't think a punch in the head is going to hurt you, unless it's, you know, a sick thing where a guy pummels a guy into the ice and things like that. (p. 62)

There are, of course, more elaborate folk theories in circulation. Apologists are prone to claiming, for example, that hockey fisticuffs are safety valves for aggressive impulses (usually described as "frustration") which inevitably accumulate due to the speed, the contact, the very nature of the game. Because these aggressive urges must be vented, the argument goes, if not one way then another, prohibiting fistfighting would result in an increase in the more vicious and dangerous illegal use of the stick. In the words of John Ziegler, President of the National Hockey League (*Toronto Star*, December 13, 1977):

> We put men on the ice who are skating at full speed; the use of the body is an important part of the game; the players are surrounded with hard boards and they play at an intensity that, when they're out on the ice, is not demanded by any other sport. I do not find it unacceptable in a game where frustration is constant, for men to drop their sticks and gloves and take swings at each other. I think that kind of outlet is important for players in our games.

Belief in the inevitability of hockey violence generally is so entrenched, one of the judges in the famous Ted Green-Wayne Maki assault trials (stemming from a stick-swinging duel during a 1969 game in Ottawa which nearly ended Green's life) concluded, the game "can't be played without what normally are called assaults." Both players were acquitted, needless to say (*New York Times*, September 4, 1970, p. 31).

As for public opinion, several polls, now somewhat dated but still of interest, have revealed that a substantial minority finds the hockey fistfight more or less acceptable. Just months after the Green-Maki episode, almost 40% of the respondents in a Canada-wide survey sponsored by *Macleans* magazine said they "liked to see fighting at a hockey game"; among males the figure was 46% (Marshall, 1970). In a 1972 *Canadian Magazine* reader survey (over 30,000 returned questionnaires), 32% of all respondents and 38% of the male respondents thought NHL players should *not* be given automatic game penalties for fighting (Grescoe, 1972). Two years later a Gallup poll (1974) on minor hockey violence reported that 20% of Canadians disagreed with the statement, "there is too much violence in minor hockey"; 20% had no opinion. In the United States a statewide survey of Minnesota residents conducted by Mid-Continent Surveys of Minneapolis, shortly after the 1975 assault trial in Minnesota of Boston hockey player David Forbes, found that 61% thought punishment for fighting in professional sports should be left to the leagues, 26% preferring court punishment, and 5% preferring both (Hallowell & Meshbesher, 1977).

Do players themselves perceive fans as wanting to see fights? Asked "Are there any situations you can imagine in which spectators at your games would approve of a minor hockey player punching another player?," 67% of a random sample of 604 Toronto minor hockey players interviewed in 1976 said "Yes" (Smith, 1979b). Most of the professional players mentioned earlier considered it an obvious question when asked if they thought their spectators wanted fights. Said one: "Everybody has that insecure feeling that if he doesn't act as the roughest guy in the League then the owner's not going to want him. The owners believe that is the thing that sells the tickets, and they're right." A former "goon" ("I used to be the policeman on the team, but now I'm the meter maid. Ha ha.") paints a picture of the crowd which leaves little doubt that hockey practitioners of his ilk, at least, orient their behavior to what spectators seem to want, albeit perhaps via the expectations of owner or coach (Smith, 1979b):

> In my first game in the NHL, I played Chicago. We're losing the game 6-3, third period. I hadn't got out on the ice. I was called up so people started yelling, "We want Jackson [not his real name]. You brought him up. Play him." So I get on the ice, my first shift, I take a penalty, nine seconds, I two handed Mikita and I go off. I come back and I run at Hull, and I knock Hull out, and people just go crazy. The next day in the paper in New York you pick up the paper, it was hard to tell what the score was of the hockey game. All it was was "Bob Jackson fights Hull, Jackson this, Jackson that." Next game in Madison Square Garden, we play there, the signs are all over: "Bob Jackson, Pier Six." (p. 120)

Quasicriminal Violence

Quasicriminal violence is that which violates not only the formal rules of a given sport, but to a significant degree the informal norms of player conduct. It usually results, or could have resulted, in serious injury, which is what brings it to the attention of top league officials and generates public outrage in some quarters. This in turn puts pressure on legal authorities to become involved. League-imposed penalties for quasicriminal violence usually go beyond the contest in question and range from suspensions from several games to lifetime bans, depending on the sport; each league seems to decide how much and what types of violence it will tolerate. Increasingly, civil legal proceedings follow, though perhaps less often than thought; up to 1978 only about 10 civil suits involving personal injury in the National Football League took place; in the National Basketball Association, perhaps two (Horrow, 1980). Criminal proceedings, rare in the past, are occurring more frequently, but convictions remain few and far between. In 1976 the Attorney-General of Ontario, after several public warnings, ordered a crackdown on violence in amateur and professional sport in the province. According to an internal memorandum provided by the Director of Regional Crown Attorneys, 68 assault charges were laid in less than a year (67 in hockey, 1 in lacrosse), but only 10 convictions were obtained, although 16 cases were still pending at the time of the memorandum. Apparently all the convictions, and almost all the charges, were against amateur athletes.

Still, a small number of episodes of quasicriminal violence in professional sports have resulted in litigation, and it is these cases that have generated the greatest publicity. Several civil disputes have received continent-wide attention. One of the first in sport's modern era took place in baseball during a 1965 game between the San Francisco Giants and the Los Angeles Dodgers. Giant batter Juan Marichal felled Dodger catcher John Roseboro with his bat following an acrimonious verbal exchange. Roseboro sustained considerable injury; Marichal was fined $1,750 by the League and suspended for eight games. Roseboro filed a $110,000 civil suit for damages against Marichal and the San Francisco club, which reportedly was settled out of court for $7,500 (Kuhlman, 1975).

A decade and a half later, in 1979, Houston Rocket basketball player Rudy Tomjanovich was awarded a whopping $3.3 million in a civil suit for injuries received from a single, devastating punch thrown by Kermit Washington of the Los Angeles Lakers during a 1977 game. Tomjanovich suffered a fractured jaw, nose, and skull, a puncture of the brain cavity, a torn tear duct, and was not surprisingly out for the season. The League Commissioner suspended Washington for 60 days and fined him $10,000. The jury, in making an award of more than half a million dollars above what Tomjanovich's attorneys had demanded, found that Washington had acted "intentionally," "maliciously," and "with reckless disregard for the safety of others." The Lakers as an organization were deemed negligent because they "failed to adequately train and supervise Washington," even though they were aware "he had a tendency for violence while playing basketball" (Horrow, 1981, p. 12). The Lakers paid.

The way now seems fairly clear for a professional sports team, as an employer, to be held accountable under civil law for the actions of the players, its employees. Perhaps the most interesting case is one which began in 1975, *Hackbart* v. *Cincinnati Bengals, Inc.* This litigation arose out of an incident in a National Football League game in 1973 in which the plaintiff, Dale Hackbart of the Denver Broncos, was given a forearm blow on the back of the head by an opposing player, Charles Clark of the Cincinnati Bengals, in a "malicious and wanton" manner 5 seconds after the play had been whistled dead. Hackbart suffered a spinal fracture which ended his career. After circulating throughout the judicial system for several years (a lower court ruled that Hackbart took an implied risk by playing a violent game and that "anything" happening to him "between the sidelines" was part of that risk), an Appeals Court finally was legally permitted to consider the question of the employer's (i.e., the Cincinnati Bengals') accountability. New civil proceedings have apparently been scheduled.

In none of the above cases were criminal charges laid. Why this near-immunity to criminal prosecution and conviction? First, from the players' point of view, most seem reluctant to bring charges against another athlete. Based on a mail survey of major-league basketball, football, and hockey players, Horrow (1980) concludes that professional athletes, in particular, tend to believe that player disputes are best settled privately and personally on the field of play; that team management does not appreciate "troublemakers" who go "outside the family" (i.e., the league) for justice and that contract difficulties or worse probably await such individuals; that the sheer disruptiveness of litigation can ruin careers, and so on. Bolstering these beliefs is the apparent willingness of some players to dismiss virtually any during-the-match assault, short of using a gun or knife, as part of the game.

From the point of view of the law, says Horrow, based on a survey of United States county prosecutors, many officials are reluctant to prosecute sports violence because they believe that they have more important things to do, like prosecuting "real" criminals; that the leagues themselves can more efficiently and effectively control player misbehavior; that civil law proceedings are better suited than criminal for dealing with an injured player's grievances; that most lawyers do not have the expertise to handle sports violence cases; and that it is almost impossible to get a guilty verdict anyway.

There are several other more subtle, nonlegal reasons for the hands-off policy of criminal justice systems. One is the "community subgroup rationale." As explained by Kuhlman (1975), this is the tacit recognition by law-enforcement authorities that certain illegal activities by members of some social groups ought more or less to be tolerated because they are widespread within the group and because group members look upon them as less serious than does society in general. Furthermore, it would be unfair to single out and punish an individual member when everyone else in the group behaves similarly. In other words, the illegal conduct is rendered less criminal because everybody does it. This rationale sometimes arises in connection with the issue of differential law enforcement for minority groups. In some tough police jurisdictions in large cities, for instance, police rarely make an arrest for felonious assaults involving family members and neighbors, even though such assaults are frequent. Police in these areas tend to define domestic violence as mere "disturbances" whereas officers in other jurisdictions are more inclined to define it as genuine violence. It seems that certain assaultive behaviors in sport are looked upon with the same benevolent tolerance. At the very least, the severity of the penalties for violence provided by the law are widely regarded within the sport community, and to a considerable degree outside it, as out of proportion to the seriousness of the illegal acts.

The "continuing relationship rationale" applies in assault cases where offender and victim have an ongoing relationship. Legal authorities may wish to avoid straining the relationship further by prosecuting one or both parties. Husbands and wives may wish to continue living together; neighbors may have to; athletes typically compete against each other at regular intervals (Kuhlman, 1975). Criminal prosecution in sport could exacerbate already present hostility to the point where league harmony is seriously threatened. The 1976 prosecutions on various assault charges of three Philadelphia Flyers hockey players, arising out of a game in Toronto, caused considerable strain between the Philadelphia and Toronto Maple Leafs hockey clubs, and even in a public squabble between the Philadelphia District Attorney and the Ontario Attorney-General (*Toronto Star*, April 22, 1976). The assumption underlying this rationale is that society has an interest in maintaining such social relationships, that professional sport, say, serves some socially useful purpose.

Finally, there is the premise of "legal individualism"—the notion that the individual is *wholly* responsible for his or her own acts—which has resulted in a virtual immunity to criminal charges of sports organizations in cases where an individual member of the organization has been indicted for assault. The leading case is *State* v. *Forbes*.

On January 4, 1975, in Bloomington, Minnesota, an altercation occurred during a National Hockey League game between David Forbes of the Boston Bruins and Henry Boucha of the Minnesota North Stars. Both players were sent to the penalty box where Forbes repeatedly threatened Boucha verbally. As they left the box at the expiration of the penalties—Boucha first and Forbes seconds later—Forbes skated up behind Boucha and struck him with the butt end of his stick just above the right eye. Boucha fell to the ice stunned and bleeding (with a badly damaged eye it turned out). Forbes jumped on him, punched him on the back of the head, then grabbing him by the hair, proceeded to pound his head into the ice. Eventually another Minnesota player separated the two. The President of the NHL suspended Forbes for 10 games, but shortly afterwards a Minnesota grand jury charged him with the crime of Aggravated Assault by Use of a Dangerous Weapon. Forbes pleaded not guilty. The jury, after a week and a half of testimony and 18 hours of deliberation, was unable to reach a unanimous verdict. The court declared a mistrial, and the case was dismissed (Flakne & Caplan, 1977).

Described in law journals as a "landmark" case because it focused so much legal and public attention on the issue of violence in sport, *State* v. *Forbes* also raised the important and still unanswered question of legal individualism as it applies to the occupational use of violence, namely: Who should be held responsible in such cases, the individual or the group? Should not only Forbes, but the Boston Bruins and even the National Hockey League, have been on trial? Was Forbes merely doing his job, his duty, as a good hockey soldier? The defense counsel tried to ask these questions during the trial, to instruct the jury to consider for instance the "context" in which the assault took place, but the judge demurred, insisting the indictment applied only to Forbes, the individual (Hallowell & Meshbesher, 1977).

The public, too, is divided on legal individualism, if an opinion poll conducted shortly after Forbes' trial regarding accountability in the trial of Lieutenant Calley of My Lai Massacre notoriety is any indicator. As reported by Hallowell and Meshbesher (1977), 58% of the respondents in this survey disapproved of criminal sanctions being applied to an individual acting in a legitimate role and following what that individual believed to be "at least implicit orders" (p. 28). Are orders to perform acts of violence implicit in professional hockey? The question should be: How explicit are such orders?

As for legally raising, not to mention demonstrating, criminal liability on the part of the employer in sports violence disputes, Kuhlman (1975) suggests that although problems of "proof" are substantial (the burden of proof on the prosecution in a criminal trial is heavier than in a civil trial), the most promising route is probably via the statutes on conspiracy; that is, the prosecution should attempt to prove that the organization and the individual conspired to commit an assault. Owners, coaches and teammates—all members of the "system"—are thus potentially implicated; sociological reality becomes legal fact.

By the way of a footnote to *State* v. *Forbes*, this writer was engaged in 1980 by the Detroit law firm of Dykema, Gossett, Spencer, Goodnow and Trigg as a consultant and "expert witness" in a civil suit being brought by Boucha against the Boston Bruins and the National Hockey League. (After several only partly successful eye operations, Boucha's career had ground to a halt.) The charge was in effect "creating an unsafe work environment." The case was settled out of court for an undisclosed amount two days before the trial was to begin in Detroit.

Criminal Violence

This category consists of violence so serious and obviously outside the boundaries of what could be considered part of the game that it is handled from the outset by the law. Death is often involved, as in the 1973 Paul Smithers case which received worldwide publicity. Smithers, a 17-year-old hockey player, was convicted of manslaughter after killing an opposing player in a fight in a Toronto arena parking lot following a game (Runfola, 1974). Almost always such incidents, though closely tied to game events, take place prior to or after the contest itself. (One suspects that if Smither's attack had occurred during the game he would have received a 5-minute or match penalty, and the victim's death would have been dismissed as an "unfortunate accident.") On the extreme fringe of this category are assaults and homicides only incidentally taking place in a sports setting.

An extended, first-hand account of another hockey incident provides an illustration of a typical episode of criminal violence in sport, while at the same time conveying something about the social milieu which encourages such misbehavior. This assault took place in a Toronto arena after the final game of a Midget (16-year-olds) playoff series which had been marred by bad behavior in the stands and on the ice, including physical and verbal attacks on opposing players by the assailant in question. The victim was the coach of the winning team. He had been ejected from the game for making a rude gesture at the referee and was standing against the boards some distance from his team's bench when the assault took place. He also happened to be a student of mine at the university. Three days after the incident he came to my office seeking some advice, his face barely recognizable. I suggested he lay an assault charge, which he had not yet done, and immediately write in detail his version of what happened. He did both. What follows, with his permission, is verbatim, except for changed names, from his 6-page account (the offending player was later convicted of assault):

> At the final buzzer the parents applauded their sons' victory and the players of our team all left the bench to congratulate the goalie who was down at our end. Out of the corner of my eye I picked up Jones making a wide circle in our end and heading over directly towards me. My only thought was that he would skate over and continue his usual swearing and animal-like antics. I was wrong. He let his stick drag behind him and with the stick

in his left hand he took a full swing with it and made contact across my face. This, in my opinion, was the result of the total release of pent-up frustration on Jones' part, since his attempts at intimidation had not succeeded. He must have viewed me as a symbol of my team's success, and his failure.

The force of the blow was further increased by the heavy heel-end of the stick, which made contact across my nose, just below my eyes. I went partially down against the seat. Some parents came to my aid, while others, including a couple of impartial fans went on the ice after the boy, along with my players. Parents from both teams tangled as everyone seemed intent on getting to Jones. I was mostly concerned with the safety of my players and getting them into the dressing room. While I stood bleeding profusely from a widely gashed and multiple-fractured nose, I was approached by an impartial spectator, James Turner, who stated that he had seen the whole incident along with Al Sommers and that he was going to call the police. He stated that if charges were laid he would be a witness stating the whole story as he saw it as an unbiased observer. There is also at least one other impartial witness, along with almost all the parents and some friends of our players. A linesman saw the whole incident also, and the referee supervisor of the league told my assistant coach, who was coaching the team at the time, that it was the "most brutal thing he's ever seen."

After answering the questions of the police who arrived approximately 20-30 minutes after the incident, and telling my version of the incident, I was rushed to North York General Hospital where I was examined first by a nurse and then by the doctor in emergency at the time. He ordered x-rays, which showed a compound fracture of the nose. After stitching the cuts across my nose and under my eye, he showed his disgust and anger at such incidents by informing me that he hoped charges were laid and law suits following. Charges of assault causing bodily harm have now been laid. He really shook me up by telling me that I was actually a very lucky person, because if I had turned my head perhaps a half-inch either way, I might very likely have been killed by such a blow to the temples or forehead.

He informed me that the usual procedure for this type of fracture was to wait for 3-5 days for the swelling to go down and then have it set by a plastic surgeon. Later he suggested I come in that morning at 8:00 A.M. to see the head of plastic surgery, Dr. Charles Palmer, who must have thought that it was quite serious, in fact serious enough to set it right at that time. I have an appointment to see him next Tuesday, April 4th.

Ever since the incident, I have had little if any sleep, a constant headache, a case of bad nerves, constant shaking, mental strain, and depression has begun to set in due to my thoughts about upcoming exams and activities at school. I have been unable to eat and at this point in time feel like a physical wreck, and the thought of almost being killed in such an incident has loomed on my mind a great deal.

The fact that no apology has been offered by the player, parents or organization, let alone concern for my health, leaves me also with a bitter feeling for those involved or associated with this assault. I don't feel the boy is as much to blame as the coach who sanctioned and reinforced this type of behavior, the parents who didn't attempt to discourage him from playing this style of hockey, and the Wallbury organization which seems to condone this type of play throughout their organization. The fact that the boy's father was drunk at this incident only leaves me feeling more sorry for this boy and the environment he has been a product of.

Conclusion

What is called violence and what is not is no trivial matter. The extent to which a behavior is perceived as violence has a great deal to do with what people are willing to do about it. As philosopher Robert Audi (1974) puts it in his essay *Violence, Legal Sanctions, and the Law*: "Misnaming the disease can lead to the use of the wrong medicine or none at all" (p. 38). I think we are close to being able to say with some clarity what sports violence is. Perhaps soon we shall know with greater certainty what to do about it.

References

Audi, R. Violence, legal sanctions, and the law. In S. M. Stanage (Ed.), *Reason and violence*. Totowa, N. J.: Littlefield Adams, 1974.

Betts, J. R. *America's sporting heritage: 1850-1950.* Reading, Mass.: Addison-Wesley, 1974.

Davis, P. H. *Football: The American intercollegiate game.* New York: Charles Scribner's Sons, 1911.

Flakne, G. W., & Caplan, A. H. Sports violence and the prosecution. *Trial*, 1977, *13*, 33-35.

Grescoe, P. We asked you six questions. *Canadian Magazine*, January 1972, *29*, 2-4.

Hallowell, L., & Meshbesher, R. I. Sports violence and the criminal law. *Trial*, 1977, *13*, 27-32.

Hechter, W. Criminal law and violence in sports. *Criminal Law Quarterly*, 1977, *19*, 425-433.

Horrow, R. B. *Sports violence: The interaction between private law-making and the criminal law.* Arlington, Va: Carrollton Press, 1980.

Horrow, R. B. The legal perspective: Interaction between private lawmaking and the civil and criminal law. *Journal of Sport and Social Issues*, 1981, *5*, 9-18.

Kuhlman, W. Violence in professional sports. *Wisconsin Law Review*, 1975, *3*, 771-790.

Marshall, D. We're more violent than you think. *Macleans*, August 1970, 14-17.

Philo, H. M., & Stine, G. The liability path to safer helmets. *Trial*, 1977, *12*, 38-42.

Rovere, G. D., Gristina, A. G., & Nicastro, J. Medical problems of a professional hockey team: A three-season experience. *The Physician and Sports Medicine*, 1978, *6*, 59-63.

Runfola, R. T. He is a hockey player, 17, black and convicted of manslaughter. *New York Times*, October 17, 1974, 2-3.

Smith, M. D. Hockey violence. *Canadian Dimension,* 1979, *13*, 42-45. (a)

Smith, M. D. Towards an explanation of hockey violence. *Canadian Journal of Sociology,* 1979, *4*, 105-124. (b)

Stagg, A. A. *Touchdown!* New York: Longmans, Green and Company, 1927.

Tatum, J., & Kushner, B. *They call me assassin.* New York: Everest House, 1979.

Toronto Star, April 22, 1976; December 13, 1977; November 25, 1981.

Underwood, J. *The death of an American game.* Boston: Little Brown, 1979.

Chapter 5

Athletic Aggression: A Moral Concern

Brenda Jo Bredemeier

Athletic aggression: Is it character-building and valuable or, perhaps, destructive and repugnant? Sport is an arena of human interaction where aggression and violence are sometimes idolized, sometimes condemned, but most often legitimated and at least tolerated. In this chapter the phenomenon of athletic aggression will be examined from social-scientific and ethical perspectives which have been informed by the study of moral development.

The Ambiguity of Violence

The term "violence" has many meanings and this plurality of understandings has itself produced practical as well as theoretical difficulty.[1] Hannah Arendt (1969) states that

> our terminology does not distinguish among such key words as "power," "strength," "force," and, finally, "violence"—all of which refer to distinct, different phenomena and would hardly survive unless they did. . . . To use them as synonyms not only indicates a certain deafness to linguistic meanings, which would be serious enough, but it has also resulted in a kind of blindness to the realities they correspond to. (p. 7)

When the same word can mean both intentionally destructive acts and constructively assertive acts, it becomes easier for the former to be justified by appeal to the positive qualities of the latter.

A number of social scientists have contributed to this semantic confusion by adhering to a global definition of aggression, viewing it as any forceful action which has as its purpose the restructuring of power. Proponents of this perspective make a distinction between destructive aggressiveness, characterized by activities which are

---

[1] This critique does not extend to the relationship between the terms "violence" and "aggression." Although some theorists have made a distinction between violence, the physical injury of others, and aggression, the psychological harm of others (Goldstein, 1975), the two terms are used interchangeably in this chapter.

hurtful to others, and constructive aggressiveness, a virtue encompassing such qualities as self-assertion and self-affirmation, physical and social courage. It is from within this conceptual framework that athletic aggression is equated with such diverse success-oriented behaviors as assertiveness, competitiveness, and forcefulness. The determination of what constitutes constructive and destructive aggression is usually based upon criteria of legality and effect. If the aggressor's act is within the formal rules or informal norms of the contest, and if the recipient of the aggressive act does not sustain an injury beyond what would be considered "appropriate," then the aggressive act may be deemed constructive.

In contrast to this global understanding, other social scientists, including this writer, advocate the use of a more parsimonious description, defining aggression as the initiation of an overt act with the intent to bring psychological or physical harm to another. Further delineation of aggressive motives serves to differentiate two forms of aggression (Bredemeier, 1975). Reactive, or hostile, aggression is an emotional response employed for the sake of injury itself, and is considered to be a common consequence of the frustration inherent in competitive sport, particularly in contests where contact is legitimated. Berkowitz (1970) has labelled this form of aggression "angry aggression" because the aggressor is often perturbed with the target of the act.

A second form of aggression is instrumental or goal aggression and is described as the attempt to inflict pain or injury for some goal other than that of injury itself. In sport, an orientation toward personal success and team victory, magnified by commercialization effects, promotes the utilization of instrumentally aggressive tactics to provoke, intimidate, or "take out" opposing players. Both reactive and instrumental aggression involve the intent to injure, and both are acknowledged, especially in contact sports, to be in the "nature of the game."

Because the construct of athletic aggression contains both overt and covert components, it is difficult to distinguish between reactive and instrumental forms of aggressive acts, and to differentiate aggressive acts from other competitive acts. For example, without knowing the intent of the player, it would not be possible to label an exceptionally vicious football tackle as an act of reactive aggression, instrumental aggression, or assertion. Attempting to clarify the distinction between aggressive and assertive acts, Silva (1980) has characterized forceful, physical, goal-directed behavior as proactive assertion when there is no intent to harm, thus differentiating it from reactive and instrumental aggression. Despite efforts to clarify the linguistic and conceptual ambiguities associated with athletic aggression, the study of this phenomenon remains confounded by a lack of consensus about basic definitions. Consequently, the inclusion of a wide variety of behaviors in the category of aggressive acts calls into question the validity of aggression instrumentation and investigation. Unless social scientists reach consensus on a parsimonious operational definition of athletic aggression, "confusion will be the epitaph of this research area" (Silva, 1980, p. 200).

As Arendt (1969) has emphasized, the ambiguity which shrouds violence also tends to blur our understanding of its practical implications. Because sport practitioners and participants have not learned to perceive and name aggressive behavior accurately, violence has come to be justified as assertion, and assertion inappropriately interpreted as aggression. The terms aggression and violence have been misused and abused, an occurrence which has functioned to render their meaning indistinct from other competitive behaviors, confounding research efforts and camouflaging the moral dimension of what has come to represent conventional sport behavior. On another level, these linguistic ambiguities function to reflect and buttress the cultural valuing of violence as a legitimate means of self-assertion and self-affirmation.

The Valuing of Violence

The valuing of violence among athletes has many causes. These causes can be identified on societal, institutional, and personal levels. Writing in a report to the National Commission on the Causes and Prevention of Violence, historian Richard Maxwell Brown (1969) has presented a sobering commentary on American violence:

> The first and most obvious conclusion is that there has been a huge amount of it. We have resorted so often to violence that we have long since become a "trigger happy" people. . . . It is not merely that violence has been mixed with the negative features of our history such as criminal activity, lynch mobs, and family feuds. On the contrary, violence has formed a seamless web with some of the noblest and most constructive chapters of American history. . . . We must realize that violence has not been the action only of roughnecks and racists among us but has been the tactic of the most upright and respected of our people. Having gained this self-knowledge, the next problem becomes the ridding of violence, once and for all, from the real (but unacknowledged) American value system. (pp. 75-76).

Another historian, Peter Levine (1981), has linked the violence permeating American society with the violence interwoven in the socio-structural context of sport. He suggests that "there is a positive relationship between a society's cultural, social and geo-political framework, the place of organized sport in that setting, and its preference, toleration or abhorrence of sports prone to high levels of violence" (p. 26). To illustrate this contention, Levine has correlated America's increasingly aggressive and often violent foreign policy of the early 1900s with the promotion of sport as a means of preserving the "savage instinct" in Americans. He reasons that because the close of the western frontier had deprived Americans of their violent testing ground, sport came to be viewed as the means through which character, drive, and aggressiveness could be nurtured, thus insuring the development of those virtues supposedly required to maintain American democracy.

The valuing of violence in contemporary sport is also evidenced within the organization of the sport teams themselves. Coakley (1981) has elaborated sport-specific reasons for the advocacy of athletic aggression:

> The commercialization of sport has led to an emphasis on heroic values (including violence) for the purpose of generating and maintaining spectator interest. And violence has come to be used as an effective tactic in winning games and enhancing the commercial reputation and popularity of individual athletes.

Player violence is also rooted in the structure and organization of sport teams themselves. The represssive control systems characteristic of so many contact teams leads players to define violence as not only an expected part of their experience, but as something necessary to maintaining their identities and self-esteem as athletes. Violence becomes a means through which athletes cope with the social psychological deprivations they experience as team members.

The socialization experiences of athletes in many sports includes the learning of violent tactics. The approval of these tactics by significant others in the lives of young athletes serves to intensify the extent to which they incorporate violence into their own sport behavior. (p. 52)

While there may be many causes for a positive valuation of violence in sport, there has also been a growing concern over its occurrence. Perceived consequences of athletic aggression have caused many to call into question the ambivalent response to sport violence and the realities to which it corresponds. This phenomenon is depicted rather cynically in a Tank McNamera cartoon which portrays a sports-medicine physician suggesting that tackling and blocking with a football helmet should be banned. A hot-eyed coach responds, "It's a game for men, Ace, not for girls! Best way to stop a man is to hit him with that helmet. Second best, actually. Best way is with a .38, but they'd penalize you for sure. . ." In the next cartoon panel, the coach continues, "Sure football is a violent game, but putting on those pads and going out there knowing you're going to get hit builds men with the character this country needs." And in the last panel, he adds, "A little paralysis seems like a small price to pay for America's future" (cited in Underwood, 1979, p. 56).

The cartoonist has captured the paradoxical situation in which we now find ourselves. Athletic aggression has in fact been valued partly because it has been seen to reflect qualities perceived as desirable in our culture. But serious ramifications of athletic aggression, including both physical and psychological harm, have exposed those values as morally questionable.

The central focus of this chapter is the presentation of a theoretical and practical understanding of the meaning and value assigned to athletic aggression by individuals involved in sport. Athletic aggression will be conceptualized as a moral issue, and will be considered from within a cognitive developmental framework. Before trying to understand the moral aspects of athletic aggression, however, we need to gain a clearer theoretical perspective of the nature of morality and of athletic aggression.

The Psychological Nature of Morality

Though the psychological nature of morality is not yet well understood, there are three dominant theoretical perspectives that offer insight into moral development. In the first two approaches, psychoanalytic and social learning, moral development is conceived as a process of enculturation or socialization of the individual by significant others. This "moralization" incorporates the learning of socially acceptable behavior and the internalization of values attached to those behaviors. In the third approach, cognitive-developmental, it is maintained that moral development is not the internalization of values, but the progressive construction of judgments guided by autonomous moral principles.

Psychoanalytic Approach

The earliest theoretical perspective offering a comprehensive understanding of moral development was Freud's psychoanalytic theory. Freud posited that moral prohibitions of an individual's aggressive and sexual instincts function to maintain the social system. The superego was seen to control primitive and hedonistic impulses in response to internalized parental and societal values, and to operate as a more or less rigid censor of pleasure-seeking instincts (the id) and personal thoughts and decisions (the ego). The regulation of internalized standards was understood as occurring through the internalized sanction of guilt, defined as aggressive instinctual energies directed toward the self.

According to Freud (1933), the critical event in moral development is the child's resolution of the oedipal complex. In this resolution, she or he identifies with the same-sex parent, internalizing the parent's superego prohibitions and ideals. Thus the child's resolution of the oedipal complex promotes conformity to support family harmony and fulfill societal expectations.

Social Learning Approach

More recently, social learning theory has offered an alternative view of the development of moral behavior. Like psychoanalytic theorists, social learning theorists view morality as equivalent to social norms and expectations; moral values are seen to be directly derived through identification with a socializing agent or representative of the social environment, and thus morality is defined as culturally relative convention. The theories diverge, however, in their view of the processes by which the internalization of social norms occurs. While psychoanalytic theory highlights internal dynamic processes tied to id, ego, and superego, social learning theorists point to the role of socializing agents and situations. Such mechanisms as operant conditioning (Aronfreed, 1968), reinforcement (Mischel & Moore, 1973), and modeling (Bandura, 1969) are seen as determinative. But how are social or personal norms to be evaluated? This problem is particularly acute for sport psychologists because the social norms of sports morality are frequently unclear and often permit physical and psychological harm.

Cognitive-Developmental Approach

The most recent approach to the understanding of moral development is the cognitive-developmental perspective. In contrast to the first two approaches, cognitive-developmentalists do not see moral development as equivalent to conformity to societal standards. In their view, the developing child is not shaped by the group, but rather, through interactions with others, forms conceptions about the social environment. Moral development incorporates a gradual and continual construction of moral meaning, and morality is seen as equivalent to the principles which are used to make judgments about actions which impact on human welfare.

The cognitive-developmental approach makes an important distinction between the structure of moral reasoning and the content of moral thought. To illustrate, let us imagine an investigator asking an athlete whether or not she values nonviolence, and if so, why. The answer would reflect the specific contents of her belief system about morality. Now let us suppose that the investigator tells a sport story in which nonviolence comes into conflict with another value, that of achievement. The interviewer then asks the athlete to choose between the potentially competing values and to explain her reasoning. With additional probing, the interviewer will uncover a patterned way of ordering and coordinating moral values. Cognitive-developmentalists have found that there is striking regularity in the underlying structures of moral reasoning which evolve as an individual develops.

The underlying structure which gives order to the content of moral thought is called a stage. While particular contents of moral thought may vary considerably from one context to another, the stage of reasoning is quite stable. Cognitive-developmentalists have posited that moral reasoning evolves through an invariant sequence of stages. Thus, learning not only increases quantitatively through learning more and more pieces of information, but also undergoes qualitative transformations in the way that the information is internally organized. Each higher stage represents a more complex and adequate organization of information.

Jean Piaget (1932/1965) was the first to study moral development from a cognitive-developmental perspective. *The Moral Judgment of the Child* was published in 1932 and featured Piaget's attempts to delineate stages of moral reasoning in children. Just as he observed stage development in children's understanding of natural events, so too did he find that their conception of morality underwent structural transformations. By observing children as they played marbles and talking with them about their understanding of the rules, Piaget came to view the development of a child's moral orientation as moving from an attitude of unilateral respect for adult authority to relationships of mutual respect among equals. These two broad stages in children's moral development were identified as the heteronomous stage and the autonomous stage. At the heteronomous stage, children were constrained by non-mutual, unilateral respect for adult authority and expressed rigid beliefs that game rules are unalterable and must be followed. At the autonomous stage, an orientation toward mutual respect and cooperation with peers had superseded conformity to adult constraints, and rules were viewed as flexible products of mutual agreement, serving to facilitate cooperative interaction in play.

Tracing the development of moral understanding in the microcosm of children's play, Piaget concluded that moral judgment progresses from the concept of fairness as equal retribution (an eye for an eye) in the heteronomous stage, toward the understanding of distributive justice as democratic fairness in the autonomous stage. He found that around the ages of 11 and 12, the cognitive and affective aspects of morality merge in a fusion of justice and love as unilateral respect is superseded by mutual respect which is finally mediated by generosity. Thus, in Piaget's view, moral judgment becomes contextually relative, enabling the child to take into account the reality of individual and situational differences.

In the late 1950s Lawrence Kohlberg modified and extended Piaget's work; through this and subsequent studies, he posited that moral development follows an invariant six-stage sequence. The six stages are organized into three levels: preconventional, conventional, and postconventional levels. The levels reflect egocentric, societal, and universal, or principled, perspectives, respectively. For sport illustrations of Kohlberg's stages see Table 5-1.

Moral growth, for Kohlberg, takes place as a result of "cognitive disequilibrium." He proposes that when a moral conflict situation arises, we attempt to resolve it using our present stage of reasoning. Sometimes, because the stage does not represent a thoroughly consistent organization, conflicting answers are possible. As we gain in ability imaginatively to take the role of others, the inadequacy of our own reasoning becomes apparent and slowly new principles are formulated to guide moral reasoning at the next level.

Justice is the key to morality according to Kohlberg, and each subsequent stage represent a more adequate understanding of the way justice can resolve moral conflicts. At the final stage, reached by only a few, the principle of justice is the ultimate arbitrator in all moral conflicts. When faced with a moral conflict, a person reasoning at Stage 6 engages in "ideal role-taking," imaginatively weighing everyone's moral claims as if behind a "veil of ignorance" (Rawls, 1971) which hides all personal attributes and even awareness of one's own identity. Thus the principle of justice represents an abstract, deductive, and logically consistent way of structuring moral values.

Kohlberg's theory of formal moral judgment, which represents the process of deducing logical moral solutions from imperative rules, may be contrasted with Haan's (Haan, Bellah, Rabinow, & Sullivan, 1983) interactional formulation. In Haan's view, cognitive-developmentalists such as Kohlberg place too much emphasis on abstract reasoning in their theoretical and empirical understanding of morality, while social-learning and psychoanalytic theorists overemphasize the importance of society. In her interactional theory, Haan proposes that morality is best understood by analyzing individuals' reasoning within specific social contexts. She contends that every individual is a moral actor, or agent, who continually enters dialogues of major or minor import to negotiate moral claims and achieve or reestablish moral balance with others. Thus, Haan's theory of interaction posits that moral solutions are achieved through dialogues among moral actor-agents who personalize and particularize their evaluations of moral information as they strive for balanced agreements.

Haan et al.'s (1983) theoretical conceptualizations and empirical findings have implications for moral formulations that are both unusual and intriguing:

1. Moral decisions are created and jointly achieved in actual of imagined dialogues instead of being drawn by single persons from principles or learned generalizations.
2. The reasoning involved is practical, not formally logical.
3. General self-interest is always a legitimate claim but a particular self-interest may or may not be legitimized in the dialogue and its resolution.
4. Moral decisions are not always expected to be perfect, absolute solutions.
5. Children are expected to engage in moral dialogues at a very early age; they are not seen as morally primitive.

Table 5-1. Kohlberg's Moral Stages with Sports Illustrations[a]

Stage 1:	*The punishment-and-obedience orientation.* The physical consequences of action determine its goodness or badness, regardless of the human meaning or value of these consequences.
Illustration:	When asked about whether or not a pitcher should use an illegal pitch, one player reasons "no, it's wrong; it can get the pitcher expelled from the game."
Stage 2:	*The instrumental-relativist orientation.* Right action consists of that which instrumentally satisfies one's own needs and occasionally the needs of others.
Illustration:	Two runners make a deal to each false-start twice in an attempt to tire out a third competitor.
Stage 3:	*The interpersonal concordance or "good boy-nice girl" orientation.* Good behavior is that which pleases or helps others and is approved by them.
Illustration:	In the third quarter, when his team is far ahead, a football coach removes his best players since that is appropriate sportsperson-like behavior.
Stage 4:	*The "law-and-order" orientation.* Right behavior consists of doing one's duty, showing respect for fixed rules and authority, and maintaining the given social order for its own sake.
Illustration:	A boxer refuses to throw any "kidney punches," even though he is sure he could get away with it, because one ought to fight by the rules.
Stage 5:	*The social-contact, legalistic orientation.* Right action, aside from what is constitutionally and democratically agreed upon, is a matter of personal "values" and "opinion."
Illustration:	When it becomes apparent that certain "legal" drugs are being used to improve athletic performance even though the long-range effects of the drugs are unknown, a group of athletes join to seek a change in the rules so that their use will be forbidden. The athletes reason that drug use violates the spirit of the game and is not in keeping with their rights as individuals.
Stage 6:	*The universal-ethical-principle orientation.* Right is defined by the decision of conscience in accord with self-chosen ethical principles appealing to logical comprehensiveness, universality, and consistency.
Illustration:	In a very close gymnastics meet, the leading gymnast on the losing team decides he is going to attempt a routine he has been working on but has not yet done without safety apparatus. When the judge learns of the gymnast's intention, he refuses to allow the performance, reasoning that all persons have an unforfeitable right to life and safety and that forfeiting basic human rights cannot be justified by an appeal to lesser goods associated with athletic victory.

[a]Moral level and stage typing is a difficult and involved process. While these illustrations are typical of the level indicated, no claim is made that the information provided is adequate for definitive moral scoring.

6. Morality is therefore always self-chosen even early in life; moral skill gradually develops but not by stages.
7. All aspects of people's functioning, including their moral thought, emotions and motivations, are brought into play during the dialogue and influence their eventual decisions.
8. Levels of moral actions can be expected to vary depending on the demands and stresses of the immediate social context.

The theory of interactional morality focuses upon the interaction of cognitive reasoning and social environment, and seems to be an especially appropriate framework for examining the moral aspects of intentions to do harm within a sport context. For a brief description of Haan's levels and sport illustrations of them, see Table 5-2.

The Psychological Nature of Aggression

Early psychological theories sought to explain aggressive behavior principally in terms of instinctual force. Although Freud (1933) viewed aggression as inevitable, he proposed that extreme interpersonal aggressiveness could be curtailed by the development of emotional ties between people and by the provision of opportunities for discharging pent-up Thanatos. In contrast, drive theorists subscribe to an energy model of aggression in which drives rather than instincts are the internal impellers of action. Dollard, Doob, Miller, Mowrer, and Sears (1939) reasoned that frustration, interference with goal-directed activity, inevitably induces an aggressive drive which motivates behavior designed to injure the person against whom it is directed. In a more recent version of drive theory, Feshbach (1972) has argued that the ultimate goal of an individual's drive to aggress is not the infliction of injury on others, but the restoration of the aggressor's self-esteem and sense of power. Other social scientists and philosophers have underscored the interrelationships of power/powerlessness and violence. May (1972) proposes that violence arises "not out of superfluity of power but out of powerlessness" (p. 23), and Arendt (1969) affirms that "violence is the expression of impotence" (p. 32).

Though instinctual and drive theorists diverge in their conceptions of aggressive motivational forces as innately supplied or externally stimulated, the researchers' understandings promote a similar valuing of sport experience. Since frustration is omnipresent in our society, sport may be seen by theorists of both approaches as a safety valve, an opportunity to reduce aggressive tendencies by releasing aggressive energy in a socially desirable way.

Conversely, social learning theorists argue that violent sport behavior, rather than purging sport participants' desire for aggressive behavior or exhausting their capacity for it, will serve to increase tendencies for future athletic aggression. Contemporary learning theorists regard aggressiveness as a behavior which is acquired and expressed because of social learning processes. Proponents of this perspective

Table 5-2. Haan's Moral Levels with Sports Illustrations[a]

Level 1:	At this level there is no real view of moral interchange between people. The moral balance is seen as an exchange of power: the person of greater power thwarts the person of lesser power. All are entitled to what they can get.
Illustration:	An athlete is ordered to the showers by an angry umpire.
Level 2:	Balances at this level are established by the self-making trade-offs to get what is desired. It is assumed that the self and others want similar things and that others, like the self, are after their own benefit.
Illustration:	A football lineman intentionally injures another player because "that's just the way the game is played."
Level 3:	The person now thinks of herself or himself as part of a human collectivity. This appreciation for social existence leads to the assumption that everyone recognizes the need for good faith and moral responsibility. The person naively assumes others will behave morally and so tries to create moral balances that consist of harmonious exchanges of good.
Illustration:	A shot-putter fails to call the official's attention to a shot that has not been weighed-in because she assumes that no one would try to cheat.
Level 4:	The naive assumptions of Level 3 inevitably result in disappointment and harm to the self. The person reasoning at Level 4 structures the moral balance through attempts to regulate it with external, impartial formulations that assign everyone the same rights or duties. It is thought that the "common interest" of all is best secured by submitting to external regulation, or systematized structured exchange.
Illustration:	A new curfew rule is strictly enforced—no exceptions—because it is in the best interest of the whole team that everyone get a good night's sleep.
Level 5:	At the final level, the individuality of persons and the complexity of social life are given full consideration. The external regulation the "common interest" is abandoned in favor of situationally specific balances which optimize the potential of all parties in a manner consistent with the particular context. All interests are taken into account and coordinated in a way that is mindful of the participants' future lives together.
Illustration:	A coach plans a heavy and strenuous workout for her team in preparation for an important game, but after a team discussion, excuses one of her star players from part of the practice because the player needs to study for a final exam.

[a]Moral level and stage typing is a difficult and involved process. While these illustrations are typical of the level indicated, no claim is made that the information provided is adequate for definitive moral scoring.

contend that experiences with significant others in specified opportunity sets determine the aggressiveness of sports participants.

Social learning theory has significantly enhanced our understanding of interpersonal and situational factors which mediate the learning and expression of athletic aggression; yet it has not provided an adequate interpretation of athletic aggression. (My transition to a cognitive-developmental approach has been a relatively recent one. The change is dramatic, but also humorous, for my critiques of social learning theory, the perspective I previously embraced, are directed as much at my own earlier work as at that of my colleagues.) The weaknesses inherent in the social learning approach are consequences both of theoretical and empirical limitations.

Though a small number of social learning researchers empirically acknowledge specified cognitions involved in the interpersonal act of aggression (Berkowitz, 1970, 1972; Goldstein, 1975; Singer, 1970/1971), most disregard relevant personal attributes which cannot be precisely operationalized. Thus, the methodology of learning theorists has impinged on their elucidation of athletic aggression. Because researchers are restricted to the assessment of overt behaviors arbitrarily defined as aggressive, the investigation of sport participants' reasoning about their own behavior has been neglected. In the absence of theoretical and empirical analyses of the personal meaning sport participants attach to their aggressive behavior, it is difficult to gain an adequate scientific understanding of a class of overt acts motivated by the *intent* to injure.

The constraints of the social learning perspective are also made manifest in the consideration of aggression as a moral issue. Rather than focusing on reason in their study of morality and aggression, learning theorists emphasize the internalization of societal and group norms. Thus morality is seen as socialized behavior that is congruent with conventional social mandates, and athletic aggression is judged either legitimate or illegitimate (Silva, 1980; Smith, 1981), a decision that is contingent upon such visible criteria as rule prohibitions and resultant injury. For social learning theorists the moral aspects of athletic aggression are embodied in societal norms, while cognitive-developmentalists focus on the moral principles involved in the aggressors' construction of meaning.

To study sport participants' reasoning about the moral conflict and choice associated with athletic aggression is to provide a complement to our present understanding of sport violence. Unfortunately there is an amazing deficiency in cognitive-developmental research in the general area of athletic aggression, as well as in the specific study of sport violence as a moral issue. The work of Gilligan probably best reflects the cognitive-developmental integration of morality and aggression, and pertinent aspects of her model will be applied to our focus on athletic aggression.

Gilligan (1982a), a former student of Kohlberg's, has developed an alternative approach to the construction and resolution of moral problems, giving expression to a "feminine voice" of experience in cognitive-developmental theory. She argues that while for men morality may be defined as reasoning in accordance with the principle of justice, women's moral reasoning is guided by the principle of nonviolence. Gilligan, critical of theoretical perspectives which have not given adequate

expression to the concerns and experiences of women,[2] contends that women tend
to construct social reality differently than men. Her research demonstrates that
women usually define themselves in a context of human relationships, struggling to
balance their responsibilities to others with their commitment to themselves;
women see morality as a matter of interpersonal care guided by the principle of
nonviolence. Men most often define themselves as separate from others, attempting
to achieve autonomy and independence; they see morality as a matter of impersonal
justice.

Extending her research on gender differences in the imaging of relationship, Gilligan (1982a, 1982b) has found that the different ways women and men experience
connection and separation impact on their perception of danger, a potential antecedent of aggression. She conceptualizes aggression as a response to the perceived
danger of powerlessness or vulnerability, and suggests that women and men perceive
danger in different social situations and construe danger in different ways. McClelland (1975), drawing conclusions from his research on power, makes a similar point.
He reports that while men associate powerful activity with assertion and aggression,
women equate power with giving and caring. Women see danger in impersonal
achievement situations, and associate it with the aloneness that can arise out of competitive success. Men perceive danger in intimacy when they consider the accompanying potential for betrayal, loss of freedom, or rejection. Thus women see danger
in separation and men in connection. Women's activities of care have been interpreted by Gilligan as activities that help to make the social world safe because they
contribute to the prevention of aggression. Rather than seeking rules to *limit* its
extension, women try to *prevent* aggression and avoid isolation; for them, aggression is the sign of a severance of connection and communication (May, 1972), a
failure of relationship. In contrast, aggression is viewed by men as a prevalent
response to the dangers of interpersonal relations. In the words of Gilligan (1982a),

> rule bound competitive achievement situations, which for women threaten
> the web of connection, for men provide a mode of connection that estab-
> lishes clear boundaries and limits aggression, and thus appears comparative-
> ly safe. (p. 44)

Gilligan's (1977) understanding of moral development has evolved out of her
study of women contemplating the real-life moral decision of whether or not to
have an abortion. An analysis of the women's response to structured interview questions regarding the pregnancy decision functioned to delineate a developmental
sequence that parallels Kohlberg's three levels of morality: from an egocentric

---

[2] Like Haan (1977b), Gilligan has examined the limitations of Kohlberg's stage
theory of moral development, and has challenged his assertion that the abstract and
deductive principle of justice is the sole determinant of principled moral reasoning.
However, while Gilligan concurs with Kohlberg's conception of moral reasoning as
a deductive process (though she believes that, for women, moral judgments are
guided by the principle of nonviolence), Haan contends that moral formulations are
inductively created through moral dialogue. Both Gilligan's (1982a) and Haan's
(1977b) models of moral development are free of the gender-bias charges associated
with Kohlberg's theoretical approach.

Table 5-3. Gilligan's Moral Levels with Sports Illustrations[a]

Level 1:	*Self-orientation.* At the first level, the individual's moral concern is focused primarily on the needs and desires of the self. Survival and self-protection are dominant themes.
Illustration:	A basketball coach tells a recruiter from a competing institution that she is not interested in a particular athlete when in reality she has been recruiting her heavily. The coach feels justified in the deception because her job security depends upon coaching success.
Transition:	*From selfishness to responsibility.* During the transition from the first to second level, selfishness versus responsibility becomes a focal problem. The issue is one of attachment or connection to others. The person's understanding of self-interest broadens in a way that allows for an integration of responsibility and care.
Illustration:	In a one-sided basketball contest the high-scoring center begins to pass frequently to her less-experienced forward to give her an opportunity to gain experience and recognition. She does this because she feels she's been selfish in shooting so frequently.
Level 2:	*Goodness as self-sacrifice.* Whereas at the first level morality is seen as a matter of sanction imposed by a society in which one is more subject than citizen, at the second level moral judgment comes to rely on shared norms and expectations. Here the conventional feminine voice emerges with great clarity, defining the self and proclaiming one's worth on the basis of the ability to care for and protect others. The strength of this position lies in its capability for caring; its limitation is the restriction it imposes on direct expression.
Illustration:	In a close softball game an injured player risks more serious injury by returning to the game when the coach asks her to go to bat. The player does not want to let down the other players or the coach.
Transition:	*From goodness to truth.* The second transition begins with the reconsideration of the relationship between self and other, as the woman starts to scrutinize the logic of self-sacrifice in the service of a morality of care. The issue of selfishness reappears; the person wonders whether responsibility should include care of the self. To make the transition to the post-conventional level, the individual must carefully distinguish between personal needs and views from those of others. The criterion for judgment thus shifts from "goodness" to "truth" as the morality of action comes to be assessed not on the basis of its appearance in the eyes of others, but in terms of the realities of its intention and consequence.
Illustration:	A scholarship athlete decides to stop participating in extra practices for gymnastic competition even though it has been paying off in improved performance. She has decided that her participation in gymnastics has largely been to win approval from others and she would prefer to use the time to improve her grades.

Table 5-3. (*Continued*)

Level 3:	*The morality of nonviolence.* By elevating nonviolence—the injunction against hurting—to a principle governing all moral judgment and action, one is able to assert a moral equality between self and other. Care then becomes a universal obligation and the basis for a positive assertion of responsibility.
Illustration:	In a water polo match, a swimmer refuses orders to deliberately aim her goal shot at the goalie's head. She reasons that all people are entitled to a life free from deliberate harm and that she is entitled to play free from the fear of possible retaliation.

[a]Moral level and stage typing is a difficult and involved process. While these illustrations are typical of the level indicated, no claim is made that the information provided is adequate for definitive moral scoring.

through a societal to a principled orientation. But while the structural progression was similar, Gilligan discovered that her female subjects understood moral dilemmas differently from male subjects tested by Kohlberg, and that female subjects employed the principle of nonviolence rather than justice to guide their postconventional reasoning. (For a brief explanation of the levels and transitions in Gilligan's moral development model and sports illustrations of them, see Table 5-3.) Through more recent research, Gilligan (1982a,b) has discovered that, at midlife, some men suddenly become aware of the value of intimacy, relationships, and caring. Thus, the interaction of experience and thought in times of crisis and change can transform gender-related ways of understanding social reality. Gilligan concludes that both women and men are provided optimal stimulus for moral growth in situations which demand coordination of autonomy and interdependence, and of the need to care for self and for others.

Gilligan's cognitive-developmental approach to moral development can lend new insight to the interpretation of sport participants' perceptions and expressions of aggressive behavior. The meaning that women and men attach to athletic aggression is derived from their construction of social reality; such variables as gender and length and type of sport involvement may mediate participants' understandings of sport violence in ways not discernible from a social learning perspective. As an example, athletic aggression may be considered illegitimate sport behavior by a female field hockey player because (a) it's dangerous and she might get hurt (Gilligan's Level 1), (b) game rules and player norms make it clear that intentional injury is behavior outside the spirit of the game (Gilligan's Level 2), or (c) as a player she has the right and the obligation to protect herself and others from harm whenever possible (Gilligan's Level 3).

Athletic aggression has always been a feature of some forms of competitive sport. Many would argue that athletic aggression is not and cannot be a moral issue because it is behavior that occurs within the sport realm, a world considered to be separate from the "real" world, a world regulated by explicit and implicit norms of convention. The morality of this world within a world is represented by such conventions as context rules, coaches' judgments, and good sportspersonship. Sports conventions of morality and aggression are often not in conflict with each other;

they are conventions about which participants are encouraged to conform rather than reason. However, just as sportspersonship can encompass more than conventional behaviors such as shaking an opponent's hand or not talking while another golfer is putting, athletic aggression has meaning that incorporates both moral and social-conventional components.

Athletic Aggression as a Social-Conventional Issue

In this section, selected literature which focuses upon a cognitive developmental approach to social convention will be related to athletic aggression. To frame the issue, the work of Turiel, a psychologist who has theoretically and empirically differentiated between moral and social-conventional conceptual domains, will be applied to conceptions of sport behavior in general and athletic aggression in particular.

Morality and Social Convention: Distinct Conceptual Domains

If morality is conceived as a judgmental process, it must be differentiated from other forms of nonmoral judgment, such as social-conventional or personal discriminations.[3] The first two domains, however, are most relevant to the focus of this chapter. Turiel (1977, 1980) has argued most effectively that scientists investigating moral development should distinguish morality from the conventions of social systems. His research demonstrates that individuals construct moral judgments out of experiences associated with the rights or well-being of others. In contrast, conceptions of social conventions are derived through experiences in which the propriety for behavior is determined by implicit and/or explicit norms in specific societal contexts. Social conventions are defined as behavioral uniformities which coordinate the actions of individuals participating in a social system. Turiel's

---

[3] In contrast to the first two domains, the personal domain takes into account the individual's conceptions of personal issues. The personal domain is defined by the set of social actions whose import and effects are perceived to be primarily upon the actor rather than other individuals or the social structure. The issue of "right or wrong" in the personal domain is represented by the circumscribed class of actions involving preference, rather than obligation or custom. Actions within the sports realm which might be viewed as personal matters include the fitness level of one's body, an unorthodox putting technique in golf, one's choice of involvement in a particular sport, and the length of one's hair. In a recent study Nucci (1981) found that subjects ranging in age from 7 to 19 ranked rules pertaining to moral issue as more important than rules regulating social convention which, in turn, were more important than norms common in the personal domain. Subjects at all ages indicated that personal acts should not be governed by a societal rule or law, rejecting such rules as inordinate or absurd. In addition, the oldest subjects labeled the rules unjust. Conversely, moral rules were viewed as legitimate across all tested situations (including athletics), and violations of social convention were viewed to be wrong only if governing rules were in effect.

thesis, then, is that morality and social convention constitute two distinct conceptual domains which develop independently of each other, evolving through different aspects of the individual's social interactions.

The differentiation between moral and social-conventional domain has seldom been made by investigators of social development. It has been assumed that convention and morality are part of one domain and do not develop independently of each other. A failure to distinguish between the two domains is evident in each of the predominant theoretical approaches to moral development. Generally, those theorists who conceive of moral development as an internalization process (the psychoanalytic and social learning perspectives) view social behaviors and values as the incorporation of externally determined and imposed content, making no distinction between moral and conventional behaviors. Thus, the two domains—moral and conventional—are treated as one category. Theorists who maintain that moral development is not the enculturation of values, but rather the construction of judgments (the cognitive-developmental perspective), presume that social convention is a subclass of morality. Turiel argues that individuals develop the capability to reason about conventional issues in a manner that is distinct from, yet similar to, their reasoning about moral issues. His research demonstrates that children form concepts of social organization which structure their thinking about social-conventional issues, and that the development of these concepts follows an age-related sequence of seven levels (see Table 5-4). Each of Turiel's levels reflects (a) a change in the conceptualization of social systems, and (b) a change in the understanding of the connections between convention and social structure. Thus, a person's relation to nonmoral aspects of social organization is not merely one of conformity, but also entails the conceptualization of conventions.

Concepts of social convention are structured by underlying concepts of social organization; concepts of morality are structured by underlying concepts of justice. Thus, social convention forms part of the individual's descriptive understandings of systems of social interaction and is thereby differentiated from moral prescriptions. Social-conventional acts in themselves do not have an intrinsically prescriptive basis independent from the coordination of social interactions or from the symbols of social organization. As Turiel explains, "social-conventional acts are part of social order, but they do not prescribe behaviors related to the welfare of others, protection of rights, or avoidance of physical or psychological harm to others" (1977, p. 3). In other words, moral issues, in contrast to social-conventional issues, are neither arbitrary nor relative to social context.

This statement, in conjunction with empirically derived support for the contention that different types of social events may be conceptualized in different ways, provides a context for the application of Turiel's work to the scientific and practical consideration of athletic aggression. Turiel's work demonstrates that different types of social experiences produce qualitatively different individual-environment interactions, resulting in the development and utilization of distinct conceptual frameworks. This research has significant methodological implications for the study of morality in sport: the variables theorized to constitute moral judgment or behavior must represent the conceptual domain being investigated. As an example, consider the intentional basketball foul, an act which would probably not draw reasoning

Table 5-4. Turiel's Social Conventional Stages (Turiel, 1977)

Stage 1: *Convention as descriptive of social uniformity*. Convention viewed as descriptive of uniformities in behavior. Convention is not conceived as part of structure or function of social interaction. Conventional uniformities are descriptive of what is assumed to exist. Convention maintained to avoid violation of empirical uniformities.

Stage 2. *Negation of convention as descriptive social uniformity*. Empirical uniformity not a sufficient basis for maintaining conventions. Conventional acts regarded as arbitrary. Convention is not conceived as part of structure or function of social interaction.

Stage 3: *Convention as affirmation of rule system; early concrete conception of social system*. Convention seen as arbitrary and changeable. Adherence to convention based on concrete rules and authoritative expectations. Conception of conventional acts not coordinated with conception of rule.

Stage 4: *Negation of convention as part of rule system*. Convention now seen as arbitrary and changeable regardless of rule. Evaluation of rule pertaining to conventional act is coordinated with evaluation of the act. Conventions are "nothing but" social expectations.

Stage 5: *Convention as mediated by social system*. The emergence of systematic concepts of social structure. Convention as normative regulation in system with uniformity, fixed roles, and static hierarchical organization.

Stage 6: *Negation of convention as societal standards*. Convention regarded as codified societal standards. Uniformity in conventions is not considered to serve the function of maintaining social system. Conventions are "nothing but" societal standards that exist through habitual use.

Stage 7: *Convention as coordination of social interactions*. Conventions as uniformities that are functional in coordinating social interactions. Shared knowledge, in the form of conventions, among members of social groups facilitate interaction and operation of the system.

---

from the player's moral domain unless it were motivated by the intent to injure, a motive classified in the moral domain because it has an intrinsic effect upon the rights and well-being of others. Consequently, a basketball strategy incorporating assertive intentional fouls would be considered social-conventional. A violation of social convention becomes a moral issue if the formal or informal norms of the specific sport event are violated in a way that gives an advantage to the actor or the actor's team (i.e., cheating on the weigh-in before a wrestling match).

Turiel has emphasized that, in contrast to the contextual nature of the social convention domain, inclusion of acts in the moral domain is consistent across all situations, even in the absence of explicit moral norms or when the governing rules encourage immoral events. In contrast, it is commonly argued—legally, empirically, and practically—that athletic aggression is a social-conventional act. In a legal case involving an ice hockey swinging dual which almost resulted in the death of one of the combatants, a judge conceded that the game "can't be played without what morally are called assaults" (*New York Times*, September 4, 1970, p. 31). Lawyers (Horrow, 1980) and social scientists (Smith, 1981) delineate legitimate and illegitimate acts of violence, contending that athletes who choose to compete automatically "consent" to the inevitability of bodily contact, the probability of minor bodily injury, and the possibility of serious injury. In response to the expression of concern over the professional football injury epidemic caused by ruthless aggressive play, National Football League Commissioner Pete Rozelle said that the NFL "didn't feel there was anything that could be done without changing the basic character of the game" (Underwood, 1979, p. 50). Randy Cross, San Francisco Forty Niner offensive guard, remarked to a *San Francisco Chronicle* (August 20, 1982, p. 65) interviewer, "to do what I do, you've got to be nasty; the football field is the wrong place to think about ethics." The writer, Lowell Cohn, goes on to assure readers that Cross, "away from the gridiron, is the most likeable of men."

How can athletic aggression be conceived as a nonmoral, social-conventional issue if, according to Turiel, moral issues are not relative to social contexts? The classification of specific acts as personal, social-conventional, or moral is somewhat variable, acknowledge Turiel (1980) and Nucci (1981), partly because each group establishes what is a matter of convention. Within the institution of sport and the social organization of a given team, rules for personal and moral conduct are often confused with rules pertaining to social convention. This ambiguity shrouds the moral aspects of violence, creating a guise of social convention that is seen to legitimate many aggressive acts merely because they occur within the sport realm. Jean Fugett, a professional football player, explains that "on the street a rational person wouldn't conduct himself this way. He might just walk away and most people would consider him the better man for it. But in football you're forced into it. It's unfortunate, but its the nature of the game" (Underwood, 1979, p. 52).

A common understanding in most combative and contact sports is that aggression, an intrinsically moral issue, is actually an issue of social convention because it is inseparable from the explicit and implicit norms of the game. Participants learn to accommodate to the values of the sport subculture and to shield themselves from moral evaluation. They are encouraged to conform to rather than to reason about the norms of this special subculture which provides an escape from the normal constraints of human social intercourse.

The sport realm is an environment created by social convention; its boundaries are framed by contest rules and its occurrences are guided by systematized structural exchanges. The conventions of sport seem even more arbitrary than the conventions of other social institutions because they are, for the most part, sport-specific and do not permeate other aspects of everyday life. Arbitrary sport conventions serve to make the separateness and relativity of sport so visible that, ironically, it is difficult to appeal to the morality of universal human rights when evaluating the appropriateness of behavior. In contrast to morality, which is oriented toward interpersonal interaction, social convention is geared toward the regulation of people as objects in a social system. Thus, the social-conventional fiber of the sport structure encourages an understanding of people as objects and of people's actions as conventional.

Aggression leading to physical and/or psychological injury is a potential occurrence not only in contact sport, but in every sports structure including two or more participants. It is an act that contains both moral and social-conventional components. Yet, it can be congruent with the highest levels of conventional reasoning and incongruent with the highest levels of moral reasoning. To discuss how and why some people conceptualize sports violence as a moral issue while others conceive of it as a case where social convention supersedes morality, we must identify the processes through which the moral and conventional conceptual domains are coordinated and/or confused with each other.[4]

Although Turiel (1977) and others (e.g., Nucci, 1981) recognize the need to investigate processes for the perception/selection of conceptual domains, they are presently committed to developing a more complete understanding of the domains themselves. Concern about the readiness with which athletic aggression is relegated to the social-convention domain, however, has moved this author to begin a theoretical and empirical investigation of the conflict and synchrony of moral and conventional domains in sport and in everyday life.

Individuals construct moral judgments out of their experiences with the realm of social actions having an intrinsic effect upon the rights and well-being of others. Conversely, conceptions of social convention are constructed out of experiences with actions whose propriety is defined by the social context. Athletic aggression may be conceptualized within both realms, for the domains of moral concern and social convention are not mutually exclusive. The understanding of athletic aggression, then, is determined by the form of knowing employed by the individual as she or he interprets social knowledge in a sports context.

Coordination of Moral and Social-Conventional Domains

Haan (1977b) describes ego processes as "ceaseless acts of people assimilating new information about themselves and their environments and accommodating to these assimilations by constructing actions that attain and re-attain an unremitting series of dynamic equilibriums" (p. 33). In different words, ego processes can coordinate various forms of knowing; they coordinate, among others, moral and social conventional domains. Haan's model of ego processes includes coping, defending, and fragmenting functions, and though it is beyond the scope of this discussion to elaborate upon these functions, this author proposes that defensive ego processes may provide one explanation for the conceptualization of athletic aggression as conventional rather than moral behavior.

As people mature, they establish an hierarchy of ego processes, a phenomenon commonly referred to as a "choice of defense." This hierarchy assures that a particular ego process is more readily utilized than another, even when both processes are equally plausible choices. Haan has noted that different situations tend to "pull" different functions, and that when certain life conditions are consistently experienced, preference in ego function may become endemic. It may be that sport experiences encourage the preferential use of particular defensive ego processes which cause conventional reasoning to supersede moral reasoning about athletic aggression.

Defensive ego functions may be elicited from either or both of the two elements of sport identified by Stone (1955) as "play" and "display." The element of "play"

---

[4] Turiel (1978) warns against the utilization of game rules to study concepts about other types of rules, because the meaning of the game context is so different from the meaning of other contexts.

includes interpersonal concerns about the dynamics of the activity, or, as Huizinga (1955) has said, "being 'apart together' in an exceptional situation, sharing something important, mutually withdrawing from the rest of the world and rejecting the usual norms" (p. 12). The element of "display" includes action which symbolically represents the dynamics of the activity for the purpose of creating entertainment for sport consumers. Thus, as one interacts within the sport realm over time, one may develop a tendency to utilize defensive ego processes when conceptualizing athletic aggression as a result of interpersonal sport experience and/or internalization of societal and institutional norms.

Habitual defensive processing is addressed directly and indirectly by a number of social scientists. Haan (1977b) contends that both acute and chronic stress promote defensive ego processing, and notes that some people prolong their own stress by defending themselves against the implications of their own experience. Those athletes who engage in reactively aggressive sports behaviors, in particular, may accumulate a backlog of unresolved problems and vulnerabilities related to guilt; by burdening themselves with concerns about social valuation they may engender defensive processing through the stress of low self-esteem.

Social scientists might also point to defensive attribution as a process through which blame for athletic aggression may be avoided. Dodge and Frame (1982) have conducted a series of studies designed to assess the nature and limits of a known bias on the part of aggressive boys to overattribute hostile intentions to peers. This line of research has proved to be fruitful in the development of a social-information-processing model of aggressive behavior. Aggressive acts can be justified as retribution when responsibility for the behavior is attributed to opponents through the mechanisms of projection and/or displacement (i.e., "my coach said the team is out to get us," "if I don't hurt my opponent first, s/he will hurt me," "I'm only conforming to how the game is played," or "that block sure looked/felt like my opponent was trying to hurt me; I'll have to make her/him pay!").

Festinger's (1957) theory of cognitive dissonance might also be applied in a discussion of habitual defensive reasoning. Dissonance reduction occurs when one wants to preserve a decision; sport practitioners, participants, and spectators may discount the assertion that athletic aggression is a moral issue in order to maintain cognitive balance, employing such defensive functions as rationalization, repression, or denial.

We have discussed a number of explanations for the ambiguity associated with moral and social-conventional dimensions of athletic aggression, including defensiveness in our society. We have considered how a person might reason about sport violence; let us now examine how her or his reasoning might affect the actual expression of athletic aggression.

Moral Reasoning and Aggressive Behavior

Is there a relationship between the way people think about moral issues and the way they act? If not, there is not much to be gained by examining the relationship between moral reasoning and athletic aggression. The question is an appropriate one;

it should not be presupposed that moral knowledge is connected to social action. The most frequently employed methodology within a cognitive-developmental framework is designed to ascertain an individual's capacity for moral reasoning by examining the way subjects contend hypothetical moral dilemmas should be resolved. This procedure is distinct from asking subjects how they would resolve the dilemma, from asking them to resolve actual dilemmas, and from observing subjects' actual behavior. The difficulties inherent in empirically assessing the judgment-action relationship are reflected in conflicting claims about the nature of the relationship.

Much of the general moral literature contains research findings in which the predicted moral reasoning-moral behavior relations have been weak, indeterminant, or nonsignificant (Gerson & Damon, 1978). Social scientists frequently appeal to the classic studies of Hartshorne and May (1928-1930) when attempting to explain children's inconsistent moral behaviors across an array of moral situations. Proposing a "doctrine of specificity," Hartshorne and May asserted that moral behavior is a function of specific social context rather than personal moral development.

Conversely, a number of cognitive-developmentalists have discovered significant relationships between subjects' levels of moral reasoning in response to moral dilemmas and their behavioral choices in specific moral conflict situations (Kohlberg, 1969, 1970; Schwartz, Feldman, Brown, & Heingartner, 1969). These theorists examine moral behavior within the context of subjects' moral judgments. Rather than focusing primarily on an individual's behaviors as viewed by an outside observer (a technique utilized by social-learning theorists), the cognitive-developmentalist studies the ways in which individuals define the behavioral situation, and their choices in that situation. Moral reasoning is thus viewed as influencing moral behavior by providing specific interpretations of the moral aspects of the situation. The task of exposing judgment-action relationships is complex, however, because people using different levels of moral reasoning can arrive at the same behavioral choices.

A major investigation designed to assess the relationship between stage of moral reasoning and behavioral choices was conducted by Haan, Smith, and Block (1968). They studied participants and nonparticipants in the original free-speech movement sit-ins at Berkeley, demonstrations organized in response to administration attempts to control the expression of different political views on campus. On the issue of civil obedience, the stages of reasoning "fit" the observed behavior quite well. Students reasoning at Kohlberg's Stage 2 were concerned about individual rights in a conflict of power, and could support participation or nonparticipation in the sit-in, depending upon how they saw the consequences of the sit-in for personal welfare. Sixty percent of Stage 2 subjects participated in the sit-in. Conventional (Stages 3 and 4) reasoning tended to support and maintain the existing system of rules and role expectations, generally leading students not to engage in civil disobedience. Stage 5 principled reasoning was concerned with the utility of anticipated consequences, due process, and the contractual arrangement between the students and the university administration. Depending upon the perceived contingencies, Stage 5 reasoning could support participation or nonparticipation; 50% of Stage 5 subjects sat-in. Stage 6 reasoning, presumably uncontaminated by self-interest or contingencies, defined the issue as a violation of the right to free expression and 80% of them sat-in. In a subsequent investigation, Haan and Block (Haan, 1975) found that a majority of the activists used principled reasoning as a major or minor way of resolving hypothetical dilemmas; conversely, only a small percentage of the nonactivists did so.

The studies investigating moral judgment-action relationships demonstrated that particular actions in particular situations may be justified by a variety of forms of moral reasoning. Whether a specific action is mandated by a stage of reasoning depends on how situationally specific moral issues are perceived and defined and behavioral consequences are understood. These points elicit two questions directly applicable to our examination of expression by participants in the sport realm. What factors mediate the relationship between moral judgment and aggressive action? How is the development of moral reasoning related to the development of moral behavior, and more specifically, to the development of athletic aggression? These questions serve to structure the remainder of this chapter, which addresses the theoretical and empirical relationship between moral reasoning and aggressive behavior.

Moral Judgment and Athletic Aggression: Mediating Factors

The literature shows that moral reasoning influences moral behavior, and that although people at different reasoning levels may make the same behavioral choices, they do so for different reasons. Thus, understanding an athlete's reasoning about athletic aggression enhances our understanding of her or his behavior. However, a parsimonious description of the relationship between moral reasoning and behavior in general, and between moral reasoning and athletic aggression in particular, is lacking. As has been emphasized, the difficulty may be attributed in part to the complex relationship between meanings and choices. It is further complicated by other factors affecting the influence of moral reasoning on moral behavior, and by the methodology employed to explore the relationship. All of these elements must be taken into account when considering an athlete's reasoning and her or his aggressive behavior.

Gerson and Damon (1978) have developed a model which reflects their view of the relationship between moral judgment and social conduct. In their model, different types of moral and nonmoral knowledge interact in a manner that shapes both moral judgement and social conduct. The various types of knowledge derive from an individual's actions and goals within social contexts and are thus determined not only by the specific nature of the social context but also by the individual's capacity to act. This capacity, in turn, directly reflects the individual's developmental status. Therefore, to better determine moral judgment-aggressive behavior relations for sport participants, we must consider how participants at different developmental levels organize both the general and sport-specific aspects of their moral knowledge, as well as how their moral knowledge interacts with other types of social knowledge as they reason and act in the sport realm. If we are to understand, for example, the aggressive behavior of a young male ice hockey competitor, we must consider the player's specific sport knowledge as well as the ways he tailors his behavior to meet the specific demands inherent in the sport context. There is a wide range of moral and nonmoral concerns that distinguishes sport from other social institutions; through interaction in sport the ice hockey player constructs a specific social understanding of the sport world that organizes his behavior choices, including the expression of aggression. Because the player brings to each hockey experience a capacity for and manner of constructing knowledge that he has developed over time, there is both stability and contextual variety in the player's aggressive behavior. Consistency in aggressive behavior can be expected when he interprets a hockey situation as similar to past hockey experiences.

As cognitive-developmentalists, Gerson and Damon view people as goal-directed agents who purposefully and consciously guide much of their behavior, adjusting their actions to obtain freely self-constructed objectives. Advocates of this position would see the hockey player as attempting to mold his understanding of hockey situations in a way that is in accord with the objectives he has constructed. For example, imagine that the boy values good sportspersonship and that he values the recognition that often accompanies success. The player's construction of his social and moral understanding of an important tournament game will lead to the development of his objectives: demonstrating good sportspersonship and winning. While competing the player may experience a conflict in objectives, forcing him to reconstruct his understanding of the "right" behavior. Given the choice of instrumentally aggressing or avoiding an opportunity to fight, the player might adjust his moral and nonmoral concerns so that the "right" behavior is to fight. Because this resolution does not represent a true integration of the two objectives, but rather a downward shift in moral understanding so that reconciliation is possible, the resolution would be termed "reconciliation through rationalization" (Gerson & Damon, 1978).

The judgment-action model of Gerson and Damon thus identifies three critical aspects of moral behavior: capacity, context, and objectives. These interdependent judgment factors have the potential to mediate the moral reasoning-aggressive behavior relationship we are exploring. In their model, Gerson and Damon have also delineated two aspects of judgment, specifying interpretation and reasoning as interrelated components of judgment. They suggest that interpretation, the initial assessment of meaning, precedes later reasoning, which is an attempt to organize contextual specifics into a coherent argument or course of action. The interpretational process may be discrete, as in an athlete's immediate response to being pushed to the ground by an opponent, or it may be an ongoing interactive process with trial reasoning occurring as an athlete reinterprets her or his opponent's conduct. Thus social knowledge, which incorporates both interpretation and reasoning, is an interaction between the athlete's constructive activity and the salient details of the situation. If a football player cannot differentiate social-conventional and moral aspects of tackling an opponent in such a way as to risk injury, the player cannot make an unadulterated moral judgment about the tackle.

After an athlete has interpreted a sport situation to be moral, she or he may or may not follow it up with reasoning or conduct. Gerson and Damon identify four interrelated forms of moral interpretation, reasoning, and conduct that one might experience: deliberative interactions, habitual interactions, intuitive interactions, and moral-emotional interactions.

Deliberative interactions. If an athlete's interpretation of athletic aggression is followed up or modified by moral reasoning, then Gerson and Damon would describe the athlete as deliberative in the construction of her or his moral understanding. The athlete using deliberative interactions is actively considering the contextual sport variables that she or he is able to interpret, and is reasoning about whether it is moral to aggress. This is a process that intertwines the athlete's interpretation, reasoning, and behavior, for in deliberative interaction interpretation is a continuous process through which reasoning and/or conduct can lead to new interpretations of the situation. Most often, it is when the athlete is in a moral crisis or conflict that deliberative understanding is attempted. If a female basketball player competing with habitual aggressiveness causes an opponent's injury, she may be forced to come up with articulated reasoning and active justification for her interpretations and conduct. This moral deliberation may facilitate moral development, leading to a more adequate organization of moral knowledge and a change in moral behavior.

Habitual interactions. In many cases athletes are encouraged to act in an automatic, habitual way that requires minimal conscious deliberation. Slogans, strategies, and behaviors are drilled into sport participants; because split-second responses are so often required, athletes are taught to react rather than reason. Thus, athletic aggression usually becomes an immediate response involving little, if any, moral reasoning. As a habitual reaction, sport violence is expressed when an athlete interprets a sport situation as similar to one encountered in the past, has a set aggressive response to it, and acts accordingly. For many athletes, aggression in sport is equated with social convention; violence becomes an habitual duty which leads to the mistreatment of others.

Intuitive interactions. Gerson and Damon explain that like habit, intuitive moral behavior is closely interrelated with interpretation and conduct, but relies very little on reasoning. Unlike habits, intuitive interactions are not automatic responses based originally on previous moral understanding, but involve an immediate and spontaneous construction of moral behavior in the situation. An athlete often encounters a novel situation in sport which cannot be quickly related to past experience. Examples include a basketball player who is in the position to break her arch rival's fall toward the scorer's table, possibly rescuing her opponent from a serious head injury, and a football player who spontaneously decides he cannot attempt to "take out" the knee of a quarterback who is in an extremely vulnerable position. In these cases, there is no opportunity to reason about personal risks or about implications for the self or team; the immediate interpretation of a novel situation in which an opponent is endangered leads to intuitive moral behavior. Situations eliciting intuitive interactions may encourage the athlete to reason deliberatively about athletic aggression after the immediate crisis has passed.

Moral-emotional interactions. Moral emotions are those intensely felt affective reactions or appraisals that are derived through an interpretation of a specific situation; they include guilt, sympathy, and outrage. Because reactive aggression is usually an emotional response to a frustrating situation, moral emotions may more frequently serve as facilitators or inhibitors of reactive rather than instrumental aggression, which is characterized as an unemotional, objectified behavior. Moral emotions cut across other types of moral interactions and can be deliberative, habitual, or intuitive. Moral sentiments such as guilt or sympathy may play a significant role in deliberations about athletic aggression by instigating a reevaluation of the intent to injure. Also, the feelings of moral outrage accompanying the frequent sport occurrence of hostile retribution may be questioned and redefined through reasoning and conduct. Moral emotional habits may be nurtured in those instrumentally aggressive athletes who must regulate and repress automatic affective responses to aggression because the feelings do not fit into their current moral understanding of athletic aggression. If an instrumentally aggressive athlete did not carefully cultivate moral-emotional habits, an affective response such as guilt or sympathy could undermine her or his ability to aggress. Finally, in intuitive interactions, moral sentiments may spontaneously propel an athlete to aggress or to restrain aggressive tendencies.

The Gerson-Damon model represents a valuable contribution to the understanding of the moral judgment-aggressive behavior relationship. The athlete, a potential aggressor, is seen in this model as constructing an interpersonal morality that is contextual, but grounded in continuities within the self and recognized similarities within sport and between sport and everyday life. It remains difficult, however, to predict an athlete's aggressive behavior by merely examining her or his moral judgment. An individual's general capacity for moral understanding is ascertained by identifying the reasoning structures she or he uses to resolve moral dilemmas. This capacity may or may not be fully used in any particular situation. As an example, an athlete in the sport world experiences competing social concerns and objectives which interact with moral reasoning in a way that differs significantly from their interaction in a laboratory setting. It is this interaction which informs the athlete's social understanding, and from which the athlete's conduct is derived.

It seems evident that some discrepancies may occur between reasoning about a hypothetical situation and reasoning about a concrete behavioral situation in which a person is directly involved, and between these forms of moral reasoning and moral action (Gilligan, 1980). In real-life situations, the implications of a particular choice are actually experienced; variables such as stress (Haan, 1965, 1977b) and self-interest (Gerson & Damon, 1978) become more salient. The sport setting may be perceived as stressful, causing athletes to reason below their ability, or to behave below their ability to reason. Also, an instrumentally aggressive athlete who interacts habitually in sport, injuring others to contribute to team success or to achieve personal goals, may act differently as a consequence of deliberate reasoning.

When variables of stress and self-interest are imbedded in the structure of an institution, that structure may function to impede moral judgment and action. Research conducted in prisons (Kohlberg, Kauffman, Scharf, & Hickey, 1972), for example, demonstrates that inmates use lower stages of reasoning in response to prison dilemmas than when they attempt to resolve standard hypothetical dilemmas. Kohlberg et al. suggested that although the inmates were capable of using higher-stage reasoning about their concrete prison environment, the environment itself was operating at a lower level. The sport environment, where athletic aggression is perceived, for the most part, as conventional behavior, is also structured to discourage optimal moral reasoning and dialogue. Hence, if we are to assess the relationship between moral reasoning and aggressive sports behavior, we must consider potential discrepancies between hypothetical and concrete moral reasoning and between moral judgment and action.

Moral Judgment and Athletic Aggression:
Their Connection and Coordination

My colleagues and I have initiated a line of research designed to explore the relationship between moral reasoning and athletic aggression within a cognitive-developmental framework that is grounded in Haan's interactional approach to morality. From this theoretical perspective, behavior is seen as a result of the interaction between an individual's organized meaning structures and environmental factors. By viewing aggression as a moral act within the moral exchange among sport participants, a new model for the social-scientific study of athletic aggression may be developed. Such a model would analyze aggression by taking into account: (a) the person's understanding of the nature of moral exchange, that is, her or his moral level; (b) the person's typical coping and defending strategies for normal and stressful situations; and (c) environmental factors such as the rule structure of the game, formal and informal norms regulating play, level of competition, and coaching demands. Only a multifaceted approach which takes into account individual and structural capacities, processing techniques, and environmental factors can provide a differentiated understanding of athletic aggression.

To gather theoretical and empirical support for this new approach to athletic aggression a series of investigations has been initiated. The first phase of this research program is guided primarily by the following questions:

1. Do respondents use the same level of moral reasoning when responding to hypothetical dilemmas which are not sport-oriented and hypothetical dilemmas which are? Do athletes and nonathletes respond in similar ways to these two types of dilemmas?
2. How does a respondent's moral reasoning about hypothetical dilemmas differ from reasoning about her or his actual athletic aggression?
3. What is the relationship between hypothetical moral reasoning and actual athletic aggression?
4. How are moral and social-conventional dimensions of athletic aggression conceptualized and coordinated by athletes?
5. How are these questions mediated by variables such as gender and length and type of sport involvement?

The sample population in this series of interrelated studies includes female and male elementary, high school, and college students. Control sample populations are composed of individuals not involved in organized sport programs, and the experimental groups include sport participants representing a variety of sport areas. Each subject is asked to respond to a brief demographic questionnaire before engaging in an interview with a trained research assistant. During the interview the subject reasons about two of Haan's hypothetical dilemmas and two athletic aggression hypothetical dilemmas. During the last portion of the interview, the subject responds to a series of questions designed to identify the point at which she or he conceives of athletic aggression as a moral rather than a social-conventional issue, and to expose the subjects' justification for that distinction. Through the transcription and scoring of recorded interviews, subjects' levels of moral reasoning can be determined.

Sports participants' behaviors during actual sport competition are observed and recorded on a behavioral checklist and on videotape. Directly following their sport performance, participants are asked to reason about their videotaped behavior, and are asked specific questions with regard to actions which may portray the intent to inflict psychological or physical harm. Additional measures of aggression include participants' responses to two instruments designed to assess aggression, the Buss-Durkee Hostility Scale (Buss & Durkee, 1957) and the Bredemeier Athletic Aggression Inventory (Bredemeier, 1975), and coaches' ratings and rankings of athletes' aggressive behavior.

The design and methodology characterizing this cluster of interrelated studies share some commonalities with a recently conducted pilot study (Bredemeier & Shields, Note 1). One of the major features of the pilot study was the comparison of 46 collegiate basketball competitors' levels of athletic aggression, as reflected by their coaches' ratings, with the athletes' stages of moral development. Because Haanian interviewers and scorers were not available at the time of the pilot test, subjects' moral reasoning scores were assessed through the administration of the Defining Issues Test (DIT). This instrument, constructed by James Rest (1979a), was derived from Kohlberg's theoretical approach and stage scheme. The DIT provides scores for Kohlberg's Stage 2 (morality of instrumental purpose and exchange), Stage 3 (morality of interpersonal concordance), Stage 4 (morality of social system), Stage 5A (morality of social contract), Stage 5B (morality of intuitive humanism), and Stage 6 (morality of universal ethical principles). Rest has added to the DIT a P (principled morality) score which is the sum of the weighted ranks given to Stage 5A, 5B, and 6 items. This score is interpreted as "the relative importance a subject gives to principled moral considerations in making a decision about moral dilemmas" (Rest, 1979b, p. 52).[5]

The results of the pilot study largely supported stage-specific hypotheses (see Table 5-5). Subjects rated as highly aggressive by their coaches scored significantly higher on moral Stages 2 and 4 than did subjects rated low in aggression. In con-

---

[5] The DIT is a paper-and-pencil measure which presents subjects with a set of alternative responses to moral dilemmas. Because DIT repondents select and prioritize responses which have been presented to them, they are performing a recognition task rather than the production task required to reason about Kohlbergian or Haanian interviews. The implications for this distinction is that subjects consistently choose items on the DIT at higher stages than the stage at which they produce statements in Kohlberg's interviews (Rest, 1979a). Rest contends that the DIT can be regarded as tapping earlier and more tacit moral understandings of a subject, while Kohlberg's interviews tap a more consolidated understanding which the subject can put into words.

74

Brenda Jo Bredemeier

Table 5-5. The Relationship Between Moral Stage and Athletic Aggression Level

Stage	Range of possible scores	Aggression level	Mean score	Standard deviation	Level of significance
Stage 2	0-33	High aggressors	12.12	6.58	.032[a]
		Low aggressors	6.80	5.37	
Stage 3	0-87	High aggressors	15.60	7.28	.014[a]
		Low aggressors	25.14	14.15	
Stage 4	0-88	High aggressors	40.31	9.38	.011[a]
		Low aggressors	30.14	11.08	
Stage 5A	0-70	High aggressors	17.72	8.04	.681
		Low aggressors	19.20	12.55	
Stage 5B	0-27	High aggressors	4.24	4.17	.102
		Low aggressors	6.88	4.35	
Stage 6	0-33	High aggressors	2.28	2.39	.016[a]
		Low aggressors	5.50	4.95	
Stage P	0-95	High aggressors	24.24	.91	.098
		Low aggressors	31.44	1.02	

[a] Significant at the .05 level.

trast, the low aggressors scored significantly higher on Stages 3 and 6. (The Stage 6 scores also created a significant P score difference between high and low aggressors).

The personal welfare and instrumental exchange orientation of Stage 2 is theoretically congruent with high athletic aggression because personal interests take priority over concern for the rights and welfare of others. For those reasoning predominantly at Stage 3, the level of athletic aggression dramatically decreases. The Stage 3 person tends to respond to stereotypical images of "good" or "nice" behavior, and good sportspersonship rather than athletic aggression is probably a common sport theme at this stage.

Although a Stage 3 conception of the "nature of the game" would presumably be incompatible with the intentional injury of others, a Stage 4 interpretation of the game likely includes acknowledged and socially legitimated aggression. Since the social norms of competitive sport not only sanction but often encourage aggression, as do coaches, it is not surprising that high aggressors express significantly more Stage 4 reasoning than do low aggressors.

The relationships between Stage 5 moral reasoning and athletic aggression levels did not reach statistical significance, though as anticipated, low aggressors scored higher on Stages 5A and 5B than high aggressors. At Stage 5A, which is oriented toward an understanding of "social contract," it would be possible to interpret various social contracts or agreements of sport in a fashion which might facilitate the acceptance, rejection, or reluctant endorsement of athletic aggression. Generally, however, postconventional or principled reasoning would discourage aggression, for Stage 5A and 5B competitors would be sensitive to the rights of opponents as well as teammates. The failure to determine a significant relationship may have been due to the small sample size and/or relatively minor amounts of reason at Stage 5. The anticipated relationship between athletic aggression and postconventional reasoning was found to be significant at Stage 6; low aggressors scored significantly higher on this stage than did high aggressors.

While these pilot results are generally suggestive of a significant judgment-action relationship (with the exception of Stages 5A and 5B) the small sample size and the inadequacies of the pencil-and-paper DIT make interpretation difficult. As a consequence both of these considerations and of the differences between Kohlberg's and Haan's theoretical systems, hypotheses for our major research program have been derived through an integration of pilot results and pertinent research literature. An application of relevant literature serves to guide expectations for our experimental findings and to highlight their theoretical and practical implications.

Kohlberg and Kramer (1969) posit that "adult age change is not only toward greater consistency of moral judgment, but toward greater consistency between moral judgment and moral behavior" (p. 107). Indeed, research within Kohlberg's paradigm seems to support the contention that there is a developmental trend in the consistency between behavior and judgment. Individuals reasoning at higher stages have been found less likely to continue to administer shocks (Kohlberg, 1969; Milgrim, 1963) and to cheat (Schwartz, Feldman, Brown, & Heingartner, 1969), and are more likely to be altruistic (Dremen, 1976) and to engage in civil disobedience (Haan et al., 1968). Rothman (1980) makes this same point, and declares that from a developmental perspective, "an increased correspondence would be expected as one moves from one developmental stage to the next. If each successive stage is more differentiated and equilibrated than the previous stages, and each represents a more balanced interaction between the individual and the environment in resolving conflicting claims, increased coordination of judgments and behavior might be found" (p. 120).

Haan's system is even more closely tied to moral action than Kohlberg's system; thus we would expect our research to demonstrate a strong linear relationship between moral reasoning and athletic aggression. The Haanian (1977b) model of moral development was conceptualized through study of moral action, and its central concepts of moral dialogue and moral balance are intrinsically actional. Consequently, when moral reasoning is assessed according to Haan's model, action should be better predicted. Indeed, in her own research Haan (1977) found that her interactional measure of moral development was more stable between the hypothetical context of a moral judgment interview and the concrete situation of an actual moral exchange than was Kohlberg's (Haan, Stroud, & Holstein, 1973). Because Haan's system is so closely tied to actual moral exchange, the hypothesized relationship between moral judgment and moral action becomes simple: the higher the level of moral reasoning, the lower the level of athletic aggression.[6]

Rothman (1971, 1976) and Turiel (Turiel & Rothman, 1972), in their study of the influence of moral statements on children's behavior, also found support for the

---

[6] According to Haan (1977b), at Level 4 an individual tries to create moral balance in accordance with external regulations which are oriented to the maintenance of the "common interest." The integration of the idea of common interest with external regulation make it more unlikely that Level 4 people would consider aggression in sport moral.

contention that the coordination of judgment and behavior increases with developmental stage. In their investigations they presented two behavioral choices to Stage 3 and 4 subjects; subjects could choose to continue with an experiment involving taking someone's prize money in accordance with the investigator's instructions, or they could choose to stop participating. Behavioral alternatives were advocated by the investigator at levels of reasoning one stage either above or below the subjects' stage.

Stage 4 subjects chose the behavioral alternative advocated at the higher stage of reasoning, coordinating their behavioral choices with the higher stage of reasoning presented to them. Thus Stage 5 reasoning affected the behavior of children who were reasoning at Stage 4. Rothman has proposed that this occurrence may be reflective of a process through which the subjects' reasoning may be subsequently transformed. A behavioral response to Stage 5 reasoning may, in turn, facilitate the development of Stage 5 reasoning within the subject.

Rothman has posited that, just as behaving in accordance with higher stage reasoning may mediate stage transition for Stage 4 subjects, so might the conflict of Stage 3 subjects represent a transitional mechanism from Stage 3 to Stage 4. Stage 3 subjects, after listening to reasoning which justified either continuing with the experiment or stopping, chose to continue regardless of the level of reasoning at which that alternative was advocated. The subjects, however, vacillated in their behavior and displayed "behavioral ambivalence" when their actions were congruent with lower-stage reasoning. Rothman contends that the conflict experienced by Stage 3 subjects may have been reflective of an intermediate transitional phase between the initial separation and subsequent connection of behavior and higher-stage reasoning. Structural conflict and disequilibrium may have been precipitated by the presentation of higher stage reasoning.

The work of Rothman and Turiel has important theoretical and practical implications for our research program; it serves to underscore the possibilities for facilitating moral growth, and to highlight the mutual and interactive nature of reasoning and behavior in the process of developmental change. These implications also merge with the culminating themes of this chapter, enabling us to see more clearly how sport participants' experiences and conceptions provide the key to understanding athletic aggression.

Conclusions

Counterposed in this chapter to the ambiguous languaging and ambivalent valuing of sport violence is the psychological study of athletic aggression as a moral concern. The study of reasoning about athletic aggression in hypothetical and actual sports dilemmas, characterized by moral and conventional conflict and choice, is seen as a complement to the work of social learning theorists. It would appear that there is a significant theoretical and empirical relationship between moral judgment and moral action, and thus between moral reasoning and athletic aggression. Moral reasoning is hypothesized to influence athletic aggression, but in interaction with situational and personal dimensions. To understand a sport participant's decision to aggress we must ask her or him to reason about it. Although two people may use similar reasoning to justify two different choices, or use different reasoning to justify the same choice, our understanding of the structure and content of their reasoning within the sport context may enhance and/or transform our conceptualization of the relationship between moral reasoning and athletic aggression.

By relating the choice of athletic aggression to its moral and social-conventional meaning for sport participants, we are thus able to dialogue with the participants and to encourage deliberate judgment and action. Sport is structured so as to maximize the potential for exercising power in a way that does violence to others; yet sport experiences can also facilitate moral growth. If sport is to provide constructive rather than destructive experiences, moral judgment must be tied to moral action (Kroll, 1975; McIntosh, 1979; Park, 1980). Aggressive actions must be clearly defined; aggressive values must be clarified. The conscious naming and evaluating of athletic aggression can cultivate an understanding of self as a moral agent, responsive to and responsible for the actualities of choice that inhere in the use of power and impact on the welfare of others.

There is justifiable concern about the physical and psychological ramifications of violence in contemporary sport. It is not enough to control athletic aggression, to confine it to rules or to regulate it to informal norms. To attempt to thwart athletic aggression by appealing solely to external structures is to view participants as mere respondents to their environment and to justify the creation of artificial boundaries which only suppress valued violence. Participants construct personal meanings for athletic aggression as they evaluate contextual information; through deliberate definition, dialogue, and decision-making, they can develop an understanding of athletic aggression as a moral issue. Moral development and athletic aggression may be characterized by mutual interaction, creating a reciprocal relationship between moral growth and aggressive behavior. Consequently, to reduce athletic aggression effectively, transformation of both external sport structures and internal reasoning structures is required. Prescriptions for these structural transformations may be derived from an interactional approach to the conception of athletic aggression, thus contributing to the development of sport and the sport participant.

Reference Note

1. Bredemeier, B., & Shields, D. *The utility of moral stage analysis in the prediction of athletic aggression.* Manuscript submitted for publication, 1982.

References

Arendt, H. *On violence.* New York: Harcourt Brace Jovanovich, 1969.

Arendt, H. *Crisis of the republic.* New York: Harcourt Brace Jovanovich, 1972.

Aronfreed, J. *Conduct and conscience: The socialization of internalized control over behavior.* New York: Academic Press, 1968.

Audi, R. Violence, legal sanctions and the law. In M. Stanage (Ed.), *Reason and violence.* Totowa, N.J.: Prentice Hall, 1973.

Bandura, A. *Principles of behavior modification.* New York: Holt, Rinehart and Winston, 1969.

Bandura, A. *Aggression: A social learning analysis*. Englewood Cliffs, N.J.: Prentice Hall, 1973.

Bandura, A., & McDonald, F. J. The influence of social reinforcement and the behavior of models in shaping children's moral judgments. *Journal of Abnormal and Social Psychology*, 1963, *67*, 274-81.

Berkowitz, L. The contagion of violence: An S-R mediational analysis of some effects of observed aggression. In W. J. Arnold & M. M. Page (Eds.), *Nebraska Symposium on Motivation*. Lincoln: University of Nebraska Press, 1970.

Berkowitz, L. Words and symbols as stimuli to aggressive responses. In J. F. Knutson (Ed.), *Control of aggression: Implications from basic research*. Chicago: Aldine-Atherton, 1972.

Bredemeier, B. The assessment of reactive and instrumental athletic aggression. In D. Landers (Ed.), *Psychology of sport and motor behavior*. State College Pa.: The Pennsylvania State University, 1975.

Bredemeier, B. Applications and implications of aggression research. In W. Straub (Ed.), *Sport psychology: An analysis of athlete behavior*. New York: Mouvement Publications, 1978.

Brown, R. Historical patterns of violence in America. In H. Graham & T. Gurr (Eds.), *The history of violence in America: Historical and comparative perspectives*. A report submitted to the National Commission on the Causes and Prevention of Violence. New York: Praeger, 1969.

Buss, A. H., & Durkee, A. An inventory for assessing different kinds of hostility. *Journal of Consulting Psychology*, 1957, *21*, 343-348.

Coakley, J. The sociological perspective: Alternative causations of violence in sport. *Arena*, 1981, *5*(1), 44-56.

Cohn, L. The road back. *San Francisco Chronicle*, August 20, 1982, p. 65.

Damon, W. *The social world of the child*. San Francisco: Jossey-Bass, 1977.

Dodge, K., & Frame, C. Social cognitive biases and deficits in aggressive boys. *Child Development*, 1982, *53*, 620-635.

Dollard, J., Doob, L. W., Miller, N. E., Mowrer, O. H., & Sears, R. R. *Frustration and aggression*. New Haven, Conn.: Yale University Press, 1939.

Dreman, S. Sharing behavior in Israeli schoolchildren: Cognitive and social learning factors. *Child Development*, 1976, *47*, 186-194.

Feshbach, S. Reality and fantasy in filmed violence. In J. P. Murray, E. A. Rubinstein, & G. A. Comstock (Eds.), *Television and social behavior. Vol. 2. Television and social learning*. Washington, D.C.: Government Printing Office, 1972.

Feshbach, S. The function of aggression and the regulation of aggressive drive. *Psychological Review*, 1964, *71*, 257-72.

Festinger, L. A theory of social comparison processes. *Human Relations*, 1954, 7, 117-40.

Festinger, L. *A theory of cognitive dissonance*. Stanford: Stanford University Press, 1957.

Freud, S. *A general introduction to psycho-analysis*. New York: Boni & Liveright, 1920.

Freud, S. *New introductory lectures on psycho-analysis*. New York: Morton, 1933.

Freud, S. Why war? In J. Strachey (Ed.), *Collected papers of Sigmund Freud* (Vol. 5). London: Hogarth Press, 1950.

Gerson, R., & Damon, W. Moral understanding and children's conduct. *New Directions for Child Development,* 1978, *2,* 41-59.

Gilligan, C. In a different voice: Women's conceptions of self and morality. *Harvard Educational Review,* 1977, *47,* 481-517.

Gilligan, C. Justice and responsibility. In *Toward moral and religious maturity.* Palo Alto, Calif.: Silver Burdett, 1980.

Gilligan, C. *In a different voice: Psychological theory and women's development.* Cambridge, Mass.: Harvard University Press, 1982. (a)

Gilligan, C. Why should a woman be more like a man? *Psychology Today,* 1982, *16,* 68-77. (b)

Goldstein, J. H. *Aggression and crimes of violence.* New York: Oxford University Press, 1975.

Greendorfer, S. Socialization in sport. In C. Oglesby (Ed.), *Women and sport: From myth to reality.* Philadelphia: Lea & Febiger, 1978.

Haan, N. Coping and defense mechanisms related to personality inventories. *Journal of Consulting Psychology,* 1965, *29,* 373-78.

Haan, N. Moral reasoning in hypothetical and an actual situation of civil disobedience. *Journal of Personality and Social Psychology,* 1975, *32,* 255-70.

Haan, N. *A manual for interactional morality.* Berkeley: University of California, Berkeley, 1977. (a)

Haan, N. *Coping and defending: Processes of self-environment organization.* San Francisco: Academic Press, 1977. (b)

Haan, N., Bellah, R., Rabinow, P., & Sullivan, W. (Eds.), *Social science as moral inquiry.* New York: Columbia University Press, 1983.

Haan, N., Smith, M. B., & Block, J. Moral reasoning of young adults: Political-social behavior, family background, & personality correlates. *Journal of Personality and Social Psychology,* 1968, *10,* 183-201.

Haan, N., Stroud, J., & Holstein, C. Moral and ego stages in relationship to ego processes: A study of "hippies." *Journal of Personality,* 1973, *41,* 596-612.

Hart, H. Are there any natural rights? In A. Melden (Ed.), *Human rights.* Belmont, Calif.: Wadsworth, 1970.

Hartshorne, H., & May, M. *Studies in the nature of character* (2 vols.). New York: Macmillan, 1928-1930.

Horrow, R. B. *Sports violence: The interaction between private law making and the criminal law.* Arlington, Va.: Corrollton Press, 1980.

Huizinga, J. *Homo ludens: A study of the play element in culture.* Boston: Beacon Press, 1955.

Kohlberg, L. Stage and sequence: The cognitive-developmental approach to socialization. In D. A. Goslin (Ed.), *Handbook of socialization theory and research.* Chicago: Rand McNally, 1969.

Kohlberg, L. Education for justice: A modern statement of the Platonic view. In N. F. Sizer & T. R. Sizer (Eds.), *Moral education: Five lectures.* Cambridge, Mass.: Harvard University Press, 1970.

Kohlberg, L. From is to ought: How to commit the naturalistic fallacy and get away with it in the study of moral development. In T. Mischel (Ed.), *Cognitive development and epistemology*. New York: Academic, 1971.

Kohlberg, L., & Gilligan, C. F. The adolescent as philosopher: The discovery of the self in a postconventional world. *Daedalus,* 1971, *100*, 1051-86.

Kohlberg, L., Kauffman, M., Scharf, P., & Hickey, J. The justice structure of the prison: A theory and an intervention. *The Prison Journal,* 1972, *51* (2).

Kohlberg, L., & Kramer, R. Continuities and discontinuities in childhood and adult moral development. *Human Development,* 1969, *12*, 93-120.

Kohlberg, L., & Turiel, E. Moral development and moral education. In G. S. Lesser (Ed.), *Psychology and educational practice*. Glenview, Ill.: Scott Foresman, 1971.

Kroll, W. *Psychology of sportsmanship*. Paper presented at the American Alliance of Health, Physical Education, Recreation and Dance convention, Atlantic City, New Jersey, 1975.

Levine, P. The historical perspective: Violence in sport. *Arena Review: The Institute for Sport and Social Analysis,* February 1981, *5*(1).

Lickona, T. (Ed.). *Moral development and behavior*. New York: Holt, Rinehart and Winston, 1976.

Lorenz, K. *On aggression*. New York: Harcourt Brace Jovanovich, 1966.

May, R. *Power and innocence: A search for the sources of violence*. New York: Dell, 1972.

McClelland, D. *Power: The inner experience*. New York: Irvington, 1975.

McIntosh, P. *Fair play: Ethics in sport and physical education*. London: Heinemann, 1979.

Milgram, S. Behavioral study of obedience. *Journal of Abnormal and Social Psychology,* 1963, *67*, 371-378.

Mischel, W., & Moore, B. Effects of attention to symbolically presented rewards upon self-control. *Journal of Personality and Social Psychology,* 1966, *3*, 390-396.

Nucci, L. Conceptions of personal issues: A domain distinct from moral or societal concepts. *Child Development,* 1981, *52*, 114-21.

Nucci, L., & Turiel, E. Social interactions and the development of social concepts in preschool children. *Child Development,* 1978, *49*, 400-407.

Park, R. Citius, altius, fortius. *The academy papers* (No. 14). Reston, Va.: The American Academy of Physical Education, December 1980.

Piaget, J. *The moral judgment of the child*. Glencoe, Ill.: Free Press, 1965.

Piaget, J. *The child and reality*. New York: Grossman, 1973.

Rawls, J. *The theory of justice*. Cambridge, Mass.: Harvard University Press, 1971.

Rest, J. *Development in judging moral issues*. Minneapolis: University of Minnesota, 1979. (a)

Rest, J. *Revised manual for the defining issues test*. Minneapolis: Minnesota Moral Research Projects, 1979. (b)

Rothman, G. R. *An experimental analysis of the relationship between level of moral judgement and behavioral choice*. Unpublished doctoral dissertation, Teacher's College, Columbia University, 1971.

Rothman, G. R. The influence of moral reasoning on behavioral choices. *Child Development*, 1976, *47*, 397-406.

Rothman, G. The relationship between moral judgment and moral behavior. In M. Windmiller, N. Lambert, & E. Turiel (Eds.), *Moral development and socialization*. Boston: Allyn and Bacon, 1980.

Schwartz, S., Feldman, K., Brown, M., & Heingartner, A. Some personality correlates of conduct in two situations of moral conflict. *Journal of Personality*, 1969, *37*, 41-57.

Scott, J. Sport and aggression. In G. Kenyon (Ed.), *Contemporary psychology of sport*. Chicago: Athletic Institute, 1970.

Shaver, K. G. Defensive attribution: Effects of severity and relevance on responsibility assigned for an accident. *Journal of Personality and Social Psychology*, 1970, *14*(2), 101-113.

Silva, J. Assertive and aggressive behavior in sport: A definitional clarification. In C. Nadeau, W. Hathwell, K. Newell, & G. Roberts (Eds.), *Psychology of motor behavior and sport*. Champaign, Ill.: Human Kinetics, 1980.

Singer, B. D. Violence, protest and war in television news: The U.S. and Canada compared. *Public Opinion Quarterly*, 1970-71, *34*, 611-16.

Smith, M. Sport violence: A definition. *Arena*, 1981, *5*(1), 2-8.

Smith, M. Aggression in sport: Toward a role approach. *Journal of the Canadian Association for Health, Physical Education and Recreation*, 1971, *371*, 22-25.

Stone, G. American sports: Play and display. *Chicago Review*, 1955, *9*, 83.

Tandy, R., & Laflin, J. Aggression and sport: Two theories. In R. Suinn (Ed.), *Psychology in sports: Methods and applications*. Minneapolis, Minn.: Burgess, 1980.

Tatum, J., & Kushner, B. *They call me assassin*. New York: Avon Books, 1979.

Turiel, E. Conflict and transition in adolescent moral development. *Child Development*, 1974, *45*, 14-29.

Turiel, E. Distinct conceptual and developmental domains: Social convention and morality. *Nebraska Symposium on Motivation*. Lincoln: University of Nebraska Press, 1977.

Turiel, E. The development of concepts of social structure: Social convention. In J. Glick & A. Clarke-Stewart (Eds.), *Personality and social development* (Vol. 1). New York: Gardner Press, 1978.

Turiel, E. Social regulations and domains of social concepts. In W. Damon (Ed.), *New Directions for Child Development*. San Francisco: Jossey-Bass, 1980.

Turiel, E., & Rothman, G. R. The influence of reasoning on behavioral choices at different stages of moral development. *Child Development*, 1972, *43*, 741-756.

Underwood, J. *The death of an American game*. Boston: Little, Brown and Company, 1979.

Webb, H. Professionalization of attitudes toward play among adolescents. In G. S. Kenyon (Ed.), *Aspects of contemporary sport sociology*. Chicago: The Athletic Institute, 1969.

Chapter 6

Perceived Injustice and Sports Violence

Melvin M. Mark, Fred B. Bryant, and Darrin R. Lehman

> Numerous observers are troubled by the frequency and magnitude of violent acts and needless aggression. Many of these acts can only be understood by examining the issues of fairness and justice which underlie them. Indeed, increasing fairness and justice should reduce the occurrence of violent, aggressive acts.

The preceding comments could readily be applied to contemporary American society in general. We were referring, however, specifically to organized sports. In this chapter we examine the relationship between justice and violence in sports. Aggression, in both sports and society, is a complex phenomenon with multiple causes. It is our contention, first, that a sense of perceived injustice is an important cause of many instances of sports violence and, second, that adopting carefully considered measures which increase the perception of fairness and justice in sports could reduce excessive aggression. In this chapter, a framework is presented which describes different sources of perceived injustice in sports. Based on this framework we offer several suggestions about how to make sports fairer, and by implication, less violent. We also examine the contention that, although sports can be made more fair and hence less violent, society could learn much from sports in terms of how to construct a fair system of justice.

Some Examples of Justice-Based Sports Violence

In each of the following examples it appears that a perceived injustice led to, or contributed to, an act of sports violence:

> In November 1963 a riot occurred at Roosevelt Raceway, a harness racing track in the New York metropolitan area. Several hundred fans swarmed onto the track. The crowd attacked the judges' booth and injured one judge. They smashed the tote board, set fires in program booths, broke windows, and damaged cars parked in an adjacent lot. Several hundred policemen were called to the scene. Fifteen fans were arrested and fifteen

others hospitalized. What instigated this riot? The sixth race was the first half of a daily double, in which bettors attempt to select the winners of successive races, with potentially high payoffs. During the sixth race, six of the eight horses were involved in an accident and did not finish the race. In accordance with New York racing rules, the race was declared official. All the wagers placed on the six nonfinishing horses were lost, including the daily double bets. Many fans apparently felt that they were unjustly treated—that the race was not fair and should have been declared "no contest."

At a May 24, 1964 soccer match between Peru and Argentina, nearly 300 spectators were killed in a riot and in the ensuing panic to exit the stadium. The melee began when fans broke onto the field to attack a referee, apparently in an attempt to lynch him. The referee then suspended the match and more fans crashed through barriers onto the field. Police fired revolvers and then tear gas, and the crowd panicked. What initiated the riot and the resulting loss of life? With 2 minutes left in the contest and Argentina leading 1-0, a Peruvian player scored. This tying goal, which would probably have sent the game into overtime, was nullified by a referee because of rough play. The partisan crowd obviously "disputed" (Michener, 1976) the referee's call and felt that their team had been unfairly deprived of a chance for victory.

In 1955, fifty-five Montreal Canadiens fans made threats on the life of National Hockey League Commissioner Clarence Campbell. When the commissioner appeared at the Montreal Forum at a Canadiens-Detroit Red Wings game, he was pelted with fruit, programs, galoshes, and other missiles. A smoke bomb was exploded and many spectators fled to the exits. Because of the fans' disruptive behavior, the Montreal Fire Chief evacuated the Forum (resulting in a Canadiens' forfeit). When the fans from inside the Forum mixed with people mingling outside, a major riot ensued. Fifteen blocks of stores were looted, windows were smashed, cars were overturned, and corner newstands and street kiosks were burned down. Over 100 people were arrested. What led to this violent behavior? In an earlier game, Canadiens' star Maurice Richard struck a referee who had attempted to intervene in a fight between Richard and a Boston Bruin player. Commissioner Campbell suspended Richard for the remainder of the regular season and the playoffs. Montreal fans were stunned by Campbell's ruling. They believed the punishment was excessive and unfair.

In a fall 1981 collegiate football game, an offensive lineman swore at a referee. The official decided that this behavior was beyond the bounds of the rules and expelled the player. Leaving the field, the lineman hit the official. What caused this violent act of aggression toward the official? Earlier in the game, the player had repeatedly complained to the referee that a defender's illegal holding was going unnoticed. When the referee continually refused to penalize the opponent, the lineman evidently felt that the official was biased, and when he was ejected for demanding justice, the player was enraged to the point of physical assault.

During a professional tennis tournament in 1981, a well-known star exploded in anger. He called one of the line judges "incompetent," and smashed his racquet on the court. When several spectators laughed and booed, the player angrily swatted a ball into the stands. What precipitated this rude, aggressive behavior in a supposedly nonviolent sport? The tennis star apparently felt that the line judge had missed many line calls during the match, and with this particular "error," could take it no longer.

These examples demonstrate just how severe and violent reactions to a perceived injustice can be. They also illustrate some of the sources of perceived injustice, a topic to which we shall return when we provide a typology of perceived injustices in sports.

Overview

We began by briefly stating the three contentions that are examined in this chapter: (1) that perceived injustice is an important cause of much sports violence; (2) that steps can be taken to reduce perceived injustices in sports, and therefore to reduce sports violence; and (3) that it may be possible to learn how to construct a more just society by studying how justice is achieved in sports.

In the preceding section we presented a few examples which illustrate how perceived injustices in sports can lead to violence. In the next three sections, respectively, we define what we mean by "perceived injustice," partially review previous claims about perceived injustice and sports violence, and discuss other causes of sports violence. Then follows a typology of the sources of perceived injustice in sports and some suggestions about how to reduce these various types of injustices. We end the chapter by comparing sports and society, and by examining how elements of the justice system predominant in sports might be applied in society.

Our focus is on those acts of sports-related violence which exceed the normative rules of sport, that is, which go beyond the "rules of the game." Clearly some sports, such as football, hockey, and boxing, by their very nature require activities that would be unacceptable if they occurred outside the arena (e.g., tackles, blocks, body checks). We are not here concerned with these acts which conform to the games' normative structures. Rather, we are interested in aggression which is not a necessary part of the game: taking a hockey stick to an opposing player's eye; bench-clearing brawls in hockey or baseball; assaults against officials; spectator riots; fights between fans and sports participants; and so on.

Our discussion concerns *all* sports violence that exceeds normative bounds. In particular, we do not systematically distinguish between sports participants and fans. A more comprehensive analysis of the relationship between perceived injustice and sports violence might include such a distinction. Our belief is that the processes through which perceived injustices affect sports violence are generally the same for participants and fans, and that by omitting this distinction we have gained considerable simplicity at the cost of some accuracy. Although it might be possible to develop a more detailed model of causal chains (Brickman, Ryan, & Wortman, 1975) that considers how the behaviors of sports participants influence those of observers and vice versa, such a task is beyond the scope of the present chapter.

Definition of Perceived Injustice

Given the central role of "perceived injustice" in our analysis, we shall in this section briefly discuss this concept and distinguish it from some related constructs. Berkowitz has previously discussed two constructs that overlap partially with perceived injustice. Expanding Dollard, Doob, Miller, Mowrer, and Sears' (1939) classic formulation, Berkowitz (1972) defines *deprivation* as a condition in which a person "lacks a goal object people generally regard as attractive or desirable" (p. 79). *Frustration* is said to occur only when the person "had been anticipating the pleasure to be gotten from this object and then cannot fulfill this expectation." Thus frustration involves the blocking of a goal, the deprivation of an *expected* or anticipated outcome (though it is unclear how strong this expectation must be to produce deprivation). In other words, one compares one's current status with one's expected status and, if this comparison is unfavorable, frustration occurs.

The experience of *perceived injustice,* in contrast, entails comparison with a standard other than simple expectancies. Perceived injustice involves a discrepancy between what one obtains and what one "deserves" (Crosby, 1976), between one's outcomes and one's "entitlement" (Davis, 1959), between the "is" and the "ought" (Gurr, 1970). Perceived injustice occurs when an individual perceives a discrepancy between what happened and what "should have happened" according to the "rules of fair play." We assume that people hold standards of what ought to be, that in at least some domains there is considerable social consensus about what should be (cf. Alves & Rossi, 1978), and that when people's standards of what should be are violated, action often results, with aggression being one possible avenue of expression.

This is not to say that all those who observe an injustice are equally likely to respond aggressively. For instance, if in a basketball game a defensive player is called for fouling the shooter, we would not expect the defensive player and the shooter to be equally provoked to anger, even if both players know the call was inaccurate. It seems obvious that the defensive player is more likely to be angered by the inaccurate call. This can be explained in terms of several different research traditions. Equity theorists report that those who are inequitably disadvantaged (or underrewarded) will respond with anger; the inequitably advantaged (or overrewarded) will respond otherwise, perhaps with guilt (Walster, Berscheid, & Walster, 1973). Research on relative deprivation demonstrates that people feel more angry about a deprivation the more they want that of which they are deprived (Crosby, 1976, 1982). Players and fans want officials' calls to be in their team's favor, not in their opponents' favor; it follows that players and fans will feel more anger when an injustice is to their team's disadvantage. Stated yet another way, a perceived injustice is more likely to lead to violence to the extent that it is frustrating.

The distinction we are drawing between perceived injustice and frustration may require a bit more explanation. Frustration involves a discrepancy between one's goals (or expectations) and what actually happened, while perceived injustice involves a discrepancy between what one believes *should* have happened and what actually happened. By definition, sports contests involve frustrations, for not all of everyone's goals can be obtained. Yet most of these frustrations occur in the context of fairly applied, fair "rules of the game." Such frustrations, we contend, are not nearly as likely to lead to violence as those frustrations that are further perceived as stemming from injustice. (Thus our analysis derives historically from earlier discussions of the role of arbitrariness in the frustration-aggression relationship, e.g., Pastore, 1952).

In many instances, of course, the judgment about whether a frustrating event is unfair will depend on the perspective, expectations, and goals of the person making the judgment. Thus, we refer to "perceived injustice," rather than simply to "injustice." We use the term *perceived* injustice to recognize explicitly that injustice is very much "in the eye of the beholder." In our earlier example of a college lineman who assaulted a referee, the defensive opponent would probably perceive less injustice in the situation than would the lineman, even if he actually was guilty of holding. Similarly, those whose horse won the controversial sixth race at the Roosevelt Raceway may have felt that the race was more fair than did those whose horses failed to finish. As we shall see later, recognizing that aggression is aroused by injustices *as they are perceived* leads to certain important recommendations about changes in sports justice systems that may reduce violence.

Previous Claims About Justice and Sports Violence

Other observers have noted that sports aggression frequently stems from perceived injustices. Most often this relationship has been discussed in the context of fan violence. For example, Lewis (1975; cited in Eitzen, 1981) concluded that "there is a direct relationship between the severity of sports riots and the crowds' perceptions of an officiating error." Smits (1968) states that crowd outbursts in soccer are "almost always" the result of a referee's decision—or the lack of one. Taking an empirical approach, Smith (1976) conducted a content analysis of 68 accounts of sports-related "hostile outbursts" published in a Toronto newspaper between 1963 and 1973. Except for "prior assaultive behavior" by others including players, "unpopular officials' decisions" constituted the most frequent category of precipitants. (And these prior assaultive behaviors may themselves have resulted from perceived injustice; see the following.) Presumably many if not most of these "unpopular" decisions that led to an outburst were ones which fans perceived as being incorrect and unfair.

Lang (1981) and Mann (1979) have each proposed a typology of sports spectator violence, and several of their categories involve perceived injustice. Mann's first type of sports riot, frustration-based, involves fans' reactions to "an illegitimate or unacceptable action—a capricious decision to deprive them of their sport or an erroneous decision to penalize their team and threaten it with defeat" (Mann, 1979, p. 354). Mann classifies such riots as based either on perceived injustice or on deprivation, depending on whether the source of the frustration is a referee's decision or a deprivation of a service, respectively. As instances of riots based on perceived injustice, Mann points to the 1964 soccer riot in Peru, and to the Maurice Richard-Clarence Campbell incident, described earlier. As an example of a deprivation riot, Mann recounts an incident in Cairo, Egypt, in which 49 people were killed and 47 injured. Roughly 100,000 tickets had been sold for a soccer game between a local Egyptian club and a visiting Czech team, but at the last minute organizers moved the match to a 45,000-seat stadium nearer to the center of the city. Apparently many fans felt illegitimately deprived of their right to see a game for which they held tickets. Deprivation riots can also occur when a highly touted contest turns out to be a farce, when highly paid athletes do not appear to be trying, or when a team appears to be running out the clock (McIntosh, 1979).

Two of the categories in Lang's (1981) four-part typology of sports riots usually involve a perception of unfairness. One of these types, the fanatic public, corresponds roughly to Mann's perceived injustice riot. Lang's "fanatic public" consists of "sports nuts" who respond aggressively to decisions or acts which "they define as damaging to [the] reputation or the chance" of their idolized team or player. Such reactions, Lang suggests, frequently follow "a decision defined as unfair," as in the Maurice Richard suspension. A second category in Lang's classification, the "acquisitive crowd," is somewhat comparable to Mann's deprivation riot. Lang's acquisitive crowd "acts spontaneously . . . against a decision or act it defines as against the rules of fair play and/or incurring some kind of personal damage or loss to self" (Lang, 1981, p. 418). Lang suggests that riotous outbursts from the acquisitive crowd are most likely to occur at betting events such as horse races, illustrating this type of violence with the Roosevelt Raceway daily double riot. She writes, however, that acquisitive crowd riots can occur "at a football match, at a soccer match, etc. . . . on almost any occasion, when fans feel they have been unjustly deprived their due" (p. 423).

Mann's perceived injustice riot and Lang's fanatic public correspond to the common image of how perceived injustice can lead to violence, that is, through unfair rules or seemingly inaccurate or inappropriate applications of the rules. On the other hand, Mann's frustration riot and Lang's acquisitive crowd expand our application of perceived injustice in sports. These categories remind us that fans can feel unjustly deprived for reasons other than the rules and rulings of the game, for example, when there are not enough bats on "bat day," when an expected star is absent for seemingly illegitimate reasons, or when entry to the arena is delayed or blocked. As we shall discuss later, such incidents reflect perceived injustice and not merely frustration.

In this section we have briefly reviewed some of the claims made by social scientists that perceived injustice causes sports-related violence, along with some of the empirical evidence that it does so. We should note that there is also some evidence that sports spectators themselves believe that perceived injustice is an important cause of fan violence. For example, Cavanaugh and Silva (1980) surveyed 1747 spectators at college and pro hockey games. Spectators responded to a questionnaire indicating the variables they believed facilitated fan misbehavior at sports events. After the factor "age," spectators judged "referees" to be the most important facilitator of fan misbehavior, agreeing with such items as "A referee's poor judgment often causes spectators to misbehave at events. ("Age" received the greatest *overall* endorsement as contributing to fan misbehavior, with younger fans expected to exhibit more violence; however, younger fans did not agree that age was the most important factor, and instead rated "referees" highest.)

Other Causes of Sports Violence

Though we and others emphasize the critical role of perceived injustice, it is clear that many other factors facilitate sports aggression. Tucker (1982) reports a striking example. A few years ago a woman wrote to University of Oklahoma football coach Barry Switzer shortly before the traditional Oklahoma-Texas game. The woman implored Switzer to win because "last year when we lost to Texas, my husband beat me up. I know he will again this year." Obviously this husband's violence did not stem from perceived injustice. It may even be inappropriate to cite this as an instance of sports violence. The example does clearly illustrate, though, that sports events sometimes provide a setting in which individuals predisposed toward violence can act out this behavior. Mann's "outlawry" and Lang's "licentious crowd" involve such processes. And soccer hooliganism is frequently explained in these terms (see Gaskell & Pearton, 1979).

Other facilitators of sports violence involve, not individual pathology, but rather social structural variables. With respect to fan violence, Mann's (1979) typology includes "remonstrance," or political protest associated with sports. Protest riot against games involving South African sports teams are one contemporary example. Mann also describes the "confrontation riot," which corresponds to Lang's (1981) "polarized crowd." This type of outburst occurs when preexisting hostilities between rival groups erupt during a sports event. Examples of this phenomenon include: the so-called "soccer war" between Honduras and El Salvador in 1969, which was immediately precipitated by a contested soccer match but had as less proximate causes several economic and political conflicts; the rioting that followed the black champion Jack Johnson's 1910 victory over Jim Jeffries, the "Great White Hope"; and the riot (cited in Smith, 1976) that occurred 2 years after World War II during a soccer match in Vienna between a Jewish Sports Club and the Austrian Police Club. Mann (1979) also includes as a type of fan violence "expressive riots" (considered by Lang to be a subtype of the licentious crowd), which stem from the extreme affective states associated with winning or losing.

A review of social psychological research on aggression reveals many other characteristics of sports events which may serve to increase the likelihood of aggression in both fans and participants. Indeed, in some sports, the athletic arena and grandstands seem almost as though they were designed to maximize most of these conditions: participants and spectators alike experience physiological arousal, which could conceivably be transferred into feelings of anger (Bryant & Zillmann, 1979); the arena and stands are noisy (Donnerstein & Wilson, 1976) and often moderately warm (Baron & Bell, 1976); generally sports fans are crowded together (Freedman, Levy, Buchanan, & Price, 1972), are relatively anonymous and deindividuated (Zimbardo, 1969), and many of them have consumed more than a small dose of alcohol (Taylor & Gammon, 1975); the very act of viewing an aggressive athletic event may promote hostility (Goldstein & Arms, 1971); sports participants typically compete before an audience, maximizing their ego-defensiveness regarding performance (Bradley, 1978); crowds often taunt or verbally abuse players for perceived errors (Baron, 1979); large amounts of money are sometimes at stake in what is usually a "zero-sum conflict" (Brickman, 1974). Although some of these variables apparently facilitate aggression only under certain conditions, it is clear that many factors other than perceived injustice can lead to sports violence.

Indeed, given the impressive list of factors unrelated to justice which facilitate violence—and the list could be expanded—it is perhaps remarkable that the problem of player and fan violence is not substantially more severe than it is. We contend that this relative success at controlling violence is largely attributable to the type of justice system predominant in sports. As we shall see later, this equity-based system has many advantages—it stresses the restoration of fairness after infractions occur, it penalizes all players identically for a given violation regardless of status or ability, and it successfully allows players both to feel that they have made up for their wrongdoing and to continue the game with "a clean slate." Because this justice system is not perfect, however, we also contend that in many instances the effects of these other causes of aggression are strengthened by the simultaneous perception of injustice. Perceived injustices increase the likelihood of an "expressive" or "confrontation riot," and likewise increase the tendency for deindividuation, and other arousal factors, to produce violence.

Previous observers concerned about sports violence have noted this interactive effect of perceived injustice and other causes of violence. Investigating causes of soccer riots and crowd outbursts, Smith (1975) indicates that prior assaultive behavior by players, spectators, and police is a separate and more important determinant than "unpopular referee's decisions"; nonetheless, Smith (1975) notes that "in several instances . . . player violence and unpopular referee's calls appeared to be part of an escalating series of precipitating factors" (p. 314). Referring to expressive riots after a disappointing defeat, Mann (1979) claims "it is likely that those engaged in violence are those who earlier judged that the team had been treated in a grossly unfair manner by the referee or the opposition" (p. 359).

In summary then, a variety of factors other than perceived injustice can lead to violence among sports spectators and participants. In fact, it seems a tribute to the justice system of sports that these factors do not lead to more violence than is the case. By acknowledging these other factors which facilitate aggression, we recognize that further reducing perceived injustices in sports will surely not eliminate sports violence entirely, since these other precipitating factors will remain. We are nevertheless optimistic that reducing perceived injustices will reduce sports violence, especially if as we have argued, other causal factors are most likely to result in violence when they occur in conjunction with perceived injustice.

Perceived Injustices in Sports: A Typology and Some Recommendations

As we have seen, numerous observers of sports have noted that perceived injustices play a significant role in sports violence. In this section we present a framework which describes the different types of perceived injustices that may arise in sports events. Our framework suggests that perceived injustices are most likely to occur (1) when an individual believes that one of the rules of the game is inaccurately or unfairly applied or (2) when the individual believes that a rule of the game itself is unfair, even if it were implemented accurately. Our framework includes one other category of perceived injustice, though we believe it is less frequent in sports. Perceived injustices can also be experienced in sports settings (3) when the individual feels unfairly deprived with respect to some outcome apart from the rules of the game, that is, through unfair denial of one's "rightful due."

In the present section we briefly discuss and illustrate these three types of perceived injustice. We further offer suggestions about how each type of perceived injustice could be controlled or reduced. If our analysis is correct, reducing the three types of perceived injustice should result in a concomitant reduction in sports violence.

Application of the Rules

Issues of perceived injustice appear to arise in sports most often in terms of contentions that rules are inaccurately or unfairly applied. Most of these contentions involve arguments that an official's call is in error. Such perceived officiating errors often result in fan and player violence, as Smith (1976), Smits (1968), Lewis (1975), and others have noted.

At the risk of oversimplifying, it may be said that sports officials make two types of judgments. One involves rule infractions: Did a player violate a rule or commit an illegal act that should be punished by a penalty? Examples of this kind of judgment include decisions about whether a football player clipped, whether a golfer illegally moved his ball, whether a baseball pitcher used an illegal substance on the ball, or whether a basketball player fouled an opponent. Judgments about rule infractions may also involve officials' decisions about intent on the part of the violators. The second type of judgment that sports officials make involves the outcome of play: Was a particular action successful or unsuccessful? Examples of this kind of judgment include decisions about whether a pitch was a strike or a ball, whether a wide receiver had possession of the football before he stepped out-of-bounds, and whether a tennis ball landed out-of-bounds.

Sports participants and observers can perceive that an official has erred in making either type of judgment. The tennis player described at the beginning of the chapter felt that the line judge was making inaccurate calls about the outcome of play. Fans and participants also perceive officiating errors involving rule infractions, and these can resemble either Type I (false positive) or Type II (false negative) errors. Type I officiating errors regarding infractions occur when an official penalizes a player for an infraction that did not occur. For instance, a football player might be called for roughing the kicker when in fact, unnoticed by the referee, he had actually been blocked into the kicker. Another Type I officiating error would be a basketball player who is charged with a foul, even though the player had in fact touched only the ball and not the opponent. Type II officiating errors occur when there has actually been a rule infraction but the official does not award a penalty. In football, officials may miss infractions such as holding, that typically occur in the midst of considerable action. In hockey, illegal acts often occur behind the officials' backs. We currently do not know whether the three types of perceived officiating errors we have described are equally likely to produce violence. It may be fruitful for future research to examine whether violence stems more often from bad calls about the outcome of plays or whether from either Type I or Type II errors in judging infractions. At present we can specify that an officiating error seems more likely to lead to violence the more serious the consequences of the error and the more flagrant the error (e.g., Lewis, 1975).

The officiating errors we have discussed thus far involve an official's judgment about a *specific* play or sequence of activities in a game. More serious concerns about rule applications arise when players or fans question the officiating for an entire game. Sometimes an official or officiating crew is perceived simply as "bad," that is, the officials are seen as failing to apply the rules competently, but erring equally toward both teams. In other more troublesome cases, as with the college lineman who assaulted the referee, officials are perceived to be biased. That is, officials sometimes seem to make more favorable calls toward one side than toward the other. It seems probable that players and spectators are most likely, first, to experience a severe sense of injustice and, second, to become violent when they believe that officials are biased.

Making officiating fairer. Our analysis suggests that one way in which organized sports can potentially reduce the likelihood of player and spectator violence is by improving officiating. Fair and accurate officiating reduces many perceptions of injustices that might otherwise lead to violence. Good officiating is also necessary to ensure that players do not turn to violence for instrumental reasons, as appears to be the case, for example, in hockey (see our discussion of instrumental violence which follows).

Many steps are available to obtain and maintain high-quality officiating. Some of these are already employed by various professional and collegiate sports. The selection and training of officials is obviously crucial. So is monitoring officials to ensure their continued high level of performance. Most professional sports "grade" officials and many select officials for postseason duties based on these quality ratings. Such efforts are to be applauded. We believe they should be expanded and that rigorous though fair criteria should be set for continued employment of officials. We also suggest that, if possible, evaluation of officials include checks for potential bias toward teams or players. For instance, the NBA could assess whether one official, relative to other officials, calls an unusually high number of penalities against any one particular team.

One strategy which may in some instances improve officiating is simply to increase the number of officials. Major league baseball now uses four officials and professional football seven, both representing increases in recent years. Fischler (1982) recently suggested that increasing the number of referees in NHL games would make it "unnecessary for teams to hire enforcers to neutralize enemy bullies." Fischler suggests that the current system, with one referee and two linesmen, be replaced by a system with three referees on the ice, a "spotter" in the stands, and three linesmen in raised seats. Each referee would be responsible for one-third of the playing area, and the "spotter" in the stands could relay information about misconduct not seen from the ice. We agree strongly with Fischler that the number of referees in NHL games should be increased. We are, however, somewhat skeptical about the use of an off-the-ice official.

Recommendations for the use of off-the-field officials, instant replays, or other mechanical devices are among the most controversial recommendations for improving sports officiating. Wimbledon has used sensors to detect whether a tennis ball is out, and similar sensors can detect whether a serve strikes the net. Professional football seems set on a long debate about the value of televised replays in settling difficult calls or in overruling seemingly inaccurate calls. Some proposals would allow each coach to appeal a specified number of plays per game to the off-the-field official monitoring the instant replay. It is easy to imagine using similar systems in other sports such as hockey or soccer; alternatively a "spotter" such as Fischler proposes could be used. One can even imagine an electronic sensor system used to judge strikes and balls in baseball, perhaps coupled with a microcomputer which would automatically set the appropriate strike zone for each batter.

We strongly believe such possibilities should be explored. Limited trials should be encouraged for these and other supplements to traditional officiating. Many sports have periods of preseason play that would be well suited to such trials. Despite our wholehearted endorsement for limited trials of off-the-field officials, instant replays, and mechanical sensors, we caution against the hasty official implementation of these or other supplements to the traditional sports official. Policy changes often have unanticipated consequences and it is important to try to determine in advance what if any these might be. For instance, current officiating practices generally do not interrupt the natural tempo of the contest. It would be difficult for an off-the-field official watching replays from several angles to achieve this unobtrusiveness. Care must also be taken to ensure that the supplements function properly and do in fact improve officiating decisions. Indeed, players questioned the accuracy of the automated judges used at Wimbledon. Similarly, considerable research is required to determine what camera positionings are necessary for instant replays to yield superior judgments in different sports. Furthermore, mechanical supplements and off-the-field officials must not only add to the accuracy and fairness of officiating, but they must also lead to the perception of fair, accurate officiating.

Making officiating seem fairer. Making officiating better should in principle reduce perceived injustice and hence reduce sports violence. An important possible qualification to this effect, however, relates to our earlier statement that injustice is "in the eye of the beholder." Specifically, the effectiveness of steps to improve officiating may be limited by the perceptual distortions or defensive reactions occurring among sports participants or committed fans. In other words, spectators may "see" officiating errors where none exist (perceptual distortion), or after defeat may defensively attribute failure to poor officiating (ego-defensive bias). Although it seems reasonable to assume that sports participants also have such reactions, they have been examined primarily among fans.

In a classic study bearing on this issue, Hastorf and Cantril (1954) had Princeton and Dartmouth students watch a film of a controversial football game that had previously taken place between the two schools. Students from both schools felt that their opponents had committed more violations than their own team. Hastorf and Cantril interpreted this result in terms of perceptual bias produced by team loyalty.

Exploring the same issue, Mann (1974) interviewed spectators after two South Australian Football League (soccer) grand finals. He found that, relative to non-partisan spectators and to supporters of the winning team, fans of the losing team were more likely to: judge that their team received fewer free kicks (i.e., beneficial penalty calls) than their opponents; state that the outcome was due to external factors (poor officiating or bad luck); and respond that dirty play had occurred, usually initiated by their opponents. In addition, after one game fans of the losing team gave poorer ratings to the umpire than did fans of the winning team (this latter difference was not statistically significant for the other game). Mann argues that these differences represent defensive rationalizations on the part of the disappointed fans of the losing team. Mann also suggests that the Hastorf and Cantril (1954) findings could be accounted for largely in terms of losing fans' defensive reactions to the outcome of the game—the Princeton and Dartmouth students knew the outcome of the game (it had taken place several weeks earlier) and distortion was apparently greater on the part of the losing Dartmouth fans. (Although the defensive attribution and perceptual bias explanations lead to similar recommendations, they do have somewhat different implications. Errors resulting from the defensive attributions should lead to violence only when a contest is over or the outcome is apparent. Perceptual distortions, on the other hand, could lead to increased violence at any time throughout the game. Our own observations lead us to hypothesize that perceptual distortion occurs during sports events, but that defensive reactions account for the differential salience and recall of misperceived officiating errors.)

Whatever the process underlying distortions of officiating quality, it is clear that besides improving officiating it is also important to improve how officiating is *perceived*. One step in this direction is to publicize efforts to improve officiating. If players and fans are aware of the extensive efforts to train, monitor, and supplement officials, they may find it less reasonable to believe that officials are biased. If participants' or spectators' expectations about officiating quality are raised to unreasonable levels, they may be disappointed even if officiating improves. If a tennis player believes that because an electronic sensor is being used, there should be *no* erroneous line calls, a single error might lead to a hostile outburst, even though the player might have commended an official who missed only one call.

A second way to enhance the perception that officiating is fair is to improve the communication officials have with players and fans. Controversial decisions or unusual rulings should be explained to both players and fans. Football has attempted to do this by having officials use microphones to explain their decisions. Alternatively, information about controversial or unusual rulings could be posted on scoreboards. Mann (1979) has further suggested that actual statistics about the number of penalties assessed against each team be displayed on scoreboards. Mann suggests this could reduce the potential dangers of distortion, because people could not overestimate the number of penalties assessed against their team.

While stadium scoreboards can be used in these ways to reduce perceived injustice, the modern, large scoreboards with instant replay capability may have a greater capacity to increase perceived injustice and instigate violence. When close or questionable calls against the home team are replayed on such scoreboards, fans may experience outrage and become violent. Indeed, the Baseball Umpires' Association recently asked the Atlanta Braves to stop televising instant replays on their stadium scoreboard, after fans violently disrupted a game in which the scoreboard replay clearly revealed an officiating error.

Fairness of the Rules

A second way in which individuals may perceive injustices in sports is by seeing a rule itself as unfair, even if the rule was perfectly implemented. Spectators at Roosevelt Raceway reacted violently even though New York racing rules were accurately applied; they simply felt that, if a rule declared official a race in which only two of eight horses finished, then the rule itself was unfair.

Our discussion focuses on those rules that concern violations or infractions, although it could be extended to other rules (such as the rule applied at Roosevelt Raceway). We begin our discussion of fairness and rules by describing two types of penalties that may be applied to rule infractions, equity-based penalties and deterrent-based penalties. We then briefly discuss the connection between the fairness of rules and instrumental violence. Finally, we discuss possible ways of improving equity-based and deterrent-based penalties.

Equity-based versus deterrent-based penalties. Even though frequent rule violations occur in many games, sports usually do not break down in disarray. In fact, by some standards the frequency of violence in sports is relatively low (Smith, 1982), especially considering, as we have seen, that sports events often occur in a context particularly facilitative of violence. Brickman (1977) suggested that rule violations cause only a relatively low level of disruption in sports because most deviance in sports occurs in the context of an equity-based rather than a deterrent-based penalty system.

The purpose of equity-based penalties is to restore fairness after infractions have occurred. The purpose of deterrent-based penalties is to prevent the incurrence of infractions. Consistent with their divergent goals, the two types of penalties also differ in their magnitude: Equity-based penalties are intended to be approximately proportional to the gain yielded by the infraction (e.g., awarding extra free throws to the basketball player fouled in the act of shooting), while deterrent-based penalties are intended to be extreme in magnitude, disproportional to the gain yielded by the infraction (e.g., the forfeiture of an entire season's competition and ineligibility for postseason play applied to NCAA member teams which intentionally use an ineligible athlete). Other examples of equity-based penalties include the various loss-of-yardage penalties in football, the free kick awarded in soccer, and the loss of a stroke in golf. Other examples of deterrent-based penalties, which are relatively rare in sports, are probation for collegiate recruiting violations, ejection from the game for striking an umpire, and forfeiture of the match for moving one's ball in golf or for hitting below the belt in boxing.

Besides their different purposes, Brickman (1977) noted several other distinctions between equity-based and deterrent-based penalties. For deterrent-based penalties, the question of intention is generally critical, while it is often irrelevant in the case of equity-based penalties. If an ineligible player is played in college football or one moves the ball incorrectly in golf, the deterrent-based penalty will differ substantially depending on whether the offense was intentional or not. If unintentional, the penalty will be severe but probably limited to the game or games in question. If deliberate, the penalty will almost certainly involve an extended period of time. In contrast, if a basketball player kicks the ball, or a soccer player touches the ball with his hands, the equity-based penalty does not depend on whether the violation was intentional.

These two types of penalties also differ in the timing of their administration (Brickman, 1977). Equity-based penalties are decided upon and implemented immediately, with as little disruption of the game as possible. Deterrent-based penalties may not be implemented immediately, often requiring a hearing because of their severity.

Equity-based penalties are designed so as to disrupt neither the flow nor the balance of a competition. Instead, they are intended to restore to the contest the competitive balance in effect prior to the violation. Nor do equity-based penalties stigmatize offenders. Deterrent-based penalties, in contrast, by their nature are of such magnitude that they are likely to alter the outcome of a contest, and in many instances decide automatically that the violator loses. Deterrent-based penalties also stigmatize the offender, as when a college team is placed on the NCAA probation list.

Inadequate penalties and instrumental violence. One of the most important connections between rules and sports violence involves the inadequacy of penalties for overly aggressive action. Much of the violence among sports participants is instrumental, in that participants undertake it in an attempt to increase their chances of success. For instance, Gaskell and Pearton (1979) point to "top soccer players [who are] incapacitated in the first few minutes of the game, at times presumably on the instructions of the coach, . . . and ice hockey teams . . . [which] resort to physical violence in attempts to draw crowds and pulverize the opposition" (p. 280). Such incidents, Gaskell and Pearton claim, "are a conscious and intentional strategy on the part of the individual and team to succeed by intimidation and violence." Smith (1974) also reports that most hockey violence is of the instrumental type. Ice hockey has probably received the greatest attention in discussions of instrumental violence, with its "enforcers." However, other sports also have instances of instrumental violence: Football players have been known to exceed the rules of the game to instill "respect" in an opponent (Tatum & Kushner, 1979); baseball's "bean ball" or brushback pitches are generally intentional acts designed to keep a hitter from "digging in" and being well set for a pitch (Bouton, 1972); and basketball players are notorious for aggressive acts aimed at intimidating their opponents while "crashing the boards" to gain better position for rebounding (Hawkins, 1972).

Instrumental aggression belongs in a discussion of justice and sports violence because it is the very nature of penalties that allows violent acts to be instrumental. If penalties for a particular form of violence are sufficiently severe and the rate for detecting violations is sufficiently high (i.e., Type II officiating errors are reasonably infrequent), then that form of violence will lose its instrumentality. In baseball, the incidence of bean balls seems to have declined substantially in recent years, after rule modifications called for the removal of the offending pitcher and his manager after the second bean ball in a game. The connection between penalty levels and instrumental violence has not gone unrecognized by individuals close to sports. Commenting on the National Hockey League, Fischler (1982) stated that "inadequate refereeing inspires wanton retaliation-vigilantism." And Don Perry, coach of the Los Angeles Kings who became embroiled in controversy after allegedly ordering Paul Mulvey onto the ice to join a brawl, commented, "I don't think we will get rid of fighting entirely, but I would like to see the NHL make the rules stiff enough to get rid of most of it" (cited in Fischler, 1982). This can be accomplished by improving equity-based and deterrent-based penalties.

Improving equity-based penalties. Organized sports often adjust their equity-based penalties. For example, collegiate football recently modified its rules on offensive holding. Frequently these adjustments are made to achieve goals that sports administrators deem desirable, such as increasing the offense generated by the forward pass in football. Adjustments to equity-based penalties can also reduce the likelihood of violence if they increase players' and spectators' sense that fairness has been restored after an infraction.

We have two general suggestions as to how improvements could be made in sports' equity-based penalties. The first is that research could be undertaken to uncover inadequacies in current equity-based penalties. One strategy for this research is to examine game statistics to determine whether a particular type of infraction systematically affects a team's chances of success. What do the records indicate happens, for instance, when the defensive team in football interferes with a pass? Does the offensive team's chance of scoring remain similar to that for offensive drives when interference does not occur, or do the chances of scoring increase or decrease considerably? If a dramatic increase occurs in the offensive team's prospects, this may indicate that the present rules penalize the defense substantially more than equity would dictate.

Another type of research directed at improving equity-based penalties is at once more promising and more troublesome. It involves interviewing those active in a sport to measure what they perceive to be a fair penalty for a particular form of infraction. Similar procedures have been used to assess what individuals believe are fair punishments for crimes (Hamilton & Rytina, 1980; Rossi, Waite, Base, & Berk, 1974; Sellin & Wolfgang, 1964). If this procedure is used with care, it may detect deficiencies that interested parties perceive in the equity-based penalty structure. However, this research methodology is susceptible to various problems endemic to self-report data and would have to be interpreted and applied with great caution.

Our second general suggestion for improving equity-based penalties is based on the observation that the potential gain from rule violations varies at different times in a contest. In a basketball game, for example, the defensive team has more to gain by fouling if it is one point behind and time has nearly expired; it is possible that the offensive player will miss the resulting free throws and that possession of the ball will change. Similar contingencies could be cited for other sports. Equity-based penalties could be modified to account for the fact that violations differ in their instrumentality depending on the circumstances of the game. A precedent for this exists in basketball. The referee can award the fouled player two free throws (as opposed to the usual one-shot penalty for a nonshooting foul) if he believes a foul was intentional. Although the referee can apply this rule at any time, in practice the two-shot intentional foul is almost always called only at the end of a game when the foul has a potentially greater benefit for the offending team.

Improving and formalizing deterrent-based penalties. Though most penalties in sports are equity-based, there are also instances of deterrent-based penalties. One strategy for reducing violent acts by sports participants is to subject such acts to deterrent-based penalties. To some extent, this is consistent with the conceptualization underlying the two types of penalties. Brickman (1977) suggested that equity-based and deterrent-based penalties are generally attached to qualitatively different types of infractions. Specifically, equity-based penalties are "generally attached to inappropriate strategies or tactics . . . [which] can generally be recognized as a variant of a behavior that would under other circumstances be appropriate in the game" (p. 142-143). Deterrent-based penalties on the other hand, "are generally attached to violations of the assumptions of the game, or to behavior that would never be appropriate under any circumstances if the game . . . were to continue" (p. 143). For example, the Ladies Professional Golf Association expelled one of its touring professionals several years ago after discovering that she was secretly moving her ball closer to the hole during tournament play. Analogously, if certain forms of violent behavior are judged to be inappropriate under any circumstances, it is fitting that they be subject to deterrent-based penalties.

Some violent actions in sports are already fixed in a deterrent-based system. Hitting below the belt or butting can lead to a boxer's disqualification. In baseball, as mentioned earlier, retaliating with a bean ball in response to an earlier bean ball in the same game results in ejection of both the offending pitcher and his manager. It is easy to imagine how other, similar deterrent-based penalties could be applied. For instance, batters could face instant ejection (and perhaps a suspension of specified duration) if they crossed a given point in moving toward the pitcher's mound.

Fischler (1982) has similarly proposed an across-the-board ban against players raising hockey sticks above the waist for any purpose other than shooting. While he suggests that violations of this rule be met with a 5-minute major penalty, the magnitude of the penalty could of course be other than this. Comparable deterrent-based penalties could be assigned to other violent acts in other sports. Furthermore, deterrent-based penalties, like equity-based penalties, could be made contingent on game conditions such that greater penalties are assigned when violations are most likely to be instrumental. For example, if sports violence is more likely to occur when valuable future benefits are at stake for fans or participants (McIntosh, 1979), then stronger deterrents could be added to counteract this aggressive tendency. Interestingly, one professional baseball club recently retaliated with a bean ball in the following game of a three-game series, to circumvent the rule banning successive bean balls within the same game. Although completely "legal" according to the rule book, this act caused a violent brawl between the opposing teams in which several players were injured. Thus it may be advantageous to give referees the discretion not only to penalize a retaliatory bean ball in the *same* game, but to punish retaliatory bean balls thrown in *successive* games as well. Just as we must be flexible about modifying equity-based penalties to make the punishment fit the crime, we must provide deterrent-based penalties with this same flexibility to deter infractions effectively.

In many sports, responses to acts of excessive violence currently fall within the purview of the league commissioner. Commissioner Campbell, for example, was responsible for the decision to suspend Maurice Richard. Because that punishment seemed excessively unfair, Canadien fans reacted violently. After Dave Forbes received a 10-day suspension in 1975, four of his Boston Bruin teammates planned to boycott the NHL All-Star Game in protest, though they were persuaded otherwise by Forbes. These examples illustrate that protest reactions sometimes follow when sports officials assign punishments which are, in the eyes of many, "arbitrary" or "excessive." Such reactions can probably be avoided if the penalties for violent acts are codified and known publicly in advance. Furthermore, without such prior knowledge, it is impossible for the prospect of punishment to have a deterrent effect. However, it is still feasible to have a penalty system which allows for a range of possible penalties (as does society's criminal justice system), permitting more severe punishment if the violation is either intentional or especially severe and allowing leniency if intent is unclear.

When harsh deterrent-based penalties are contemplated, issues of due process naturally arise. This is especially true when the severity of such punishments approaches or exceeds the severity of potential punishments resulting from criminal prosecution. In this age of the millionaire athlete, suspension without pay, even for a short time, is a substantial penalty. It is crucial that sports be sensitive to issues of due process regarding deterrent-based penalties, lest their severity diminish the fairness of sports rules and exacerbate the very problems they seek to reduce. There is another reason that increases in deterrent-based penalties must be made with care: Making penalties more severe sometimes causes them to be applied less frequently. Fearing Type I (false positive) errors, officials may hesitate to impose harsh penalties unless the violation is clearly unambiguous. This tendency may be especially pronounced before large "home crowds" (Edwards, 1979), during championship play, or when such rulings would decide the final outcome of competition.

Unfair Denial of "Rightful Due"

A third way in which individuals may perceive injustices in sports involves feeling unfairly deprived with respect to some outcome apart from the rules of the game (i.e., through unfair denial of rightful due). In their typologies of fan violence, Lang (1981) and Mann (1979) discussed the acquisitive crowd and the deprivation riot, respectively. Both of these types of aggression involve fans who react violently when deprived of something which they believed they would obtain. Examples include reactions when access to a stadium is blocked, when a highly touted match on a boxing card is unexpectedly cancelled, when players are perceived not to try their hardest, and when a promotion falls short (e.g., when there are not enough bats on "bat day"). Such incidents involve perceived injustice rather than simple "frustration," when fans feel they are entitled to and deserve the object of which they are deprived.

Although Lang's and Mann's typologies describe fan outbursts, sports participants as well may sometimes feel deprived of their "just due" with respect to concerns other than the rules of the game or how these rules are implemented. For example, professional athletes probably expect locker rooms to meet certain standards. Contract negotiations sometimes include such details as the athlete having a private hotel room when traveling with the team. And, of course, that most central issue in contract negotiations and renegotiations, money, is often discussed in terms of what the player feels he or she deserves. We can only speculate about whether players who feel unfairly treated in these areas are more inclined toward violence.

The most obvious procedure for reducing this type of perceived injustice is for those responsible for sports events to strive to deliver those goods and services which fans were promised. Sports administrators should remember that satisfactory delivery of the "product" is necessary not only for the commercial success of their sport, but also for avoiding a sense of frustration and perceived injustice, and the consequent increased likelihood of violence. On those occasions when it is impossible to deliver these goods, the reasons should be communicated as clearly as possible so that deprived individuals recognize their deprivation is not for illegitimate reasons. In addition, if possible, there should be a mechanism for the deprived individual to be compensated. When he owned the Chicago White Sox, for example, the master sportsman Bill Veeck on several occasions gave free passes to fans who sat through a game during inclement weather, or when the White Sox played an unusually incompetent game.

What Society Can Learn from Sports

In the previous section, we considered improvements that could be made in the system of rules and penalties used in sports. We now turn to the ideas that an analogy can be drawn between sports and society, and that, though imperfect, the equity-based justice system predominant in sports represents a model that society could usefully imitate.

Applying Elements of Sports' Justice Systems to Society

Brickman (1977) has compared the penalty systems predominant in sports and society, and he contends that society can gain much by incorporating into its own justice system elements of the equity-based rules and penalties used so successfully in sports. Brickman noted four key features of the way sports generally react to illegal acts. In this section we review these four elements and then illustrate how society could apply them to improve its criminal justice system.

Perhaps the most essential feature of the justice system in sports is that conflict is recognized as "a central and inevitable element" (Brickman, 1974). Having recognized the inevitability of conflict, it follows that deviance in the pursuit of selfish aims is also an inevitable element of the system. By accepting that conflict is inevitable, the sports world is able to rely predominantly on equity-based penalties, which are designed to react to deviance by restoring equity, as opposed to deterrent-based penalties, which are designed to prevent conflict and deviance.

Second, the major purpose of the system of rules and penalties in sports is *restoring fairness* (not just punishing or rehabilitating wrongdoers). This goal of restoring things to how they were before any given infraction occurred is consistent with the overall aim of justice as Plato defined it—to maintain the health of the social order. Indeed, a justice system that does not restore the balance of fairness seems absurd. To illustrate this point, imagine the following situations occurring in a football game. Team A's offensive receiver is waiting for an easy 35-yard touchdown pass that is in midair, when Team B's defensive cornerback knocks him down from behind and intercepts the pass. The referee calls a pass interference penalty on the defender, but gives the defensive team (B) possession of the ball. Alternatively, Team C's defensive tackle jumps across the line of scrimmage before Team D snaps the football. The referee calls an offside penalty and, because this was the defensive tackle's third offside violation, the referee ejects him from the game and suspends him from further league play. These seemingly bizarre penalties involve rulings that fail to restore fairness, either by rewarding the offender (i.e., Team B's cornerback) or by punishing the offender excessively (i.e., Team C's tackle). They illustrate that the essence of the rules and penalties in sports is the restoration of justice. Although penalties in sports can only approximate the damage caused by fouls or infractions, they are generally viewed by participants and observers alike as serving justice satisfactorily. Admittedly, some rules and penalties in sports do seem unfair to fans and players. Often in such cases, however, a belief that over the course of the game "things will eventually even themselves out" helps participants to preserve a sense of fairness.

A third crucial feature of sports' justice systems is that in sports rule violators are treated more or less alike, regardless of their status or abilities; few special considerations are given to the better players. The sixth personal foul in professional basketball automatically banishes the offender from the game, regardless of whether he is Kareem Abdul-Jabbar or the worst player in the NBA. Similarly, tripping in ice hockey is an automatic 2-minute penalty, whether you are Wayne Gretzky or the NHL's weakest player.

Finally, after restoring fairness, the sports world successfully manages to "wipe the slate clean" for players who commit violations. The stigma of having been an offender no longer remains. In ice hockey, for instance, after a player sits out for his 2-minute tripping penalty, he skates back on the ice and is treated just like any other player; since the penalty has been successfully served, no lingering stigma remains attached to the wrongdoer.

We believe society could use elements of these four features to improve its own system of justice. As Brickman (1977) noted, society has not yet admitted the fact that conflict is a central and inevitable element of our system. If society could accept that "people are not perfectable, that certain forms of deviance in the human situation are inevitable, and that therefore we must build a system of justice whose operating ideal is a case in which deviance occurs rather than a case in which all deviance has been deterred" (Brickman, 1977, p. 151), perhaps we would be more accepting of penalties designed to restore fairness (i.e., equity-based penalties) and less eager for stronger punishments of infractions (i.e., deterrent-based penalties).

Like the football player who received no compensation after being interfered with by an opponent, victims of crime in society sometimes feel that fairness has not been restored even after the offender has been punished. Society frequently leaves victims to start over on their own, either without their property (which had been stolen) or with astronomical medical expenses from injuries, and with the psychological trauma of their victimization usually remaining. And like the football player who was ejected from the game and suspended after his third violation, criminal offenders in society sometimes feel that their prescribed punishment exceeds the magnitude of their crime. Indeed, the overcrowding, violence, and despair that plagues our prison system makes long-term sentences seem like a form of "cruel and unusual punishment." If society were to make restoration of fairness the main goal of its justice system, as does sports, then one way to achieve this would be to give criminals sentences whose purpose is to "restore both the loss that the victim had suffered and the loss that society suffered through its investment in preventing, detecting, and punishing such crimes" (Brickman, 1977, p. 152).

Numerous legal scholars, philosophers, and sociologists (e.g., Forer, 1980; Fry, 1959; Gandy, 1978; Schafer, 1970; Smith, 1965) have proposed "restitution" as an alternative system for restoring fairness. The restitution model requires that offenders work to repay both their victims and society for the physical, psychological, and financial damages caused. By working to compensate victims and society for their losses, offenders may not only experience punishment for their crimes, but may gain self-respect and responsibility for the future as well (Brickman, 1977; Eglash, 1958).

Just as sports' penalties are only approximations of the damage that violations cause, so are sentences in the criminal justice system. What sports have been able to establish, and what society should strive to attain, is a sense among its participants and observers that the sentences for crimes are satisfactory in "serving justice." Because a criminal serving time in prison does nothing to restore fairness for the victim of the crime, supporters of restitution have proposed that sentences for offenders include "labor directly concerned to recover property, repair damage, or make streets safer" (Brickman, 1977, p. 152). More generally, restitution sentences might require the criminal to contribute earnings from specified tasks to a general fund whose purpose is to compensate victims. One important difference between equity-based penalties and deterrent-based penalties is that equity-based penalties always have meaning, so that offenders (and usually victims and society) know precisely why certain things are being required of them. In contrast, deterrent-based penalties are not necessarily connected to the crime in any meaningful way, but rather are arbitrary and fixed forms of punishment. Thus, the key to an equity-based system is the idea that the penalties (i.e., restitution) are meaningfully connected to the violation in a way that punishment per se or current prison practices are not.

Penalties in sports are applied to all players relatively equally, regardless of their status or abilities. Just as the weakest player in the NBA has to sit out of the remainder of the game when he commits his sixth personal foul, so does Kareem Abdul-Jabbar. While equal justice may not be perfectly obtained in sports, the cause of justice in society would be furthered if society favored the advantaged no more than does sports. One major objection often raised in connection with restitution sentences is that the rich would be able to buy their way out of sentences that poor people would have to serve. To alleviate this problem, sentences could require offenders to make restitution by performing specific tasks for certain salaries, with only the pay earned for these tasks applying to the sentence (Brickman, 1977).

Finally, our criminal justice system has been harshly criticized for the way it stigmatizes ex-offenders. Brickman (1977) argued that what ex-convicts resent most of all is that, although society has sentenced them to imprisonment to pay their debt, society never gives them credit for having paid. Criminal sentences do not restore equity and do not wipe the slate clean. Since the status of criminal offenders is perceived as permanent, it is difficult for ex-offenders to begin anew. Thus, our criminal justice system often leads offenders to feel that society owes them a debt. Ex-offenders who feel that they have restored equity (i.e., repaid for the wrong they committed) should feel less stigma in the future, just as the hockey player who has served his penalty skates back onto the ice and becomes "just like any other player out there."

Are Sports Special?

The preceding comments suggest that society could benefit from emulating sports' predominantly equity-based approach to infractions. One response to this suggestion is the argument that sports are special, and that the special nature of sports means that equity-based penalties will succeed in sports even though they would not succeed in society.

Brickman (1977) considered and refuted four related arguments about why equity-based penalties might be appropriate in sports but inappropriate in society more generally. We shall briefly review those arguments here. We shall then consider four additional arguments. One argument that Brickman considered is that equity-based penalties are appropriate in sports but not in society because "the stakes are lower in sports." Although the consequences of being "clipped" in football or being "tripped" in hockey are usually less serious for victims than being robbed or even harassed, the stakes in professional sports are sometimes as high as in other areas of life. In both sports and society, one's income and one's self-esteem often depend on one's performance in "the game." Even in amateur sports among children the stakes are sometimes considerable. Because winning is so important, for example, star Little Leaguers often develop elbow and shoulder injuries from pitching too often before their bones have hardened (Torg, 1982).

A second argument is that sports accommodate equity-based penalties in a way that society cannot because sports are based on different values than the rest of society—values of fair play and honor above victory. Yet one of the most lengendary coaches in the history of football believed that, "Winning isn't everything; it's the only thing." Even if Vince Lombardi "did not in fact condone all means to victory, it is clear that many of those who admired him have been less discriminating" (Brickman, 1977, p. 148). From professional leagues to children's sports, competitiveness and the desire to win often overshadow the values of fair play and good sportsmanship. Although most youngsters take up sports initially just to be with their friends and to have fun, these goals are quickly subverted by a competitive societal emphasis on winning. The sports world, like society, teaches participants to value competitive success—to "play to win." This lesson quickly becomes ingrained in children. A well-known motto at a children's summer camp in Maine illustrates this point. While playing tennis, especially against another camp, kids are taught to remember, "When in doubt, call it out."

A third argument, based on assumptions contrary to the second, is that for sports contests we relax our ordinary standards and are unconcerned with behavior that would ordinarily be judged harshly. This reduces our desire to control deviance, making us accept equity-based penalties that we would otherwise reject. Admittedly, sports sometimes allows players to behave violently and spectators to admire this violence. However, to say that the sports world is unconcerned with fairness or harsh behavior is a misstatement. Although some violence can be construed as "part of the game" in certain sports, it is also true that we wish to see violent behavior punished if it is perpetrated unfairly. Our desire for fairness in sports seems to be as strong as in other areas, and in fact, "the 'sports' that most strongly feature a display of violence—the Roller Derby and Professional Wrestling—are also the strongest morality plays, with audiences deeply concerned to have the good guys triumph over the unfair tactics of the bad guys" (Brickman, 1977, p. 150).

The final argument that Brickman considered is simply that sports are special because we think of them as a "peculiar form of interaction deliberately marked off from the rest of life, with [their] own special rules" (Brickman, 1977, p. 150). Brickman's response to this argument was that sports are not peculiar parts of life but rather entail the same sorts of rules and involve the same types of social psychological processes as do other spheres of life (e.g., the home or the workplace).

In sum, sports do not seem to be a separate, distinct domain apart from the rest of society. On the contrary, the sports world is strikingly similar to and symbolic of society in terms of its values and basic assumptions. Thus, we believe that society has much to learn from sports—that the same types of improvements which have helped sports justice systems work so effectively may likewise benefit society's criminal justice system.

There are at least four additional possible differences between sports and society. These differences are more difficult to refute than those considered by Brickman. The first two involve social organizational differences between highly structured sports events, on the one hand, an an anonymous, transient society, on the other. First, in sports the participants are in direct interaction and generally must continue to interact after a rule infraction (or else the game is over); society, in contrast, must deal with infractions involving strangers or interactants whose continued activity does not depend on the presence of the other. It may be that restitution can function better, and specifically will be more meaningful to both victim and offender, when the two parties exist in an ongoing social network. An interesting analysis of this point is provided by Nader and Combs-Schilling (1975), who examine restitution from a cross-cultural perspective. We might add incidentally that the fact that crimes in society can easily occur between people who might otherwise not interact, might help explain why criminal acts are conceived largely as "crimes against society" rather than simply as crimes against the victim (also see Jacobs, 1975, and Schafer, 1970, for the history of the concept of "crimes against society").

A second difference exists between sports and society that may account for any difference between the two in terms of the effectiveness or acceptability of equity-based and deterrent-based penalties. Equity-based penalties may in fact be more likely to restore equity in sports than in society. In sports opponents interact over a period of time during the contest. This continual interaction contributes to the sense that, even if a penalty (e.g., 15 yards in football) is too large or too small for a particular single violation, or even if a particular infraction was not seen by the official, errors will even out over the course of the game and in the long run equity will be restored. If equity-based penalties were applied to criminal acts in society, people might have much less cause to believe that errors will even out. In part, this is because of perceived differences in terms of the likelihood of detection.

A third possible difference between sports and society involves how "membership" is gained and maintained in each. Not everyone must participate in organized sports. As one moves up the ladder of organized sports, from the sandlot to the professional arena, there are selection criteria, and these may function to screen out individuals prone to deviance. Further, organized sports can simply banish players for infractions. Society, in contrast, has no selection criteria for membership, and that which corresponds closest to banishment is incarceration or execution.

Finally, a fourth difference exists between sports and society which could result in equity-based penalties being less effective in society. As we have noted, sports is probably more effective in guaranteeing that all its members are treated "equally under the law." Unlike society, all sports contests begin with the score tied. Moreover, in professional sports some measure of competitiveness is required for fan interest, so mechanisms exist to avoid excessive superiority on the part of one or two teams (e.g., in player drafts teams with the worst records pick first). A somewhat radical analysis suggests that equity-based penalties may be ineffective—and in fact impossible—in the face of inequalities of outcome and opportunity. In the words of Anatole France (1907), "the law, in its majestic equality, forbids the rich as well as the poor to sleep under bridges, to beg in the streets, and to steal bread."

In sum our analysis suggests that while sports and society are generally similar in terms of values and basic assumptions, they differ in other important ways. Careful consideration of these differences may lead to a better understanding of when restitution programs in society will and will not work. They also point to structural impediments in society that may counteract the general advantages of equity-based penalties. Students of social order and social conflict may learn much more from extensive study of sports in society.

Conclusion

In this chapter we have examined the role of perceived injustice in sports violence. Our partial review of the literature revealed that numerous commentators and occasional empirical studies have noted that fan and spectator violence often are the result of some form of perceived injustice. Such observations have not been integrated, however, and have taken place in the absence of a comprehensive framework which describes the types of perceived injustice in sports. In the present chapter, we have attempted to provide such an integrative framework. Based on this framework we have also made suggestions about possible ways of reducing perceived injustices in sports. Our contention is that by alleviating perceived injustice, sports violence will be reduced.

We believe that the framework presented in this chapter can be expanded further to provide a much more complete understanding of the consequences of perceived injustices in sports. We have not been able to attend sufficiently to how participants and spectators might react differently to perceived injustices, and to how these two groups may influence each other. Nor have we analyzed rule structures on a sport by sport basis, as would be done in a more comprehensive analysis. And we have not considered the possibility that perceived injustices may sometimes lead to responses other than anger (e.g., a player may resolve to try harder, or a fan may decide that the sport is not worth watching; see Mark, 1982). In short, while the present analysis represents a substantial advance in understanding how perceived injustices affect sports violence, there are numerous conceptual and empirical advances yet to be made. In fact, a careful reading of the chapter will reveal the outline of a program of research that could be conducted to increase our knowledge about the role of perceived injustice in sports violence.

In the last part of this chapter we compared the justice systems of sports and society, extending an earlier analysis by Brickman (1977). Our comparison between sports and society may imply that society could benefit by reducing its reliance on deterrent-based penalties in favor of more equity-based penalties. Our comparison further indicates that societal justice may be partially understood through the study of justice in sports. It may be that, just as "the Battle of Waterloo was won on the playing fields of Eton," the battle for a more just society may be won partly by learning from Yankee Stadium, Soldiers' Field, and Pauly Pavillion.

Acknowledgments. This chapter is lovingly dedicated to Phil Brickman, a man of tremendous compassion, friendship, and scholarship. Phil's untimely death prevented him from being a coauthor of the chapter and we are proud to acknowledge his contribution of ideas and much more.

We would also like to thank Sheldon Alexander, Nancy Cantor, and Jon Krosnick for their helpful comments on a previous version of the chapter.

References

Alves, W. M., & Rossi, P. H. Who should get what? Fairness judgments on the distributions of earnings. *American Journal of Sociology*, 1978, *84*, 541-564.
Baron, R. A. Effects of victim's pain cues, victim's race, and level of prior instigation upon physical aggression. *Journal of Applied Social Psychology*, 1979, *9*, 103-114.
Baron, R. A., & Bell, P. A. Aggression and heat: The influence of ambient tempera-

ture, negative affect, and a cooling drink on physical aggression. *Journal of Personality and Social Psychology,* 1976, *33,* 245-255.

Berkowitz, L. Frustration, comparisons, and other sources of emotional arousal as contributors to social unrest. *Journal of Social Issues,* 1972, *28,* 77-91.

Bouton, J. *Ball Four.* Briarcliff Manor, New York: Stein & Day, 1972.

Bradley, G. W. Self-serving biases in the attribution process: A reexamination of the fact or fiction question. *Journal of Personality and Social Psychology,* 1978, *36,* 56-71.

Brickman, P. (Ed.). *Social conflict: Readings in rule structures and conflict relationships.* Lexington, Mass.: D. C. Heath, 1974.

Brickman, P. Crime and punishment in sports and society. *Journal of Social Issues,* 1977, *33,* 140-164.

Brickman, P., Ryan, K., & Wortman, C. B. Causal chains: Attribution of responsibility as a function of immediate and prior causes. *Journal of Personality and Social Psychology,* 1975, *32,* 1060-1067.

Bryant, J., Comisky, P., & Zillmann, D. The appeal of rough-and-tumble play in televised professional football. *Communication Quarterly,* 1981, *29,* 256-262.

Bryant, J., & Zillmann, D. Effect of intensification of annoyance through unrelated residual excitation on substantially delayed hostile behavior. *Journal of Experimental Social Psychology,* 1979, *15,* 470-480.

Cavanaugh, B. M., & Silva, J. M. III. Spectator perceptions of fan misbehavior: An attitudinal inquiry. In C. H. Nadeau, W. R. Halliwell, K. M. Newell, & G. C. Roberts (Eds.), *Psychology of motor behavior and sport,* 1979. Champaign, Ill.: Human Kinetics, 1980.

Crosby, F. A model of egoistical relative deprivation. *Psychological Review,* 1976, *83,* 85-113.

Crosby, F. *Relative deprivation and working women.* New York: Oxford University Press, 1982.

Davis, J. A. A formal interpretation of the theory of relative deprivation. *Sociometry,* 1959, *22,* 280-296.

Dollard, J., Doob, L., Miller, N., Mowrer, O., & Sears, R. *Frustration and aggression.* New Haven: Yale University Press, 1939.

Donnerstein, E., & Wilson, D. Effects of noise and perceived control on ongoing and subsequent aggressive behavior. *Journal of Personality and Social Psychology,* 1976, *34,* 774-781.

Edwards, J. D. The home field advantage. In J. H. Goldstein (Ed.), *Sports, games, and play.* Hillsdale, N. J.: Erlbaum, 1979.

Eglash, A. Creative restitution: A broader meaning for an old term. *Journal of Criminal Law, Criminology and Police Science,* 1958, *48,* 619-622.

Eitzen, D. S. Sport and deviance. In G. R. F. Lüschen & G. H. Sage (Eds.), *Handbook of social science of sport.* Champaign, Ill: Stipes, 1981.

Fischler, S. Thoughts on helping N. H. L. undo its seige on itself. *New York Times,* March 28, 1982, p. S-2.

Forer, L. *Criminals and victims.* New York: W. W. Norton and Co., 1980.

France, A. *Crainquebille.* Paris: Calmann-Lévy, 1907.

Freedman, J. L., Levy, A. S., Buchanan, R. W., & Price, J. Crowding and human aggressiveness. *Journal of Experimental Social Psychology*, 1972, *8*, 528-548.

Fry, M. Justice for victims. *Journal of Public Law*, 1959, *8*, 191-194.

Gandy, J. Attitudes toward the use of restitution. In J. Hudson and B. Galaway (Eds.), *Offender restitution in theory and action.* Lexington, Mass.: D. C. Heath, 1974.

Gaskell, G., & Pearton, R. Aggression and sport. In J. H. Goldstein (Ed.), *Sports, games, and play.* Hillsdale, N. J.: Erlbaum, 1979.

Goldstein, J. H., & Arms, R. L. Effects of observing athletic contests on hostility. *Sociometry*, 1971, *34*, 83-90.

Gurr, T. R. *Why men rebel.* Princeton: Princeton University Press, 1970.

Hamilton, V. L., & Rytina, S. Social consensus on norms of justice: Should the punishment fit the crime? *American Journal of Sociology*, 1980, *85*, 1117-1144.

Hastorf, A. H., & Cantril, H. They saw a game: A case study. *Journal of Abnormal and Social Psychology*, 1954, *49*, 129-134.

Hawkins, C. *Foul.* New York: Holt, Rinehart and Winston, 1972.

Jacobs, B. The concept of restitution: An historical overview. In J. Hudson & B. Galaway (Eds.), *Restitution in criminal justice.* Lexington, Mass.: D. C. Heath, 1975.

Kuhlman, W. Violence in professional sports. *Wisconsin Law Review*, 1975, *3*, 771-790.

Lang, G. E. Riotous outbursts at sports events. In G. R. F. Lüschen & G. H. Sage (Eds.), *Handbook of social science of sport.* Champaign, Ill.: Stipes, 1981.

Lewis, J. M. Sports riots: Some research questions. Paper presented at the meeting of the American Sociological Association, San Francisco, 1975.

Lipsky, R. *How we play the game: Why sports dominate American life.* Boston: Beacon Press, 1981.

Mann, L. On being a sore loser: How fans react to their team's failure. *Australian Journal of Psychology*, 1974, *26*, 37-47.

Mann, L. Sports crowds viewed from the perspective of collective behavior. In J. H. Goldstein (Ed.), *Sports, games, and play.* Hillsdale, N.J.: Erlbaum. 1979.

Mark, M. M. *The effects of relative deprivation: A test of a contingency theory.* Unpublished manuscript, The Pennsylvania State University, 1982.

McIntosh, P. *Fair play: Ethics in sports and education.* London: Heinemann, 1979.

Michener, J. A. *Sports in America.* New York: Random House, 1976.

Nader, L., & Combs-Schilling, E. Restitution in cross-cultural perspective. In J. Hudson & B. Galaway (Eds.), *Restitution in criminal justice.* Lexington, Mass.: D. C. Heath, 1975.

Pastore, N. The role of arbitrariness in the frustration-aggression hypothesis. *Journal of Abnormal and Social Psychology*, 1952, *47*, 728-731.

Rossi, P., Waite, E., Base, C. E., & Berk, R. E. The seriousness of crimes: Normative structure and individual differences. *American Sociological Review*, 1974, *39*, 224-237.

Schafer, S. *Compensation and restitution to victims of crime* (2nd ed.). Montclair, N.J.: Patterson Smith, 1970.

Sellin, J. T., & Wolfgang, M. E. *The measurement of delinquency.* New York: Wiley, 1964.

Simmons, C. H. Theoretical issues in the development of social justice. In M. J. Lerner & S. C. Lerner (Eds.), *The justice motive in social behavior.* New York: Plenum, 1981.

Smith, K. J. *A cure for crime: The case for the self-determinate prison sentence.* London: Gerald Docksworth, 1965.

Smith, M. D. Significant others' influence on the assaultive behavior of young hockey players. *International Review of Sport Sociology,* 1974, *9,* 45-58.

Smith, M. D. Sport and collective violence. In D. W. Ball & J. W. Loy (Eds.), *Sport and social order: Contributions to the sociology of sport.* Reading, Mass: Addison-Wesley, 1975.

Smith, M. D. Precipitants of crowd violence. *Sociological Inquiry,* 1976, *48,* 121-131.

Smits, T. *The game of soccer.* Englewood Cliffs, N. J.: Prentice-Hall, 1968.

Tatum, J., & Kushner, B. *They call me assassin.* New York: Everest House, 1979.

Taylor, S. P., & Gammon, C. B. Effects of type and dose of alcohol on human physical aggression. *Journal of Personality and Social Psychology,* 1975, *32,* 169-175.

Torg, J. S. *Athletic injuries to the head, neck, and face.* Philadelphia: Lee & Febiger, 1982.

Tucker, D. College sports (Part 4 of a 4-part Associated Press series). State College, Penn., *Centre Daily Times,* March 27, 1982, p. C-1.

Walster, E., Berscheid, E., & Walster, G. W. New directions in equity research. *Journal of Personality and Social Psychology,* 1973, *25,* 151-176.

Zimbardo, P. G. The human choice: Individuation, reason and order vs. deindividuation, impulse and chaos. In W. Arnold & D. Levine (Eds.), *Nebraska Symposium on Motivation* (Vol. 17). Lincoln: University of Nebraska Press, 1969.

Chapter 7

Aggressive Behavior of Soccer Players as Social Interaction

Amélie Mummendey and Hans Dieter Mummendey

Much has been written about aggression in sports, and seemingly for good reason. If aggressive behavior is conceived of as a kind of behavior that intentionally or unintentionally is directed against a person, or is performed to set other persons at a disadvantage, or even leads to the injuring or hurting of an opponent, sports seems to be a suitable field for the observation of aggressive behavior, and for the empirical investigation of its antecedents and consequences.

Soccer as a Field for Studying Aggressive Interaction

As soccer is the most popular sport in Europe, it has attracted much attention from European psychologists and sociologists writing about aggression in sports. A good deal of the empirical results considered by a research group of the German Federal Institute for Sport Science (Projektgruppe "Sport und Gewalt" des Bundesinstituts fur Sportwissenschaft, 1982) is based on studies (e.g., Schmidt, 1978) of European football (soccer), although there seem to be more empirical investigations on the aggressive behavior of fans, spectators, and hooligans than of actors interacting in sporting events (e.g., Gabler, Schulz, & Weber, 1982; Weis, Backes, Gross, & Jung, 1982).

That which is known about factors influencing the aggressive behavior of players is classified by the research group (Projektgruppe, 1982) as follows:

1. Structural factors: e.g., systems of rules due to the specific sport discipline.
2. Situational factors: home or away game, state of play (i.e., how many goals already scored by each team), importance of the result of the game, class of game (i.e., 1st or 2nd division, etc.), how many minutes already played, position of player, task of player, referee, trainer, where the foul occurred.
3. Understanding of norms and rules: e.g., informal concepts of norms that allow more aggressive behavior than is allowed by the rules.
4. Interactions of players' and audience's violence.

European football certainly seems to be a promising field for the study of aggressive behavior since, compared with everyday behavior routines, there seem to be many aggressive acts resulting in numerous, often severe, injuries. There is also much public interest and discussion in the media about players' hurting and damaging each other, and this seems especially true for the professional football leagues. A tendency toward increased aggression is implied by the apparently high level of physical injury in professional football. While the publicly discussed level of physical aggression and violence in football appears to be extraordinary to some observers, there are other interpreters who consider football aggression to be only a special case of instrumental aggression that seems to prevail in industrial societies (see Volkamer's 1971 study of football players' aggressive tendencies, interpreted in the framework of competition-oriented social systems).

Since sports are taken as a field for the scientific study of aggression, psychological studies in this field will be only as valid as the psychological theories and concepts of aggression are. If we look at books about aggressive behavior written or edited by psychologists we find no homogeneous perspective, no uniform way of dealing with the problem of what is called aggression. Consequently, authors of books on aggression normally present collections of different ethological and psychological approaches including, for example, catharsis-oriented views of aggression, learning-theory oriented interpretations, and so on. Aggressive behavior in the field of sports seems to be discussed first of all in a kind of *functional* manner: What function has competition in sports for the competing individual? What are the effects of aggressive competition in sports on the individual engaged in that particular competition? What are the effects on the spectators observing aggressive competition in sports either from their seats or on television? As for the catharsis-learning controversy: Are players or spectators more or less aggressive after their engagement in sporting competition? Are there types of sport that lead to more or less aggression in athletes or spectators? Are there different positions in a team with respect to aggressive behavior and are there relations between the respective roles and the personalities of the players?

We think that it can be noticed that all these different approaches toward aggressive behavior and violence in sport have two features in common: First, aggressive or violent behavior is treated from an *individualistic* perspective; second, the whole field of sporting activities, especially matches between individuals or teams is dealt with as if these activities were something *extraordinary* and different from normal everyday activities and interactions.

An individualistic perspective implies that psychologists are mainly concerned with the occurrence of certain *individual acts* that can be defined as aggressive. Here the interest lies in the conditions for the varying probability of the occurrence of those acts, the question of how many individuals show aggressive acts, and how often they do this. Apparently sporting activities are considered as being *special* with respect to the problem of aggression and violence—at least in the context of certain kinds of matches, such as football, soccer, ice hockey—in the sense that participants, and more and more often audiences, too, engage in extraordinarily intense and frequent aggressive behavior which seems to differ from the way people behave in other situations (e.g., in the supermarket or on the bus).

In the following considerations we argue for a more *social psychological* perspective on aggressive behavior; that means aggression and violence are conceptualized as a certain kind of *social interaction* between at least two individuals which takes place in a defined social context, the appearance and the process of this interaction are dependent on certain characteristics of the surrounding social context. Sporting matches are seen as only one example out of a larger number of contexts or *behavior settings* which all can be described with respect to common aspects having some impact upon the regulation of aggressive interactions.

Aggressive Behavior as Social Interaction

When we talk about aggressive behavior we describe incidents, in which, for example, a child hits another in order to gain possession of a favored toy, a person is wounded or killed by another's use of violence, or a football player is offended and severely hurt. What do these apparently differing incidents have in common?

There are always at least two people, or identifiable social units, taking part in the events. For one of these two people (the victim) the incident is unpleasant. Additionally, the victim maintains that the action of the protagonist is either unjust or inappropriate to the antecedent or prevailing situation, and hence considers himself justified in holding the protagonist responsible for any resulting damage. The protagonist, however, proceeds on the assumption that his action is justified by the given circumstances, and appropriate to the previous behavior of his interaction partner. In regard to the incident in question, he does not take the viewpoint of the victim into consideration. Thus, we can identify three typically conflicting positions: that of the victim, that of the protagonist, and that of any possibly available witnesses.

Although there may be agreement over what is "aggressive" in general, one can see a number of conflicting interpretations as to whether a specific incident involves aggression or not. It could be, for example, that in a dispute over the possession of a toy, one observer sees it as an aggressive quarrel, and another as harmless and just part of a game. What one person considers a swear word another may consider to be effective jesting or teasing. A militarily occupied country can consider the occupation to be an aggressive enforcement of unauthorized territorial claims, or desired assistance with internal difficulties, and this can also be directly criticized as unauthorized meddling in internal affairs. Even an apparently unequivocal fact, such as the killing of a person, can be judged in different ways. For a revolutionary, the successful assassination of a dictator is considered to be the appropriate and legitimate way to change unbearable social conditions. On the other hand, from the opposite viewpoint, the assassination is a crime, is aggressive to the highest degree, and calls for suitable punishment.

Thus, it appears to be of great interest to assume that the character of aggressive behavior is not in itself without problems. Therefore, *the final goal is not so much the descriptions of definitely identifiable behavior, but more, the final interpretation of specific interactional processes leading to the label "aggressive."* In the course of the following argument, aggressive behavior will be specified as confrontation between people. "Social interaction" will be preferred as a unit of analysis to "individual behavior." Since an aggressive act is regarded as a social interaction between individuals or groups in a specific social situation, for an adequate description and analysis of aggressive behavior it is not sufficient to confine oneself to morphological aspects (such as intensity or directedness in a behavior-theoretical sense) or criteria of inner psychic processes (such as annoyance) or aggression as a dispositional assumption. Supplementary aspects of the normative context must be interposed with, among others, *ecological* aspects of the setting. The individual construction of this social situation can be seen as determined by the observed meaning of the ecological conditions. The choice of appropriate behavior alternatives would follow from this. Such behavior regularities in interaction can be regarded as necessary preconditions to the observation of *norm disturbance*. A deviation from normative appropriateness may under certain circumstances to be investigated be judged as aggression. In such a case, the victim will, from his perspective, perceive offense to a norm. He then desires vindication and provokes reactions which may possibly be labelled as "aggression" by the new victim (the former protagonist). The reactions of the victim are influenced by the nature of the *norm offense relative to the situational context*, and by the possibility that he will interpret this in accordance with his social motivations, personal standards, his view of himself, his ideas of justice, and so on. The concept of aggressive behavior as a social interaction between various persons in a certain situation is supported by several authors (DaGloria & DeRidder, 1977, 1979; Felson, 1981; Leyens, 1977; Tedeschi, Gaes, & Rivera, 1977).

What is interesting about aggressive interaction is the rough description of sequences of reciprocal ways of behaving, namely, continuation, escalation, breaking off, or compensation for damages. The description of these phenomena requires consideration of the temporal progress of an aggressive episode. At definite times in this progression, one may recognize an aggressive quarrel through the typical opposing positions drawn up by those taking part. These positions are principally interchangeable. A protagonist and a victim interact at a definite point in time during the episode. At the same time, a third person may witness the sequence of events. Certainly, the classification of the persons involved in a concrete exchange, either in the role of the victim or protagonist, is dependent on their individually intended judgments. However, independent of this fact, there is always a protagonist position, and a related victim position, in an interaction sequence which is described as aggressive.

The circumstances in both of these positions can be regarded as a conflict like that, for example, described by Feger (1972): "Conflict behavior is directed towards either the destruction, wounding, damaging, or exerting of control over, the other party or parties. Conflict relationship exists when it is possible for one party to make (relative) gains at the expense of the other" (p. 1600; our translation).

In the case of an aggressive interaction both protagonist and victim have by definition incompatible interests. The victim wishes to avoid the consequences of the action that the protagonist provokes. Thereby, interest should be understood in the broadest sense of the given goal orientation of each person involved. It may concern itself with "conflicts of interest" as in the meaning given by Sherif (1966) or "conflicts of values" as in Tajfel (1978).

The deciding factor for the conceptualization of "aggressive" behavior is certainly not the direct or indirect harmful interest that is shown, in fact, by the protagonist, but is more the interest that the victim *imputes* to the protagonist. The victim can throughout arrive at the assessment that one of the ways of behavior to which he is object is aggressive, while at the same time the protagonist is convinced (though he may not state this as a justification after the event) that he had no intent of causing harm (Riess, Rosenfeld, & Tedeschi, 1981). Indeed, the protagonist himself may state that his goal is prejudicial to the victim, but in contrast to the victim, he judges his action to be relatively appropriate to the given circumstances, and with this assessment, stands opposed to the victim. The present conflict relationship which is judged here as an aggressive social interaction implies (at least current at the time of the choice of action) a divergence between victim and protagonist in the judgment of the action, regarding its situational normative appropriateness. Thus, a social interaction is classified as aggression if, in addition to causing injury (or assumed intent to injure), there exists with respect to situational normative appropriateness, an actual dissent between victim and protagonist.

The concept of aggressive behavior as a specific form of social interaction suggests four fundamental aspects: *mutual interpretation, situational context, divergence of perspectives* depending on specific positions (victim, actor, or observer), and *temporal progress*.

Mutual Interpretation

Aggressive interactions are, like all social interactions, conveyed by the valuations of the interaction situation and by the expectations of the persons concerned (Tajfel, 1972; Tajfel & Fraser, 1978). The interaction partners interpret and judge the respectively evoked reciprocal behavior and choose their own responses as a result of their respective definitions of situations and actions. The interpretation of an action as aggressive determines the progress of subsequent interaction. The result of such an interpretation is that the victim, corresponding to the norm of negative reciprocity, considers it his right to respond to this aggressive behavior in an "aggressive" manner, "to pay back the same with the same" (Lagerspetz & Westman, 1980). The protagonist who is judged to be aggressive is not only rejected, but must also contend with corresponding reactions and sanctions (Kane, Joseph, & Tedeschi, 1976; DaGloria & DeRidder, 1977). A protagonist who shows repentance, and supplies reasons for his behavior, does not have to face sanctions (Mallick & McCandless, 1966; Schwartz, Kane, Joseph, & Tedeschi, 1978).

Injury, intention, and norm deviation have been established as the leading interpretational criteria to define aggressive behavior (cf. Löschper, Mummendey, Bornewasser, & Linneweber, 1982).

Injury. Aggressive behavior is distinguished from any other social behavior by its apparently injurious consequences for at least one of the persons concerned. The observer's description of it as either injurious or harmless is not only based on obvious behavior and its observable consequences, but draws upon supplementary information from the whole situation (Schott, 1975). The judge draws inferences to describe an incident as injurious from many different sources. An offense such as rape would be classified as more or less injurious, depending on the social group to which the victim belongs (Jones & Aronson, 1973), or the sort of attitude held by the judge (Malamuth, 1981). In order to describe an incident or stimulus result as injury, the judge must have standards that enable him to determine deviations from norms. The perception of injury, and the definition of behavior as aggressive, is a judgment process which, along with descriptions, also involves attributions and valuations (Tedeschi & Riess, 1981). The goal or purpose of an injurious action is an essential part of the description of the critical behavior. Since the aims of a behavior, or the motives of a protagonist, cannot always be directly observed in his behavior, they must be integrated by the judge and attributed to the protagonist.

The injury variable has been considered as a substantial part of scientific definitions and operationalizations of aggression (Berkowitz, 1962; Buss, 1961). Inquiries into the perception of aggressive behavior have established that, beside other definition criteria, the factor of injury is significant (Rule & Nesdale, 1976). The willingness of judges to impose sanctions is clearly influenced by the extent of injury that has occurred (Nesdale, Rule, & McApa, 1975; Shaw & Reitan, 1969).

Intention. In a definition of critical behavior, it is not only necessary to consider whether it is possible to identify a perpetrator or producer of injury but also whether this perpetrator can be held responsible for his actions and their consequences. If a protagonist is regarded as the responsible cause of a negative action sequence, this does not mean to say that he can be held responsible for it. He may have caused the incident unintentionally or through unforeseen ways. With respect to intentionality, much is determined through attribution processes (cf. Harvey, Ickes, & Kidd, 1976, 1978). The attribution of cause is not to be equated with that of responsibility (Heider, 1958). The choice of counteractions or sanctions from the judge's point of view, and therewith the further course of the interaction, is dependent upon the perceived intention of the perpetrator of the injury. Also, when an actual injury does not take place, perhaps because the protagonist's action is without success, the behavior may be defined as aggressive because of the protagonist's intent, and hostile counteractions may follow (Greenwell & Dengerink, 1973; Nickel, 1974; Schuck & Pisor, 1974). The attribution of the actor's responsibility or guilt is a necessary requirement for the imposition of counteractions or sanctions (Dyck & Rule, 1978; Shaw & Reitan, 1969). Intended aggressive behavior is judged to be more objectionable than justified aggressive acts (Briscoe, 1970; Ferguson & Rule, 1980).

Norm deviation. In prevailing debates in the realm of attribution research, it is increasingly emphasized that attribution, as a basis for deciding on appropriate counteraction, involves much more than the localization of causal factors, namely, reasons and justifications regarding social norms and rules (Buss, 1978; Pligt, 1981; Zuckerman, 1979). It has been found that action has to violate norms and rules shared by the judge in order to be defined as aggressive. Tedeschi and co-workers managed to establish in several experiments that a protagonist who intends to cause injury is only judged by witnesses to be aggressive when his behavior is also judged to be antinormative, that is, not in accord with situationally valid rules. The norm of negative reciprocity (Gouldner, 1960) may be regarded as an important regulating standard for aggressive interaction (Lagerspetz & Westman, 1980). If an "intent to injure" constitutes a reply to a previous provocation, then the protagonist is not assessed as aggressive. If the counteraction exceeds the preceding deed, if, for example, revenge is excessive, it is judged as inappropriate and aggressive (Brown & Tedeschi, 1976; Carpenter & Darley, 1978; Kane et al., 1976; Rivera & Tedeschi, 1976; Stapleton, Joseph, & Tedeschi, 1978). Perceptions of the justification or legitimacy of a frustration, applied to situationally valid standards, effect a decrease of aggressive behavior, while assaults which are interpreted as inappropriate and arbitrary increase aggressive counteractions (Burnstein & Worchel, 1962; Pastore, 1952).

Injury, intention, and norm deviation may be regarded as essential definition criteria for aggressive behavior (Tedeschi, Brown, & Smith, 1974). The abovementioned criteria determine the interpretation of behavior in reciprocal ways. For example, the extent of actual damage is irrelevant to the definition of the critical act when the judge has distinct indications of the existence of intent on the part of the protagonist, and/or the norm-offending character of the action in question. If a behavior distinctly deviates from valid norms, and the judge has unequivocal information as to the protagonist's intent to injure, then as a result it will be certain that the critical action will be defined as aggressive (Löschper et al., 1982; Mummendey et al., 1982). As norms and values exercise no continual influence on interaction, but receive situation-specific activation (Pepitone, 1976), and as in interaction situations, competing sets of norms hold validity and relevance, there are diverging judgments of the appropriateness of an action possible that are dependent on the very context in which the critical action is embedded.

Situational Context

Aggressive social interaction does not take place in a vacuum (see Tajfel, 1972; Weinstein, 1969), and for that reason should not be conceived as such. Aggressive interactions are bound to situational contexts which may be described by analogy, for example, Barker's (1968) "behavior settings" or Stokols and Shumaker's (1980) "places," in regard to their spatial and temporal dimensions. The situation context reveals whether, and in what measure, single or multiple criteria are fulfilled with regard to norm deviation. The context of a critical interaction is here defined as the network of social, spatial, normative, and temporal circumstances, and those concerned with the development of interaction. These circumstances are brought by a judging individual into the (psycho)logical context (Mummendey & Linneweber, 1981). Context aspects are accentuated in the judgment of the incident (cf. the concept of "environmental props," Forgas, 1978). It is, therefore, more the context than the behavior itself which determines the definition (Tedeschi & Lindskold, 1976). Norms and rules are made available by the surrounding social system. They are codified (e.g., as explicit behavior instructions, orders, etc.), or they exist as implicit conceptions, expectations, and so on. The actual context of a particular interaction thereby exists as subjective representations, constructions, and a selection of objective factors. These certainly stand not in an arbitrary but in an analyzably regulated relationship to reality. A particular interaction is consequently judged not in an arbitrary manner, but by criteria of appropriateness specific to the situation, that is, by normative criteria which are superindividually considered to be valid in the specific situation (cf. Linneweber, Mummendey, Bornewasser, & Loschper, 1982).

Divergence Between Protagonist's and Victim's Perspectives

The particular judgment of a behavior in respect to its situational appropriateness, and more extensively, to its aggressive character, is thus variable but not arbitrary. The specific perspective of a judge may be regarded as an essential determiner of appropriateness judgments. It is assumed that with aggressive interactions, a divergence arises in perceived appropriateness between the protagonist and the victim. The victim maintains that the protagonist's way of behavior is inappropriate, for instance, in regard to standards that are subjectively considered to be valid. He comes to this opinion by assessing the preceding interaction and by considering the conceivable behavior alternatives. At the time of his choosing to act, and actually executing his action, the protagonist makes a positive judgment of them, adequate to his definition of the situation. He considers his action to be appropriate (or he would not have executed it).

Investigations of attribution theory show a divergence in attributions of cause between victim and protagonist (Jones & Nisbett, 1971; Nisbett, Caputo, Legant, & Maracek, 1973; Storms, 1973; Regan & Totten, 1975). Contradictory attributions of cause characterize and promote conflict (Forsyth, 1980; Horai, 1977; Orvis, Kelley, & Butler, 1976). Aggressive interactions are not distinguished by a consensus of opinion, but by a conflict of interpretations and situation assessments. Corresponding to this, hints are found in several investigations of aggressive behavior—just as in everyday life—that there is a basic divergence between protagonist and victim in the judgment of critical actions (DaGloria & DeRidder, 1977; Felson, 1978; Tedeschi et al., 1974). Hamilton (1978) emphasizes that attributions of responsibility always contain a comparison of the action in question with valid behavior expectations and standards. Buss (1978) offers the theory that protagonists not only deal with situational attributions, but always deliver explanations for their own behavior which represent a justification in regard to the social norms and rules of social behavior. In the protagonist-observer divergence, it is increasingly evident that evaluative or motivational processes are efficacious, especially for the attributions that deal with socially undesirable or negative behavior (Pligt, 1981; Zuckerman, 1979).

Aggressive Interaction as a Process

A social-psychological perspective on aggressive interactions rejects a static approach in favor of a process-oriented one. Aggressive quarrels are characterized by the fact that the victim and the protagonist, at a given point in time, diverge in the judgment of the critical incident. Thus, interaction sequences may be understood as the linking together of separate segments in which the respective positions of victim and protagonist, and the corresponding situation definitions, change. Segmentation, corresponding to taking a particular position, may be worked out, not only from the point of view of (scientific) observers, but the persons involved also structure and punctuate the course of the interaction (Newtson, 1976). In reply to the victim's biased interpretation of the protagonist's action as aggressive, the interaction may be continued and possibly escalated, stopped, or compensated by the protagonist himself. The different types of progress, breaking off, continuation, escalation, or compensation, result from different subjective balance developments. For instance, the breaking off of an interaction chain is to be expected when both the involved interaction partners come to a unanimous judgment of the situation as being not unpleasant and well balanced, or from the viewpoint of the person who is at that particular time in the role of victim, his personal counteraction would be unsuitable or too expensive with regard to the present social and personal standards (Mummendey, Bornewasser, Loschper, & Linneweber, 1981).

Aggressive Interaction and Its Evaluation in Professional Soccer: Two Case Studies

Above we have outlined some principles or aspects according to which a social interaction is classified as more or less aggressive. In the following we shall give some examples for our assumption that interpretations and evaluations of interactions in soccer follow the same principles. By this it will be shown that violence in sports can be regarded as being as relative to judgmental conditions as violent acts in other areas of everyday life.

For this purpose we looked at a selection of recent sentences passed by the Federal Court of the German Football Confederation (members of this court are professional judges doing this kind of work honorarily). As examples two typical sentences are selected and partly quoted below. Each case is concerned with the judgments made at appeal proceedings: In each case the accused had made an appeal against his conviction by a sports court. The real names of football clubs and players have been changed.

Case 1

In the spring of 1981, S-town football club played at home against H-town football club in a round of the football league championship. The guests were favored to win, as S-town were placed in the lower half of the league table. Unexpectedly, S-town won the game. The national player, A, was positioned as center forward for H-town. His opposite was the practically unknown S-town defender, B. The game was played into the second half without the occurrence of any unsportsmanlike fouls. Also, the referee saw no grounds whatsoever to admonish or caution player B because of unfair play towards player A. As the game was drawing to an end, H-town's defeat became increasingly probable. Player A wanted to take advantage of a free kick awarded to his team in order to score a goal. To achieve this, he had to get rid of his "marker," player B, who up to now had always successfully prevented him from shooting a goal. After having once again futilely tried to get past player B, player A positioned himself with his back in front of player B during another prolonged break in the game made necessary because an S-town player stayed too close to the ball while it was placed ready for a free kick. While player B unsuspectedly gave his attention to the correct strategic possibilities of the free kick that were being attempted by the other players and the referee, player A decided upon an apparently more favorable position. He then struck out with his right arm, and drove his elbow backwards with full force into the stomach region of the completely unsuspecting player B's abdomen. While player B collapsed on the field, nerve-paralyzed like a boxer hit in the solar plexus, and was in a state of shock with acute suspension of breathing, player A, unmarked and free, ran past him in order to take personal advantage of the further development of the game. After treatment lasting some minutes, and recuperation, player B was able to resume play.

The accused player A admitted to the objective fact of the assault. He at first claimed to have hit out with his left arm, "as a blow with the right elbow could have had disastrous consequences." After being shown the television recording, during his interrogation by the supervising committee, he admitted to having struck out with his right arm. He claimed however that he had only struck out because player B had physically obstructed him.

The assault made by player A is exceptionally reprehensible. It exceeds average unsportsmanlike behavior that is on occasion characteristic of an assault. In its gravity and degree of blame, it is typified by brutal violence, pronounced ruthlessness, and malice. The accused player A, who is evidently superior to the injured player B in terms of body size, weight, and strength, struck out, and in a calculating manner took full advantage of the effect of a pointed elbow joint.

The extreme danger of injury to his fellow player left him cold. Apart from the disruption of the function of the solar plexus, the related suspension of breathing, and the general shock suffered by player B, such a blow to the abdominal region as was made by the accused, brings with it a real and dangerous possibility of a ruptured liver or spleen, and stomach surgery. As a result of shock, and the suspension of breathing there is also the danger of disturbed circulation in the brain, with the consequence of brain cell damage.

It is also widely known that liver or spleen ruptures, and also stomach surgery, are dangerous. The fact that the injured player B recovered directly, and eventually could rejoin the game, takes nothing away from the accusation of brutal violence in regard to the assault made by player B.

The claim made for previous fighting between the two players cannot be justified. The event here being tried took place during an interruption of play, and it is not necessary to take previous episodes of play into account.

The assault committed by player A shows behavior of criminal nature (brutality, dangerousness, malice, and ruthlessness). In addition, there is also the circumstance that the act took place during an interruption of play and behind the back of the referee. Thereby the act is particularly reprehensible, showing a low level of decent and moral behavior, and while taking part during a sporting activity, blatantly adverse to the ideals of sport.

Injury. The injuries that B sustained as a result of A's actions (nerve paralysis, suspension of breathing, real danger of serious internal injury, and danger of disrupted blood circulation in the brain), are impressively described in the court's verdict. In this situation, the court, as observer, takes the perspective of the victim. The actor first describes his action as being one particularly designed to avoid a serious injury. When this interpretation can no longer be maintained, he offers another interpretation that no longer tries to qualify the degree of injury.

Harm intent. The harm intent (A, having not been able to get rid of his bothersome "marker" by fair means, wants to do so with an aimed blow when no one is watching him) is portrayed in such a way that the court takes the viewpoint of the victim. The verdict does not prove whether or not the actor denies the intent of his action.

Norm deviation. The behavior of A is defined by the court not only as a serious violation of football regulations, but also as even criminal and immoral, in that A, unprovoked and only for his own advantage, had inflicted a potentially serious injury on a defenseless person. The actor, on the other hand, interpreted his behavior as a reaction to unfair behavior by B (obstruction), that is, he justified his behavior with the aid of a norm of negative reciprocity or retaliation so that his behavior appears to be comparatively suitable.

Situation context. H-town and S-town were playing in a round of the football league championship. H-town team were favored to win, but in the course of the game their defeat became more and more probable. As center forward, A's special task was to shoot goals. The free kick awarded to H-town gave A a particularly favorable chance to score a goal. The task of shooting a goal was of the greatest importance from H-town team's point of view.

Perspective divergence. The above cited arguments of the court against player A clearly reveal that it takes the perspective of player B, that is, the victim, as its own, and considers the behavior of the accused to be extremely unsuitable. The verdict says very little about the opinion of the accused A. Nevertheless, the fact that A had made an appeal against the first judgment that had been unfavorable to him, supports the notion that he has a more positive view of his action.

Process characteristics. The game had proceeded without any exceptionally unfair play up until the moment of the critical action. In particular, B did not conspicuously make any unfair play in regard to A or any other members of the H-town team. The court considers that the blow that B received from A was for him as victim, unexpected and unprovoked, that is, A is seen as the initiator. On the other hand, the actor identifies his behavior as being a result of unfair behavior by B.

Case 2

In the 85th minute of a football league championship game between B-town and H-town in February 1979, player X, by committing a foul, caused player Y to fall down. The referee stopped play, and awarded a free kick to H-town. In his fall, player Y rolled against the legs of player Z, entangled himself with him, and thereby became involved in a tussle with player Z, from whom he felt himself to be injured. As he picked himself up, he consequently hit player Z in the face with his left hand. Apart from the fact that player Z felt the blow, no injuries were sustained. Player Z immediately took his revenge by kicking player Y's feet. This was witnessed by the referee who ordered player Z off the field. The referee had not seen the directly antecedent behavior of player Y towards player Z. These facts were accepted as proved by the court through the defense statement of player Y as far as this could be taken into account, by the statements of the witnesses, player Z, and the referee, as well as a television recording of the proceedings.

The defense of player Y, that he had wanted to make a conciliatory gesture to player Z with his left hand, was considered by the court to be disproved by the evidence, and therefore an implausible evasive defense. Player Z had, according to his credible statement, felt without doubt that player Y's left hand darted out very quickly, and that player Z reacted just as quickly in an attempt to jerk his head out of the way. Such behavior is not an expression of a conciliatory attitude, but rather of an aggressive attitude, or an attitude anticipated to be aggressive.

The court is of the opinion that player Y should receive no subsequent punishment for his offense, although he had committed an assault when he hit his opponent in the face, and the referee would possibly have sent him off if he had noticed the assault. It is the conviction of the court that, as shown by the situation of the game, it is indeed, from the point of view of intent and consequence, a comparatively light blow that obviously can be explained by the player's annoyance with the injury he had sustained, and it is not to be interpreted as if it were a calculated intent to injure the opponent player Z. For beforehand, player Y was so irregularily assaulted by his opponent player X that he fell down, and because of this the referee interrupted the game. Only because of this foul, did player Y get involved in the tussle with player Z that drove him to the blow. Player Y's assault thus took place in direct association with the events in the game, and is therefore not to be seen as an exceptional case that should subsequently be punished for being particularly reprehensible, without due consideration of the setting of the offense.

Injury. For both court and victim (Z took his revenge by kicking Y's feet) the injury consisted of a perceivable, but relatively light blow to Z's face. On the other hand, the accused Y appears to have received absolutely no recognizable injury.

Harm intent. In the opinion of the victim Z, the intention of Y to injure Z is suggested by Y's gesture, Z's reaction, and the situation as a whole. In the opinion of the court, there is no direct intent to injure Z, but rather a rash reaction of Y to X's behavior. On the other hand, the accused Y attributes a completely different prosocial intention to his action.

Norm deviation. The court certainly regards the behavior of Y to be unsportsmanlike, and therefore unsuitable. However, it interprets the behavior as understandable in the sense of the norm of retaliation. On the other hand, the actor perceives no deviation whatsoever in his behavior (in his opinion a conciliatory gesture).

Situation context. The critical event took place close to the end of a championship game. The critical action was part of a sequence of hostile interactions. The referee had already interrupted the game because of X's assault on Y.

Perspective divergence. Both victim and court perceive Y's gesture as an assault, while the actor perceives it as a conciliatory gesture. With regard to the assessment of suitability, the court partially takes the perspective of the accused.

Process characteristics. In the opinion of the accused, the victim, and the court, the accused had first of all been unfairly attacked just before the critical action, and then subsequently could have felt himself to be encroached upon by the tussle. In reaction to the critical action, the victim attacked the new victim by kicking him. This action was punished by the referee.

In case 1, the high court of the German football league dismissed player A's appeal, and imposed an 8-week suspension and a fine. In case 2, player Y's appeal was granted, and the previous court sentence (a suspension for six games) was reversed. Both cases dealt with behavior that was against the rules. However, the courts' judgments turned out very differently. The justification for very differing judgments was clearly made with reference to the criteria for judging an action to be aggressive that have been introduced here. While in case 1 the critical behavior was interpreted as unprovoked, intentionally injurious, and so forth, the behavior in case 2 was construed to be provoked, not carried out with intent to injure, and so on. Because of these different interpretations, totally divergent actions are thought to be suitable.

The Referee's Power of Interpretation

Those incidents in football that are conspicuous because of their aggression (e.g., blows to the stomach or face), are obviously identified in accordance with the same judgment patterns that are effective in other less spectacular areas of everyday life. Unlike many other areas of life, however, there is always in football a person who has "power of definition": the referee. Only the referee's interpretation is decisive as to whether behavior is aggressive and against the rules or not. Referee's interpretations, however, are laid down in a generally binding catalog of regulations that are above individual interpretation. There are 17 main regulations, and a few dozen special ones, for football (compare Ebbersberger, Malka, & Pohler, 1980). The main parts of this catalog serve to specify and differentiate among the categories "forbidden play," "dangerous play," and "unfair play." It is thereby noticeable that intent to harm functions as an essential criterion for this differentiation. "Intention" means here thoughtlessness, inconsiderate play, lack of foresight and prudence, and so forth (and thus is used in a broader sense; a behavior is called "intended" if the player is seen as responsible for it, e.g., if he hits another player instead of the ball).

In this way it becomes clear that in football, unlike many other areas of behavior, there exists a good precondition for classifying ways of behavior as "aggressive" and sanctioning them. As this is possible in a way that is less "fuzzy" than in other areas of behavior, it may be a reason for the fact that in football there is a greater unanimity over what sort of behavior is unsuitable and needing to be sanctioned. On the other hand, the fact that the referee, as a single individual, possesses the power of interpretation in the concrete situation, is a guarantee that the decision on whether behavior is aggressive and needing to be sanctioned, remains the result of subjective interpretation processes. This in turn provides sufficient flexibility for divergence of judgment, as the referee favors only one out of several possible perspectives.

Conclusions

It is continually pointed out that in soccer football there is an extraordinarily high number of spectacular assaults that often lead to serious injury. Which conditions are responsible for aggressive behavior in football is a question that is being continually reflected upon. In our opinion it is meaningful to describe such aggressive behavior as a specific form of social interaction. Such interactions are characterized by the following fundamental aspects: mutual interpretation of the critical act, surrounding situation context, differences of interpretation and evaluation from specific positions (actor/victim/observer), and temporal interaction processes. Examples from football jurisdiction show that those judgment and assessment processes effective for the definition of behavior as unsuitable and sanctionable agree with the same processes that have been worked out for other areas of everyday life. Unlike other areas of life, football is mostly concerned with physical interactions, so conflicts are settled predominantly by physical means. Therefore the total level of conflict settlement between the interaction partners appears to be far more spectacular. It nevertheless becomes apparent that the use of criteria for the differentiating judgments of such conflicts, as is undertaken by members of the social system "football," agrees well with those criteria used in everyday life. In this way it could, for example, happen that a blow to the face would be considered to be a comparatively unimportant assault, though this is a judgment that would not necessarily be accepted in other social contexts.

Acknowledgments. The authors are deeply indebted to Willi Essing and Wilhelm Hennes for information about football court decisions, and to Volker Linneweber, Gabi Löschper, and Manfred Bornewasser for cooperation in formulating the central features of an interactional approach to aggressive (cf. Mummendey, Bornewasser, Löschper, & Linneweber, 1982).

References

Barker, R. G. *Ecological psychology*. Stanford, Ca.: Stanford University Press, 1968.
Barker, R. G., & Wright, H. F. *Midwest and its children*. Evanston, Ill.: Row, Peterson, 1955.
Berkowitz, L. *Aggression: A social psychological analysis*. New York: McGraw-Hill, 1962.

Briscoe, M. E. *Attribution of responsibility and assignment of sanctions for violations of positive and negative norms.* Unpublished doctoral dissertation. University of Florida, 1970.

Brown, R. C., & Tedeschi, J. T. Determinants of perceived aggression. *Journal of Social Psychology*, 1976, *100*, 77-87.

Burnstein, E., & Worchel, P. Arbitrariness of frustration and its consequences for aggression in a social situation. *Journal of Personality*, 1962, *30*, 528-540.

Buss, A. H. *The psychology of aggression.* New York: Wiley, 1961.

Buss, A. R. Causes and reasons in attribution theory: A conceptual critique. *Journal of Personality and Social Psychology*, 1978, *36*, 1311-1321.

Carpenter, B., & Darley, J. M. A naive psychological analysis of counter-aggression. *Personality and Social Psychology Bulletin*, 1978, *4*, 68-72.

DaGloria, J., & DeRidder, R. Aggression in dyadic interaction. *European Journal of Social Psychology*, 1977, 7, 189-219.

DaGloria, J., & DeRidder, R. Sex differences in aggression: Are current notions misleading? *European Journal of Social Psychology*, 1979, *9*, 49-66.

Dyck, R. J., & Rule, B. G. Effect on retaliation of causal attributions concerning attack. *Journal of Personality and Social Psychology*, 1978, *36*, 521-529.

Ebersberger, H., Malka, J., & Pohler, R. *Schiedsrichter im Fussball. Ein Lehrbuch für Schiedsrichter, Trainer und Spieler.* Bad Homburg: Limpert, 1980.

Feger, H. Gruppensolidaritat und Konflikt. In C. F. Graumann (Ed.), *Handbuch der Psychologie. Vol. 7: Sozialpsychologie.* 2. Halbband, Göttingen: Hogrefe, 1972.

Felson, R. B. Aggression as impression management. *Social Psychology*, 1978, *41*, 205-213.

Felson, R. B. An interactionist approach to aggression. In J. T. Tedeschi (Ed.), *Impression management: Theory and social psychological research.* New York: Academic Press, 1981.

Ferguson, T., & Rule, B. G. The effect of inferential set, outcome severity, and basis for responsibility on children's evaluations of aggressive acts. *Developmental Psychology*, 1980, *16*, 141-146.

Forgas, J. P. Social episodes and social structure in an academic setting: The social environment of an intact group. *Journal of Experimental Social Psychology*, 1978, *14*, 434-448.

Forsyth, D. R. The functions of attributions. *Social Psychology Quarterly*, 1980, *43*, 184-189.

Gabler, H., Schulz, H.-J., & Weber, R. Zuschaueraggressionen—Eine Feldstudie über Fussballfans. In G. Pilz et al. (Eds.), *Sport und Gewalt.* Schorndorf: Karl Hofmann, 1982.

Gouldner, A. W. The norm of reciprocity: A preliminary statement. *American Sociological Review*, 1960, *25*, 161-178.

Greenwell, J., & Dengerink, H. A. The role of perceived versus actual attack in human physical aggression. *Journal of Personality and Social Psychology*, 1973, *26*, 66-71.

Harvey, J. H., Ickes, W. J., & Kidd, R. F. (Eds.). *New directions in attribution research* (Vol. 1). Hillsdale, N. J.: Erlbaum, 1976.

Harvey, J. H., Ickes, W. J., & Kidd, R. F. (Eds.). *New directions in attribution research* (Vol. 2). Hillsdale, N.J.: Erlbaum, 1978.

Heider, F. *The psychology of interpersonal relations.* New York: Wiley, 1958.

Horai, J. Attributional conflict. *Journal of Social Issues,* 1977, *33,* 87-100.

Jones, C., & Aronson, E. Attribution of fault to a rape victim as a function of respectability of the victim. *Journal of Personality and Social Psychology,* 1973, *26,* 415-419.

Jones, E. E., & Nisbett, R. E. *The actor and the observer: Divergent perceptions of the causes of behavior.* Morristown, N. J.: General Learning Press, 1971.

Kane, T. R., Joseph, J. M., & Tedeschi, J. T. Person perception and the Berkowitz paradigm for the study of aggression. *Journal of Personality and Social Psychology,* 1976, *33,* 663-673.

Lagerspetz, K. M. J., & Westman, M. Moral approval of aggressive acts: A preliminary investigation. *Aggressive Behavior,* 1980, *6,* 119-130.

Linneweber, V., Mummendey, A., Bornewasser, M., & Löschper, G. *Klassifikation feld- und verhaltensspezifischer Interaktionssituationen: Der Kontext aggressiver Interaktionen in Schulen.* Bielefelder Arbeiten zur Sozialpsychologie, No. 89, Universität Bielefeld, 1982.

Löschper, G., Mummendey, A., Bornewasser, M., & Linneweber, V. *Die Beurteilung von Verhaltensweisen als aggressiv und sanktionswurdig: Der Einfluss der zentralen und typisch konfigurierten Definitionskriterien Absicht, Schaden und Normabweichung auf das Aggressionsurteil.* Bielefelder Arbeiten zur Sozialpsychologie, No. 91, Universität Bielefeld, 1982.

Malamuth, N. M. Rape proclivity among males. *Journal of Social Issues,* 1981, *37,* 138-157.

Mallick, S. K., & McCandless, B. R. A study of catharsis of aggression. *Journal of Personality and Social Psychology,* 1966, *4,* 591-596.

Mummendey, A., Bornewasser, M., Löschper, G., & Linneweber, V. Aggressive Interaktionen in Schulen. Unveröffentlichter Forschungsbericht (II) über ein Projekt im Rahmen des Schwerpunktprogrammes der DFG "Psychologische Ökologie." Psychologisches Institut der Universität Münster, Münster, 1981.

Mummendey, A., Bornewasser, M., Löschper, G., & Linneweber, V. Aggressiv sind immer die anderen. Plädoyer für eine sozialpsychologische Perspective in der Aggressionsforschung. *Zeitschrift für Sozialpsychologie,* 1982, *13,* 177-193.

Mummendey, A., & Linneweber, V. Systematisierung des Kontextes aggressiver Interaktionen: Beziehungen zum behavior setting-Konzept. *Bielefelder Arbeiten zur Sozialpsychologie,* 1981, *78.*

Nesdale, A. R., Rule, B. G., & McApa, M. Moral judgments of aggression: Personal and situational determinants. *European Journal of Social Psychology,* 1975, *5,* 339-349.

Newtson, D. Foundations of attribution: The perceptions of ongoing behavior. In J. H. Harvey, W. Ickes, & R. Kidd (Eds.), *New directions in attribution research* (Vol. 1). Hillsdale, N. J.: Erlbaum, 1976.

Nickel, T. W. The attribution of intention as a critical factor in the relation between frustration and aggression. *Journal of Personality,* 1974, *42,* 482-492.

Nisbett, R., Caputo, C., Legant, P., & Maracek, J. Behavior as seen by the actor and as seen by the observer. *Journal of Personality and Social Psychology*, 1973, *27*, 154-164.

Orvis, B. R., Kelley, H. H., & Butler, D. Attributional conflict in young couples. In J. H. Harvey, W. Ickes, & R. F. Kidd (Eds.), *New directions in attribution research* (Vol. 1). Hillsdale, N. J.: Erlbaum, 1976.

Pastore, N. The role of arbitrariness in the frustration-aggression hypothesis. *Journal of Abnormal and Social Psychology*, 1952, *47*, 728-731.

Pepitone, A. Toward a normative and comparative biocultural social psychology. *Journal of Personality and Social Psychology*, 1976, *34*, 641-653.

Pligt, J. van der. Actors' and observers' explanations: Divergent perspectives or divergent evaluations? In C. Antaki (Ed.), *The psychology of ordinary explanations of social behavior*. London: Academic Press, 1981.

Projektgruppe "Sport und Gewalt" des Bundesinstituts für Sportwissenschaft. Gutachten "Sport und Gewalt." In G. Pilz, D. Albrecht, H. Gabler, E. Hahn, D. Peper, J. Sprenger, H.-F. Voigt, M. Volkamer, & K. Weis (Eds.), *Sport und Gewalt*. Schorndorf: Karl Hofmann, 1982.

Regan, D. T., & Totten, J. Empathy and attribution: Turning observers into actors. *Journal of Personality and Social Psychology*, 1975, *32*, 850-856.

Riess, M., Rosenfeld, P., & Tedeschi, J. T. Self-serving attributions: Biased private perceptions and distorted public descriptions. *Journal of Personality and Social Psychology*, 1981, *41*, 224-231.

Rivera, A. N., & Tedeschi, J. T. Competitive behavior and perceived aggression. *Perceptual and Motor Skills*, 1976, *42*, 181-186.

Rule, B. G., & Nesdale, A. R. Moral judgment of aggressive behavior. In R. G. Geen & E. C. O'Neal (Eds.), *Perspectives on aggression*. New York: Academic Press, 1976.

Schmidt, W. *Aggression und Sport. Längsschnittuntersuchung sozialpsychologischer Determinanten beim Fussball in unterschiedlichen Belastungssituationen*. Ahrensburg: Czwalina, 1978.

Schott, F. Was ist Aggression? In H. Selg (Ed.), *Zur Aggression verdammt? Ein Überblick über die Psychologie der Aggression*. Stuttgart: Kohlhammer, 1975.

Schuck, J., & Pisor, K. Evaluating an aggression experiment by the use of simulating subjects. *Journal of Personality and Social Psychology*, 1974, *29*, 181-186.

Schwartz, G. S., Kane, T. R., Joseph, J. M., & Tedeschi, J. T. The effects of post-transgression remorse on perceived aggression, attributions of intent, and level of punishment. *British Journal of Social and Clinical Psychology*, 1978, *17*, 293-297.

Selg, H. *Diagnostik der Aggressivitat*. Göttingen: Hogrefe, 1968.

Shaw, M. E., & Reitan, H. T. Attribution of responsibility as a basis for sanctioning behavior. *British Journal of Social and Clinical Psychology*, 1969, *87*, 217-226.

Sherif, M. *Group conflict and cooperation: Their social psychology*. London: Routledge & Kegan Paul, 1966.

Stapleton, R. E., Joseph, J. M., & Tedeschi, J. T. Person perception and the study of aggression. *Journal of Social Psychology*, 1978, *105*, 277-289.

Stokols, D., & Shumaker, S. A. People in places: A transactional view of settings. In J. Harvey (Ed.), *Cognition, social behavior and the environment.* Hillsdale, N. J.: Erlbaum, 1980.

Storms, M. D. Videotape and the attribution process: Reversing actors' and observers' point of view. *Journal of Personality and Social Psychology,* 1973, *27,* 165-175.

Tajfel, H. Experiments in a vacuum. In J. Israel & H. Tajfel (Eds.), *The context of social psychology: A critical assessment.* London: Academic Press, 1972.

Tajfel, H. The achievement of group differentiation. In H. Tajfel (Ed.), *Differentiation between social groups.* London: Academic Press, 1978.

Tajfel, H., & Fraser, C. (Eds.). *Introducing social psychology.* Harmondsworth: Penguin, 1978.

Tedeschi, J. T., Brown, R. C., & Smith, R. B. A reinterpretation of research on aggression. *Psychological Bulletin,* 1974, *81,* 640-662.

Tedeschi, J. T., Gaes, G. G., & Rivera, A. N. Aggression and the use of coercive power. *Journal of Social Issues,* 1977, *33,* 101-125.

Tedeschi, J. T., & Lindskold, S. *Social psychology.* New York: Wiley, 1976.

Tedeschi, J. T., & Riess, M. Verbal strategies in impression management. In C. Antaki (Ed.), *The psychology of ordinary explanations of social behavior.* London: Academic Press, 1981.

Weinstein, N. D. The development of interpersonal competence. In D. Goslin (Ed.), *Handbook of socialization theory and research.* Chicago: Rand-McNally, 1969.

Weis, K., Backes, P., Gross, B., & Jung, D. Zuschauerausschreitungen und das Bild vom Fussballfan. In G. Pilz et al. (Eds.), *Sport und Gewalt.* Schorndorf: Karl Hofmann, 1982.

Volkamer, M. Zur Aggressivität in konkurrenzorientierten sozialen Systemen. Eine Untersuchung an Fussball-Punktespielen. *Sportwissenschaft,* 1971, 33-64.

Zuckerman, M. Attribution of success and failure revisited, or: The motivational bias is alive and well in attribution theory. *Journal of Personality,* 1979, *47,* 245-287.

Chapter 8

Social Bonding and Violence in Sport: A Theoretical-Empirical Analysis

Eric Dunning

Introduction

It is widely believed that we are living today in one of the most violent periods in history. Indeed, it is probably fair to say that, in Western societies at least, the fear that we are currently undergoing a process of "decivilization"—with regard to physical violence if not in other respects—is deeply imprinted in the contemporary *zeitgeist*, one of the dominant beliefs of our time. Eysenck and Nias (1978), for example, refer to "a number of acknowledged facts" which, they claim, "have helped to persuade many people that the civilization in which we live may be in danger of being submerged under a deluge of crime and violence." The psychologist Peter Marsh (1979), similarly contends that recent attempts to eradicate violence have led to a decline in opportunities for socially constructive ritual violence—what he calls "aggro"—with the consequence that uncontrolled and destructive violence has increased. There has been, he writes, "a drift from 'good' violence into 'bad' violence. Men are about as aggressive as they always were but aggression, as its expression becomes less orderly, has more blood as its consequence."

A not insignificant part of the belief that we are living in an excessively violent age is the widespread feeling that violence is currently increasing in, and in conjunction with, sports. Yiannakis, McIntyre, Melnick, and Hart (1976), for example, write that: "There can be little doubt that both crowd and player violence in sport are increasing at an alarming rate." The German sociologist, Kurt Weis (1976), appears to agree with this diagnosis. He argues that the putative trend towards growing violence on the sports field and among sports spectators represents at least a partial disconfirmation of Elias's theory (1978a, 1982) of the "civilizing process." It is with this issue—the implications of this putative trend for Elias's theory—that I shall concern myself in this chapter. For reasons that will emerge, I disagree with the view that contemporary sports and contemporary society are, unambiguously and in some simple sense, growing more violent. I also disagree with the idea that this supposed trend represents a partial disconfirmation of the theory of Elias. At the same time, however, I want to argue that the issue of violence in contemporary sports and contemporary society raises a number of complex problems and that it will only be possible to tackle these problems more adequately than has been done in the past by developing the relevant aspects of the theory of the civilizing process beyond the level reached by Elias himself. That is the goal I have set myself in this chapter. In order to move towards it, it will be necessary to raise a number of wider sociological issues. More specifically, what I shall do is:

1. Attempt to advance beyond Elias by distinguishing between types of human violence.
2. To argue, along with Elias, that a long-term civilizing transformation with respect to violence has taken place in the industrially most advanced societies of Western Europe. I shall try to move beyond Elias by conceptualizing this transformation as a change in the balance between some of the forms of violence distinguished in the typology.
3. Suggest that the change in the balance between forms of violence that can be empirically observed is attributable in large measure to an observable transformation in the forms of social bonding. I shall use the concept of social bonding in the *sociological* sense introduced by Durkheim and elaborated by Elias, and not in the "sociobiological" sense introduced, for example, by Tiger (1969) and Fox (1977). That is, I shall use it to refer to different forms of relationships that are *observably socially produced* and not to their production by some *hypothetical* but as yet *undiscovered* gene pattern that *may* have been laid down during mankind's prehistoric past. My first task, however, is to lay the foundation for a typology of violence.

Towards a Typology of Human Violence

The types of violence engaged in by human beings, in sports and elsewhere, are diverse and complex. It seems reasonable, however, to suppose that a degree of purchase on the problem can be obtained by drawing distinctions among its separable forms and dimensions. I shall distinguish between types of violence in terms of: (a) the means employed; (b) the actors' motives, especially with reference to the forms and levels of intentionality involved; and (c) some of the social parameters which help to distinguish forms of violence from one another. As an aid in the execution of this task, I shall draw upon a modification of some aspects of Weber's typology of action. It seems that at least eight distinctions can be provisionally made among the forms of human violence, namely:

1. Whether the violence is actual or symbolic, that is, whether it takes the form of a direct physical assault or simply involves verbal and/or nonverbal gestures.
2. Whether the violence takes a "play" or "mock" form, or whether it is "serious" or "real." This dimension might also be captured by means of the distinction between "ritual" and "nonritual" violence, though it has to be noted that, *pace* Marsh and his colleagues (1978), ritual and play can both have violent content.
3. Whether or not a weapon or weapons are used.
4. Where weapons are used, whether or not the assailants come directly into contact.

5. Whether the violence is intentional or the accidental consequence of an action sequence that was not intentionally violent at the outset.
6. Whether one is dealing with violence that is initiated without provocation or with a retaliatory response to an intentionally or unintentionally violent act.
7. Whether the violence is legitimate in the sense of being in accordance with a set of socially prescribed rules, norms, and values, or whether it is nonnormative or illegitimate in the sense of involving the contravention of accepted social standards.
8. Whether the violence takes a "rational" or "affective" form, that is, whether it is rationally chosen as a means for securing the achievement of a given goal, or engaged in as an emotionally satisfying and pleasurable "end in itself." Another way of conceptualizing this difference would be to distinguish between violence in its "instrumental" and "expressive" forms.

Some sociologists would call these distinctions "ideal types" but it is better to conceptualize them in terms of interconnected polarities and balances. But let me become more empirical and apply this mode of conceptualization systematically to some of the problems of violence in sports. I shall start by considering some general issues and then make some observations about the development of modern sports.

Sports and Violence in Developmental Perspective

All sports are inherently competitive and hence conducive to the arousal of aggression and violence. In some, however, for example, rugby, soccer, and boxing, violence in the form of a "play fight" or "mock battle" between two individuals or groups is a central ingredient. Such sports are enclaves for the socially acceptable, ritualized expression of physical violence and I shall concern myself in this context solely with sports of this kind. It is important in this connection to note that, just as the real battles that take place in war can involve a ritual component—for example, the battles of tribal groups such as the Dani of New Guinea (Gardner & Heider, 1974). So the mock battles that take place on a sports field can involve elements of, or be transformed into, nonritual violence. This may occur when, perhaps as a result of social pressures or the financial and prestige rewards involved, people participate too seriously in a sport. As a result, the tension level may be raised to a point where the balance between friendly and hostile rivalry is upset in favor of the latter. In such circumstances, the rules and conventions designed to limit the violence and direct it into socially acceptable channels may be suspended and the people involved may start to fight in earnest. Thus, in soccer and rugby, they may play with the aim of inflicting physical damage and pain. Or in boxing where the infliction of damage and pain is a legitimate part of the contest, they may fight after a round has finished or after the contest as a whole has been brought to an end. However, the standards governing the expression and control of violence are not the same in all societies. And in our own society, they differ between different groups and different sports and have not been the same in all historical periods (see Chapters 2 & 3). In fact, I want to argue that a central aspect of the development of modern sport has been what Elias would call a "civilizing process" regarding the expression and control of physical violence. Centrally involved in this process—whatever short-term fluctuations there may have been—has been a long-term shift in the balance between "affective" and "rational" violence.

To start with, it is worth recalling some relevant aspects of Elias's theory. In a nutshell, he holds that there has occurred in Western Europe a long-term decline in people's propensity for obtaining pleasure from directly engaging in and witnessing violent acts. He refers in this connection to a dampening of *Angriffslust,* literally to a decline in the lust for attacking, that is, in people's desire and capacity for obtaining pleasure from attacking others. This has entailed, firstly, a lowering of the threshold of repugnance (*Peinlichkeitsschwelle*) regarding bloodshed and other direct manifestations of physical violence; and secondly, the internalization of a stricter taboo on violence as part of the "superego." A consequence of this is that guilt feelings are liable to be aroused whenever this taboo is violated. At the same time, there has occurred a tendency to push violence increasingly behind the scenes and, as part of it, to describe people who openly derive pleasure from violence in terms of the language of psychopathology, punishing them either by means of hospitalization or imprisonment. However, this same social process has increased people's tendency to plan, to use foresight, and to use longer-term, more rational strategies for achieving their goals. It has also entailed an increase in socially generated competitive pressure. Consequently, I want to suggest that it has contributed to an increase in people's propensity in specific situations to use violence in a calculated manner. Let me illustrate this complex process by reference to the development of rugby football.

Modern rugby is descended from a type of medieval folk game in which particular matches were played by variable, formally unrestricted numbers of people, sometimes considerably in excess of 1,000. The boundaries of the playing area were only loosely defined and limited by custom, and games were played both over open countryside and through the streets of towns. The rules were oral and locally specific rather than written and instituted and enforced by a central controlling body. Despite such local variation, the folk antecedents of modern rugby shared at least one common feature: They were all play struggles that involved the customary social toleration of a level of physical violence considerably higher than is normatively permitted in rugby and comparable games today. It must be enough in the present context to substantiate this point by reference to a single example, the Welsh game of "knappan" as described by Owen in 1603.

According to Owen (1603/1892), the number who took part in knappan matches sometimes exceeded 2,000 and, just as in other folk games, such as Cornish "hurling," some of the participants played on horseback. The horsemen, said Owen, "have monstrouse cudgells, of iii foote and halfe longe, as bigge as the partie is well able to wild (wield)." As one can see from the following extract, knappan was a wild affair:

> at this playe privatt grudges are revendged, soe that for everye small occasion they fall by the eares, wch beinge but once kindled betweene two, all persons on both sides become parties, soe that sometymes you shall see fyve or vi hundred naked men, beatinge in a clusture together, ... and there parte most be taken everyeman with his companie, so that you shall

see two brothers the one beatinge the other, the man the maister, and frinde against frinde, they . . . . take upp stones and there with in theire fistes beate theire fellowes, the horsemen will intrude and ryde into the footemens troupes, the horseman choseth the greatest cudgell he can gett, and the same of oke, ashe, blackthorne or crab-tree and soe huge as it were able to strike downe an oxe or horse, he will alsoe assault anye for privatt grudge, that hath not the Knappan, or cudgell him after he hath delt the same from him, and when on blowe is geven, all falleth by the eares, eche assaulting other with their unreasonable cudgells sparinge neyther heade, face, nor anye part of the bodie, the footemen fall soe close to it, beinge once kindled with furie as they wholey forgett the playe, and fall to beatinge, till they be out of breathe, and then some number hold theire hands upp over theire heades and crye, ... peace, peace and often times this parteth them, and to theire playe they goe a newe. Neyther maye there be anye looker on at this game, but all must be actours, for soe is the custome and curtesye of the playe, for if one that cometh with a purpose onlye to see the game, ... beinge in the middest of the troupe is made a player, by giveinge him a *Bastonado* or two, if he be on a horse, and by lending him halffe a dozen cuffs if he be on foote, this much maye a stranger have of curtesye, although he expecte noethinge at their handes. (Owen, 1603/1892)

There is ample evidence to show that games of this type were played in various parts of Britain from at least the 14th to the 19th century. Moreover, the wildness so vividly depicted by Owen is amply confirmed by other accounts (Dunning & Sheard, 1979). That is what one would expect in a type of game characterized by the following constellation of features: large, unrestricted numbers of players; loosely defined and locally specific oral rules; some participants playing on horseback while others played on foot; the use of sticks to hit other players as well as the ball; control of matches by the players themselves rather than by a referee; and the absence of an outside, controlling organization to establish the rules and act as a court of appeal in cases of dispute.

Not all of these features were present in all cases but most of them were. As a result, such games were closer to "real" fighting than modern sports. As Riesman and Denney (1971) pointed out, modern sports are more "abstract," more removed from "serious" combat. The folk antecedents of modern rugby may have been mock battles in the sense that the lives and life chances of the contending groups were not directly at risk and that the infliction of serious injury and death was not their central aim. Nevertheless, their relatively high level of open violence and the opportunity they afforded for inflicting pain may have constituted one of their sources of enjoyment. After all, the people of preindustrial Britain enjoyed all sorts of pastimes—cock-fighting, bull- and bear-baiting, burning cats alive in baskets, prizefighting, watching public executions—which appear "uncivilized" in terms of present-day values. Such pastimes reflected what Huizinga (1924) called "the violent tenor of life" in Europe during the "autumn" of the middle ages and which continued until well into what historians regard as "modern" times. They also reflected the comparatively high "threshold of repugnance" with regard to witnessing and engaging in violent acts which, as Elias has shown, is characteristic of people in a society that stands at an earlier age in a "civilizing process" than our own.

By contrast with its folk antecedents, modern rugby exemplifies a game form that is civilized in at least four senses that were lacking in the ancestral forms. It is typical in this respect of modern combat sports more generally. Modern rugby is civilized by:

1. A complex set of formally instituted written rules which demand strict control over the use of physical force and which prohibit it in certain forms, for example, "stiff-arm" tackling and "hacking," that is, kicking an opposing player off his feet.
2. Clearly defined intragame sanctions, that is, "penalties," which can be brought to bear on offenders and, as the ultimate sanction for serious and persistent rule violation, the possibility of exclusion from the game.
3. The institutionalization of a specific role which stands, as it were, "outside" and "above" the game and whose tack is to control it, that is, that of "referee."
4. A nationally centralized rule-making and rule-enforcing body, the Rugby Football Union.

This civilization of rugby football occurred as part of a continuous social process. Two significant moments in it were: (a) the institution, at Rugby School in 1845, of the first written rules. These attempted, among other things, to place restrictions on the use of hacking and other forms of physical force, and to prohibit altogether the use of "navvies" (the iron-tipped boots which had formed a socially valued part of the game at Rugby and some of the other mid-19th century public schools); and (b) the formation in 1871 of the Rugby Football Union. The Rugby Union was formed partly as a result of a public controversy over what was perceived as the excessive violence of the game. One of its first acts was to place, for the first time, an absolute taboo on hacking. What happened at each of these moments was that the standards for controlling violence in the game advanced in two senses: firstly, it was demanded that players should exercise a stricter and more comprehensive measure of self-control over the use of physical force; and secondly, an attempt was made to secure compliance with this demand by means of externally imposed sanctions.

To speak of rugby as having undergone a "civilizing process" is not to deny the fact that, relative to most other sports, it remains a rough game. Features such as the "ruck" provide the opportunity for kicking and "raking" players who are lying on the ground. The scrum offers opportunities for illegitimate violence such as punching, eye-gouging, and biting. Given the close packing of players that the scrum involves, it is difficult for the referee to control the interaction. Nor is the contention that rugby has undergone a limited civilizing development inconsistent with the fact that it has probably grown more violent in specific respects in recent years. It has certainly grown more competitive as is shown by the introduction at all levels of cups and leagues. Growing competitiveness means that the importance of victory has increased, and this elevation of the success goal has involved an erosion of the old amateur ethos. It has, for example, diminished considerably the significance of the idea that taking part is more important than winning. It has probably simultaneously increased the tendency of players to play roughly within the rules and to use illegitimate violence in pursuit of success. In short, it seems a priori likely that the use of *instrumental* violence in the game has recently increased.

To say this is not to claim that, in the past, the violence of the game was entirely nonrational and affective but rather that the balance between rational and affective violence has changed in favor of the former. That is because the structure of modern rugby, together with the relatively civilized personality pattern of the people who play it, mean that pleasure in playing is now derived far more from the expression of skill with the ball, in combining with teammates and from more or less strictly controlled and muted forms of physical force, and far less from the physical intimidation and infliction of pain on opponents than used to be the case in its folk antecedents and in the mid-19th-century public schools when hacking and the use of navvies remained central and legitimate tactics. But the social and personality structures that have given rise to the modern game have simultaneously increased the incidence of instrumental violence in it—for example, players who are able to gain satisfaction from the comparatively mild forms of physical force that are permitted in the modern game and who do not find pleasure in inflicting pain on others, are constrained to use violence, both legitimately and illegitimately, in an instrumental fashion. They do not gain pleasurable satisfaction from such violence per se. It is not engaged in as an end in itself but as a means for achieving a long-term goal, that of winning a league or cup.

The growing competitive pressure that leads to the increasing *covert* use of rational violence, is simultaneously conducive to *overt* violence, namely that which occurs when sportsmen momentarily lose their self-control and strike an opponent in retaliation. The fact that the tactical use of instrumental violence often forms a trigger leading to such a loss of self-control shows yet again how one kind of violence can be rapidly transformed into another.

How is this apparently paradoxical development—that a game has grown less violent in certain respects and simultaneously more violent in others—to be explained? I should like to hypothesize that it is principally a consequence of a long-term shift in the pattern of social bonding, of the manner in which the members of our society are related to one another. Let me start to illustrate what this means by returning to Elias's theory of the civilizing process.

Violence and the Transformation of Social Bonds

Although Elias does not express it in these terms, it is, I think, fair to say that a central aspect of the civilizing process—the lengthening of interdependency chains—involved a change in the pattern of social bonding comparable to the one described by Durkheim as the transition from "mechanical" to "organic" solidarity. In order to distance the analysis from the evaluative connotations implicit in Durkheim's terminology and to convey the idea that both concepts refer to forms of interdependence, I propose to describe this aspect of the process as one in the course of which "segmental" bonding gradually came to be replaced increasingly by "functional" bonding. Centrally involved in this transformation was a process in which the significance of the ascriptive ties of family and residence grew gradually less,

Table 8-1. Segmental and Functional Bonding and Their Structural Correlates

Segmental bonding	Functional bonding
1. Locally self-sufficient communities, only loosely tied into a wider, proto-national framework; relative poverty.	Nationally integrated communities, tied together by extensive chains of interdependence; relative affluence.
2. Intermittent pressure "from above" from a weak central state; relatively autonomous ruling class divided into warrior and priestly sections; balance of power skewed strongly in favor of rulers/authority figures both within and between groups; little pressure generated structurally "from below"; power of rulers simultaneously weakened, for example, by rudimentary state apparatus and poor means of transport and communication.	Continuous pressure "from above" from a strong central state; relatively dependent ruling class in which the secular and civilian sections are dominant; tendency towards equalization of power through the generation of multipolar controls within and between groups; intense pressure generated structurally "from below"; power of rulers simultaneously strengthened, for example, by relatively efficient state apparatus and relatively efficient means of transport and communication.
3. Close identification with narrowly circumscribed groups united principally by means of ascribed kinship and local bonds.	Identification with groups that are united principally by means of achieved bonds of functional interdependence.
4. Narrow range of occupations; homogeneity of work experience both within and between occupational groups.	Wide range of occupations; heterogeneity of work experience both within and between occupational groups.
5. Low social and geographical mobility; narrow experiential horizons.	High social and geographical mobility; wide experiential horizons.
6. Little social pressure to exercise self-control over physical violence or to defer gratification generally; little exercise of foresight or long-term planning.	Great social pressure to exercise self-control over physical violence and to defer gratification generally; great exercise of foresight and long-term planning.
7. Low emotional control; quest for immediate excitement; tendency towards violent mood swings; high threshold of repugnance regarding violence and pain; pleasure from directly inflicting pain on others and from seeing others suffer; violence openly displayed in everyday life; low guilt feelings after committing violent acts.	High emotional control; quest for excitement in more muted forms; relatively stable temperament; low threshold of repugnance regarding violence and pain; vicarious pleasure from watching "mimetic" violence but not "real" violence; violence pushed "behind the scenes"; high guilt feelings after committing violent acts; rational recourse to violence in situations where it is perceived as undetectable.

Table 8-1. (*Continued*)

Segmental bonding	Functional bonding
8. High degree of conjugal role segregation; "mother-centered" families; authoritarian father with low involvement in the family; high separation of male and female lives; large numbers of children.	Low degree of conjugal role segregation; "joint," "symmetrical," or "egalitarian" families; father with high involvement in the family; low separation of male and female lives; small numbers of children.
9. High physical violence in relations between the sexes; male dominance.	Low physical violence in relations between the sexes; sexual equality.
10. Loose and intermittent parental control over children; violence central in early socialization; spontaneous, affective violence of parents towards children.	Close and continuous parental control over children; socialization principally by nonviolent means but limited, planned recourse to rational/instrumental violence.
11. Structurally generated tendency for "gangs" to form around the lines of social segmentation and for them to fight other local gangs; emphasis on "aggressive masculinity"; ability to fight the key to power and status in the gang and the local community.	Structurally generated tendency for relationships to be formed through choice and not simply on a local basis; "civilized" masculine style, expressed, for example, in formal sport; chances for more than local power and status; status determined by occupational, educational, artistic, and sports ability.
12. "Folk" forms of sport, basically a ritualized extension of fighting between local gangs; relatively high level of open violence.	"Modern" forms of sport, that is, of ritualized play-fights based on controlled forms of violence but strong social pressure to use violence in its rational/instrumental forms.

while that of achieved ties determined by the division of labor grew gradually more important.

The differences between these two types of social bonding can be expressed, provisionally and formally, by means of the polar models set forth in Table 8-1. They attempt to depict, not only the two contrasting types of social bonding but also the distinctive types of overall social figuration within which, respectively, segmental and functional bonding are (or were) generated and which, reciprocally, they help (or helped) to maintain.

These two models are a rather crude attempt to express some of the central structural differences between the societies of medieval Europe and those of modern times. The models are, however, very general and thus obscure differences such as those between social classes. They also ignore the existence of empirical overlaps between the two types and, to the extent that it is based on extrapolation from observable trends, the model of functional bonding exaggerates, for example, the degree of sexual equality that has so far been achieved in societies which approximate to that type.

Nor do I wish to imply by this analysis that the trend towards the increasing pre-dominance of functional bonding has been a simple, unilinear process or that it will necessarily continue into the future. A number of interrelated preconditions facili-tated such a development in the past, central among them, continuing economic growth, the ability of the state to retain an effective monopoly over the means of violence, and, despite the fact that they have often offered stiff resistance, a willing-ness over the long term on the part of ruling groups to compromise and grant con-cessions as the power of subordinate groups has grown. But such complexities are less germane for present purposes than the manner in which such types of social bonding and their wider structural correlates produce, on the one hand, a tendency towards violence with a high emotional or affective content and, on the other, a high degree of individual and social control over violence together with a tendency towards the use of violence of a more rational kind. It is to that issue that I shall now, very briefly and schematically, address myself.

Segmental Bonding and the Sociogenesis of Affective Violence

The structure of a society in which segmental bonding is the dominant type is con-ducive to physical violence in human relations in a number of mutually reinforcing ways. Expressed in terms of a cybernetics analogy, one could say that the various elements of such a social structure form a positive feedback cycle which escalates the tendency to resort to violence at all levels and in all spheres of social relations. The weakness of the state, for example, means that such a society is prey to outside attacks. That places a premium on military roles and that, in turn, leads to the con-solidation of a predominantly warrior ruling class, a class trained for fighting and whose members, because of their socialization, derive positive satisfaction from it.

Internal relations in such a society work in the same direction. Fighting, with or without weapons, is endemic, largely because "in-groups" are narrowly defined with the consequence that even ostensibly similar groups from the same locality are defined as "outsiders." So intense are the feelings of pride and group attachment generated within particular kin and local segments that conflict and rivalry are virtu-ally inevitable when the members of two or more of them meet. And their norms of aggression, coupled with the lack of social pressure to exercise self-control, mean that conflict between them leads easily to fighting. Indeed, fighting, both within and between such groups, is necessary for the establishment and maintenance of reputations in terms of their standards of aggressive masculinity. The best fighters tend to emerge as leaders and all the members of such groups have to fight in order to feel and prove to others that they are "men."

The fighting norms of such segmentally bonded groups are analogous to the ven-detta systems still found in many Mediterranean countries in the sense that an indi-vidual who is challenged or feels himself slighted by one or more members of an out-sider group feels that his group honor, and not simply his own, is at stake. Corres-pondingly, he is liable to seek revenge, not simply by retaliation against that or those particular members but against *any* member of the offending group. On both sides, furthermore, there is a tendency for others to come to the aid of the initiators of the conflict. In that way, fights between individuals tend to escalate into feuds between groups, often long-lasting ones, thus providing a clear indication of the very great degree of identification under such social circumstances of individuals with the groups to which they belong.

The endemic violence characteristic of societies of this type, together with the fact that their structure consolidates the power of a warrior ruling class and generates an emphasis on male aggressiveness and strength, is conducive to the general dominance of men over women. In its turn, male dominance leads to a high degree of separateness in the lives of the sexes and, with it, to families of the mother-centered type. The relative absence of the father from the family, coupled with the large family size which is typical in societies of this type, means that children are not subjected to close, continuous, or effective adult supervision. That, in its turn, has two principal consequences. First, because physical strength tends to be stressed in relations among children who are not subjected to effective adult control, it further increases the violence characteristic of such communities. The tendency of children in segmentally bonded communities to resort to physical violence is also reinforced by its use by their parents as a means of socialization and by the adult role models available to them in the society at large. Second, the relative lack of close adult supervision of children is conducive to the formation of gangs which persist into early adult life and which, because of the narrowly defined group allegiances characteristic of segmental bonding, come persistently into conflict with other local gangs. The sports of such communities—for example, the folk antecedents of modern rugby—are ritualized expressions of the "gang warfare" typically generated under such conditions, an institutionalized test of the relative strengths of particular communities which grows out of, and exists side by side with, the perpetual and more serious struggles between local groups.

The postive feedback cycle by means of which high levels of violence are generated in a society characterized by segmental bonding is illustrated schematically in Fig. 8.1.

Functional Bonding, Civilizing Pressures and the Sociogenesis of Rational Violence

Empirical societies which approximate closely the model of functional bonding are, in most respects, diametrically opposite to those where segmental bonding is the dominant type. Like the latter, such societies are subject to a positive feedback cycle but, in this case, the cycle performs, on balance, a civilizing function, serving mainly to limit and restrain the level of violence in social relations. This does not mean necessarily that it reduces the *rate* of violence but rather that it leads to the predominance of violence in more muted forms. However, the structure of such societies simultaneously generates intense competitive pressure and a tendency for rational means to be used in goal achievement. In its turn, this combination generates a tendency for illigitimate violence and other forms of rule violation to be used rationally or instrumentally in specific social contexts, for example, in high competitive combat sports. Let me elaborate on this.

A key structural feature of a society where functional bonding is the dominant

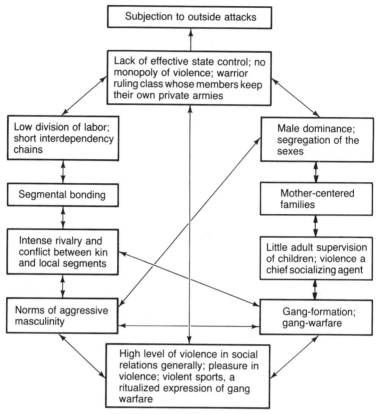

Fig. 8-1. Social dynamics of violence generation under conditions of segmental bonding. Arrows indicate main directions of influence in positive feedback cycle.

type is the fact that the state has established a monopoly on the right to use physical force. To the degree that its monopoly is stable and effective, the division of labor is permitted to grow—that is, the chains of interdependence in it lengthen—and that, reciprocally, augments the power of the state, for example, because central control becomes increasingly necessary as the social structure grows more complex. Both the state monopoly on physical violence and the lengthening of interdependency chains exert, on balance, a civilizing effect. The former exerts such an effect directly because the state is able to prevent citizens from openly carrying arms and to punish them for using violence illegitimately, that is, in situations where it claims a monopoly for its own agents. The latter exerts such an effect indirectly because the division of labor generates what Elias calls "reciprocal" or "multipolar" controls. That is, bonds of interdependence allow the parties to a division of labor to exert a degree of control over one another mutually. In this sense, the division of labor exerts an equalizing or "democratizing" effect. Such an effect is civilizing for at least two reasons: (a) because the reciprocal controls generated by interdependence are conducive to greater restraint in interpersonal relations; and (b) because a complex system of interdependencies would be subject to severe strain if all or even some personnel failed to exercise continuously a high degree of self-control. In that way, self-control is an essential precondition for the maintenance and growth of the differentiation of functions.

A society of this type is highly competitive because a complex division of labor also generates an achievement ideology and a tendency for roles to be allocated on the basis of achievement rather than ascription. This intensification of competition leads to a general increase in rivalry and aggressiveness in social relations but, to the extent that the state effectively claims a monopoly on the right to use physical force, it cannot be expressed in the form of openly and directly violent behavior. The dominant standards generated in such a society work in the same direction by decreeing that violence is wrong and, to the extent that such standards are internalized in the course of socialization, men and women come to have a low threshold of repugnance with regard to engaging in and directly witnessing violent acts.

But, while the dominant tendency in such a society is towards a comparatively high and effective level of control over violence, competitive pressure, coupled with the fact that long chains of interdependence and the correlative pattern of socialization constrain people to use foresight, to defer immediate gratification and to use rational means of goal achievement, means that there is a parallel tendency towards the planned or instrumental use of violence by ordinary citizens in specific social contexts, most notably, in crime, in sports, and, to a lesser extent, in the socialization and education of children. Only the use of instrumental violence in sports need concern us here.

The first thing to note in this connection is the fact that, in a society where a high degree of functional bonding exists, combat sports such as rugby, soccer, and boxing form a social enclave in which specific forms of violence are socially defined as legitimate. Such sports are ritualized and civilized play fights in which the use of physical force is hemmed in by rules and conventions, and controlled, immediately, by specific officials such as referees and, at a higher level, by committees and tribunals set up by national and international ruling bodies. But, to the extent that the competitive pressure in such sports increases, either because their practitioners are competing for extrinsic rewards such as financial remuneration or the honor of winning a trophy, or because they are subject to pressure to win from the local or national groups whom they represent, there will be a tendency for the significance of victory to be raised and, correspondingly, for players to break the rules as a deliberate tactic. As part of this, there will be a tendency for them to use violence illegitimately in situations where they perceive the likelihood of detection to be low or where they take a calculated risk that the penalties incurred upon detection will not detract significantly from the achievement of their own or their team's long-term goals.

The positive feedback cycle by means of which low levels of general violence are generated in a society characterized by functional bonding, together with the generation in such a society of a tendency for people to resort to rational or instrumental violence in specific situations, is illustrated schematically in Fig. 8.2.

Of course, the tendency towards the rational use of violence in modern sport is counteracted, on the one hand, by general values and sport-specific norms but, on the other, because it is liable to provoke retaliation, it serves simultaneously to increase the general level of sporting violence. The complexity of the picture is

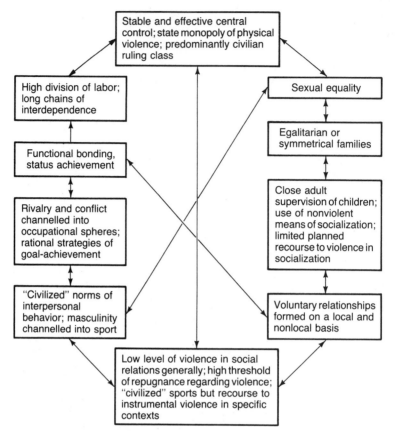

Fig. 8-2. Social dynamics of violence limitation and recourse to instrumental violence under conditions of functional bonding. Arrows indicate main directions of influence in positive feedback cycle.

further increased when one takes into account the fact that this discussion is based on a model that exaggerates the degree to which functional bonding has in fact developed in modern Britain. In particular, the model of segmental bonding still seems to be approximated fairly closely in certain sections of the British working class. It is reasonable to suppose that bonds of that type play a part in generating the norms of violent or aggressive masculinity that can be observed, for example, in the fighting of football (soccer) hooligans.

Segmental Bonding in the Working Class and the Sociogenesis of Football Hooligan Violence

It is commonly believed that football hooliganism first became a "social problem" in Britain in the 1960s. Research, however, shows that no decade in the history of the game has gone by without the occurrence of disorderliness on a substantial scale. In fact, its incidence has tended to follow a U-shaped curve, being relatively high before World War I, falling between the wars and remaining relatively low until the late 1950s. Then, in the 1960s, it increased, escalating fairly rapidly from the mid-1960s onwards, coming to form an almost "normal" accompaniment of the professional game. Despite such variations in its incidence over time, a recurrent feature of football hooliganism is physical violence. This can take the form of assaults on players and referees, or of clashes between rival fan groups. It is clashes with rival fan groups, often with the police involved as well, that are the dominant form of football hooligan violence in its present phase. Sometimes, such violence involves the use of weapons, either in direct, hand-to-hand combat or in the form of aerial bombardment with missiles from a distance. Marsh, Rosser, and Harré (1978) suggest that football hooliganism is a form of "ritualized aggression" and that is not usually seriously violent except to the extent that official intervention distorts it and prevents it from taking its "normal" form. They evidently think of ritualized and "serious" violence as mutually exclusive, for it is difficult to conceive of throwing coins, darts, beer cans, and, as has happened recently at matches, petrol bombs, as "ritualized aggression." To say this is not to deny the possible effect that official intervention may have on the forms that football hooliganism takes. The penning and segregation of rival fans, for example, have probably increased the incidence of aerial bombardment. But what Marsh and his colleagues seemingly wish to deny is the fact that such groups evidently wish to inflict serious injuries on one another of the kind, for example, that are liable to be caused by coins, darts, and petrol bombs. Alternatively, the Oxford research group may mean to imply that, independently of their violent intentions, football hooligans are restrained by instinctive mechanisms as is the case, for example, with wolves, according to the findings of ethologists such as Lorenz. But, despite Marsh's (1979) attempts to distance himself from the cruder sorts of sociobiological speculations, it is reasonable to conclude that the Oxford analysis involves too close an identification of their human subjects with animals lower on the evolutionary scale. Hence it underestimates the degree to which human behavior is normatively, that is, socially, and not instinctively controlled.

I should like to hypothesize that the violent behavior of football hooligans—whatever elements of ritual it may contain—is centrally connected with norms of masculinity that: (a) place an extreme stress on toughness and ability to fight; (b) are, in that respect, different in degree—though not in kind—from the masculinity norms that are currently dominant in society at large; and (c) that tend, as a result, recurrently to incur condemnation from socially dominant groups. In fact, such norms are reminiscent in many ways of the masculinity norms which were general in British society at an earlier stage of its development, more specifically, or the norms of manliness which, if the analysis presented earlier is correct, were generated by the medieval and early modern forms of segmental bonding and their correlates in the wider social structure.

There are at least four aspects of present day football hooliganism which suggest that its core features may be generated by segmental bonds, namely:

1. The fact that the groups involved appear to be as, and sometimes more, interested in fighting one another as they are in watching football. Indeed, their own accounts suggest that they derive positive enjoyment from fighting and that, for

them, ability to fight forms the principal source of both individual and group prestige.

2. The fact that the rival groups appear to be recruited principally from the same level of social stratification, that is, from the so-called "rough" sections of the working class. This means that, in order to account for it, one has to explain the fact that their fighting involves *intra-* as opposed to *inter*-class conflict. Segmental bonding can explain that fact, though it is necessary to state clearly that, to say this is not to deny either the fact that such groups engage in forms of inter-class conflict—for example, that they fight regularly with the police who are the representatives of the dominant classes—or the fact that they are exploited victims of socially more powerful groups.

3. The fact that the fighting of such groups takes a vendetta form in the sense that, independently of any overt action they may take, particular individuals and groups are set upon simply because they display the membership insignia of a rival group. The long-standing feuds which develop between rival groups of hooligan fans, and which persist despite the turnover of personnel that occurs within such groups, point in the same direction, that is, they are an indication of the very great degree of identification of particular hooligans with the groups to which they belong.

4. The remarkable degree of conformity and uniformity in action that is displayed in the songs and chants of football hooligans. A recurrent theme of these songs and chants is enhancement of the masculine image of the in-group, coupled with denigration and emasculation of the out-group. It is difficult to conceive of the members of more individualized groups either wishing to or being capable of engaging in such complex uniform actions and it is, accordingly, reasonable to suppose that the homogenizing effects of segmental bonding may lie at their base.

Sociological research (Bott, 1957; Parker, 1974; Willis, 1978; Wilmott & Young, 1957) suggests that "rough" working-class communities are characterized by all or most of the following constellation of social attributes: (a) more or less extreme poverty; (b) employment of members in unskilled and/or casual jobs, coupled with a high susceptibility to unemployment; (c) low levels of formal education; (d) low geographical mobility except for some males who travel occupationally, for example, in the army or in connection with unskilled work in the building and construction trades; (e) mother-centered families and extended kin networks; (f) a high degree of conjugal role segregation and separation of the lives of the sexes generally; (g) male dominance, coupled with a tendency for men to be physically violent towards women; (h) little adult supervision of children, coupled with frequent resort to violence in socialization; (i) comparatively low ability of members to exercise emotional control and defer gratification; (j) a comparatively low threshold of repugnance towards physical violence; (k) the formation of street-corner "gangs" which are led by the best fighters and within and between which fighting is frequent; and (l) intense feelings of attachment to narrowly defined "we-groups" and correspondingly intense feelings of hostility towards narrowly defined "they-groups."

The different aspects of such figurations tend to be mutually reinforcing. That is, like their preindustrial counterparts, working-class communities constitute a positive feedback cycle, one of the principal consequences of which is aggressive masculinity. However, these modern forms of segmental bonding are not identical with the pre-industrial forms because they are located in a society with a relatively stable and effective state, and in which there exists a complex network of interdependencies. As a result, the segmentally bonded local groups of today are subjected to "civilizing" pressures and controls from two main sources: (1) from the policing, educational, and social work agencies of the state; and (2) from functionally bonded groups in the wider society. Pressure in the latter case occurs partly by means of the direct actions that are taken by such groups, and partly by means of the influence they are able to bring to bear on the mass media and official agencies.

In short, segmental groups in modern society are subjected to restraint *from the outside* but not, to anything like the same extent, *from within*. Internally, their members remain locked in social figurations that are reminiscent in many ways of the preindustrial forms of segmental bonding and that correspondingly generate acute forms of aggressive masculinity. The intense feelings of in-group attachment and hostility towards out-groups of such segmentally bonded groups mean that rivalry is virtually inevitable when their members meet. And their norms of aggressive masculinity and comparative inability to exercise self-control mean that conflict between them leads easily to fighting. Indeed, much as was the case with their preindustrial counterparts, fighting within and between such groups is necessary for the establishment and maintenance of reputations in terms of their standards of aggressive masculinity. As a result, particular individuals take positive pleasure in performing what is, for them, a socially necessary role.

Football has become a setting for the expression of such standards partly because norms of manliness are intrinsic to it. That is, it, too, is basically a play fight in which masculine reputations are enhanced or lost. Its inherently oppositional character means that it lends itself readily to group identification and the enhancement of in-group solidarity in opposition to a series of easily identifiable out-groups, the opposing team and its supporters. To the extent that some fans are drawn from communities characterized by segmental solidarity, football hooliganism in the form of fighting between gangs of rival supporters is a highly likely result. Indeed, it is probably correct to say that football hooliganism is a present day counterpart to the folk antecedents of modern football, though superimposed on and intermingled in a complex manner with the more differentiated and "civilized" association game.

Acknowledgment. I am grateful to Johan Goudsblom for his helpful comments on an earlier version of this paper.

References

Bott, E. *Family and social network*. London: Tavistock, 1957.

Carew, R. *The survey of Cornwall*. London, 1602.

Dunning, E., Maguire, J., Murphy, P., & Williams, J. The social roots of football hooligan violence. *Leisure Studies*, 1982, *1*, 139-156.

Dunning, E., & Sheard, K. *Barbarians, gentlemen and players: A sociological study of the development of rugby football*. Oxford: Martin Robertson, 1979.

Elias, N. *The civilizing process: The history of manners*. New York: Urizen; Oxford: Blackwell, 1978. (a)

Elias, N. *What is sociology?* London: Hutchinson, 1978. (b)

Elias, N. *State formation and civilization*. Oxford: Blackwell, 1982.

Eysenck, H. J., & Nias, K. D. *Sex, violence, and the media*. New York: Harper & Row, 1978.

Fox, R. The inherent rules of fighting. In P. Collett (Ed.), *Social rules and social behaviour*. Oxford: Blackwell, 1977.

Gardner, R., & Heider, K. *Gardens of war*. Harmondsworth: Penguin, 1974.

Huizinga, J. *The waning of the middle ages*. New York: Doubleday, 1924.

Marsh, P. *Aggro: The illusion of violence*. London: J. M. Dent, 1979.

Marsh, P., Rosser, E., & Harré, R. *The rules of disorder*. London: Routledge & Kegan Paul, 1978.

Owen, G. *The description of Pembrokeshire*. In H. Owed (Ed.), Cymmrodorion Society Research Series, No. 1, 1892, pp. 270-282. (Originally published, 1603.)

Parker, H. J. *View from the boys*. Newton Abbot: David & Charles, 1974.

Riesman, D., & Denney, R. Football in America: A study in culture diffusion. In E. Dunning (Ed.), *The sociology of sport: A selection of readings*. London: Frank Cass, 1971.

Tiger, L. *Men in groups*. London: Thomas Nelson, 1969.

Weis, K. Role models and the social learning of violent behaviour patterns. *Proceedings of the International Congress of Physical Activity Sciences*, Quebec, 1976, pp. 511-524.

Willis, P. *Profane culture*. London: Routledge & Kegan Paul, 1978.

Wilmott, P., & Young, M. *Family and kinship in East London*. London: Routledge & Kegan Paul, 1957.

Yiannakis, A., McIntyre, T. D., Melnick, M. J., & Hart, D. P. (Eds.), *Sport sociology: Contemporary themes*. Dubuque, Iowa: Kendall Hunt, 1976.

Chapter 9

Sports, Conflict, and Conflict Resolution: Problems of Substance and Methodology

Günther Lüschen

Introduction

In assessing the contribution of sports to international understanding, claims are manifold. Often such claims stating a positive or negative contribution lack definitional and methodological clarity. Often, they are statements of belief, of limited experience or express normative demands. Everybody will probably agree that behind all of these questions are very complex issues particularly when dealing on a political level of international relations and peace—rarely is the complexity dealt with sufficiently. Moreover, to the already difficult question of how to understand and secure international peace is added the expectation that sports serve some function in this respect.

One of the most respected authorities on matters of peace in West Germany, the physicist and philosopher Friedrich von Weizsäcker, in a recent interview (1982) stated flatly that he had no scientific solution nor theory for peace among nations, while indicating that he had probably thought out the problems of peace and international understanding as much as anybody else. For sports, conflict, and conflict resolution, Max Gluckman in 1972 summed up his experiences both as an observer of sports and as an eminent social scientist that the "balance [between conflict instigation and resolution through sport] is often delicate" and that he does not, "on present evidence agree . . . that the discharge of aggression in games might lead to games replacing war . . . indeed, the game may breed as much excitement including aggression as it releases among players and spectators." This chapter will review prominent events, major theoretical approaches, and then, after an account of substantive and methodological problems, advance praxeological suggestions for sports policy dealing with sports and conflict.

Factual Accounts and Theoretical Explanations
—A Short Review

A review of individual cases concerning sports, conflict, and conflict resolution easily generates examples for or against a function of sports for conflict resolution. To a number of accounts which this author referred to in an address to the Tblisi Olympic Congress in 1980 and in a recent article (1982) one may add two recent cases, which in their own way support the conclusion that such cases are contradictory and provide no clear insight.

In the 1982 World Soccer Championship the game between Austria and West Germany resulted in a score that deprived Algeria from advancing to the next round. German citizens, because of the unsportsmanlike conduct of their team, were so embarrassed that they apologized to the Algerian Embassy. Comments in the media stated that international relations and the general reputation of West Germany would need years to repair. This sporting event certainly was not in line with most of previous arguments and obviously had consequences in a number of ways—and not only in one direction. Perhaps by now, after the team rehabilitated itself through a victory over Spain and France, there is little impact left of this sporting event, while in the special reality of the mass media it was a major problem for days. The second example, demonstrating the limits of sport events, stems from the French Open Tennis Tournament. The final match, between Wilander and the Argentinian Vilas was barred from British television, thereby depriving a sporting event, during the war over the Falkland Islands, to ease relations between Argentina and Great Britain. But one may also ask, would it have really have had such an effect? Were not the officials of British Television assigning an importance to sport that it does not really have? Obviously, the officials thought so, and thus, one may, as a sportsman, find something positive in this incident after all.

The case of the Argentinian Vilas and British Television may provide another illustration, where problems of interpersonal relations between individuals, mainly a matter for psychological explanation, are hopelessly mixed up with intersystemic, international relations, which are mainly a matter of sociological and political science explanation. Vilas after all is very much an individual, privately and in the international tennis world, representing Argentina to only a limited degree. Famous love relationships between members of unfriendly nations occurring every now and then at international sporting events are other cases that often get credit for having consequences in terms of intersystemic relations. To be sure, there may be some slight impact over the symbolic meaning assigned to such events, but in general, arguments citing the impact of interpersonal incidents between individuals definitely lack an understanding of the difficult and entrenched nature in the relations of nation-states, which are the result of long traditions, alliances, and economic and other interests.

To add to the present unsystematic approaches and general inconclusiveness of results in terms of intersystemic relations, very often observations focus on the incidents accompanying sporting events such as conduct of fans and riotous outbreaks in and around sports arenas. What one might call the *individualistic fallacy* abounds here again insofar as explanations are mainly offered in psychological terms referring to aggression and aggression release. To a considerable degree, psychological explanations, if only implicitly, are the bases of two major groups of theoretical approach to the consequences of sporting events.

Konrad Lorenz is the major representative of a school of thought expecting catharsis as a consequence of sporting contests. His expressed belief (1963) that through sports international relations will be helped is probably more an outcome of his generally positive evaluation of aggression than it is a differentiated account of the peculiar structure of international relations.

The Sherifs may be cited as representing a school of thought that expects as a consequence of competition increased aggressiveness and a breakdown of intersystemic relations. Again, their studies (1961) and subsequent discussions (Sherif, 1972), as well as the observations of others particularly with regard to crowd behavior (Goldstein, 1979), lack a systematic accounting of intergroup and intersystemic structures. One of the few accounts within this approach is that of Arno Plack (1973), who criticizes Lorenz and others for neglecting the moral level in their dealings with sporting events that are only "seemingly harmless."

These two major theoretical approaches to be found in many variations in the bulk of discussions and research were put to an empirical test on a cross-national level. Richard Sipes (1973) did not in any detail spell out and control for quite a few variables. However, his comparative global treatment represents so far the major empirical insight with regard to the followers of Lorenz or Sherif and also with regard to the question whether sports in general are affiliated with intersystemic good relations or not. He used 20 cases of mainly tribal societies from the *Ethnographic Atlas* that could be classified as either being war-like or not and having combative sports or not. The seemingly low number is due to the fact that he needed sufficient information for both of his categories and thus was forced to eliminate quite a few from his sample. The results in Table 9-1 apparently indicate that combative sports will reinforce war-like systems. The deviant-case analysis makes this correlation even stronger; one of the two societies that was not war-like at the time of the analysis had a history of heavy involvement in warfare. The deviant case being war-like without combative sports had, as expected by Sipes, such a fragile infrastructure that it had to avoid any type of internal strife for fear of destroying its internal social fabric. While not providing any information for actual processes in response to the two cited approaches this study supports Sherif and rejects the functionality of sport for conflict resolution. Sipes also points out that

Table 9-1. Correlation of Warlikeness and Presence of Combative Sports in 20 Selected Societies from the Ethnographic Atlas[a]

| | | Combative Sport | | |
		Yes	No	Total n
Warlike	Yes	9	1	10
	No	2	8	10
Total n		11	9	20

[a]From R. Sipes (1973, p. 71), cited with permission by the *American Anthropologist* and the author.

his results suggest cultural learning and sociocultural selection rather than innate propensity for aggression as suggested by the ethologists. Heinilä, some 16 years ago, had already provided us with a careful analysis predicting intergroup conflict and hostility rather than conflict resolution through sport (1966). To this one might add a few disastrous outcomes of sporting events, most prominent among them the 318 deaths at an international soccer match in Lima, Peru in 1964. However, single incidents do not lead to final conclusions, and the fact that they are being reported in the mass media is certainly not a valid indication for scientific insight. But to overlook them is equally unscientific. And the results of Sipes are of course seemingly overwhelming evidence for the destructive potential of sports —at least, his results indicate the structural interdependence with war, a fact that Lorenz might still be able to interpret positively. Yet, it certainly runs counter to our expectations for sports providing international understanding.

One should, however, be reminded again that this result does not indicate anything about the actual process within these societies, only a guess that sports reinforces a war-like structure. Moreover, it is imperative to note that the results of Sipes are based on a selection of mainly tribal societies with a lesser level of cultural development outside such institutions as their kinship system and religion (see Chapter 11).

Norbert Elias (1971, 1976) has demonstrated that, particularly for the control of violence, throughout the history of modern societies one can observe a "civilizing process." For the history of sport he points to the fact that we have by and large the wrong perception of violence in sport in antiquity. While not generally correct for Greek antiquity (cf. McIntosh, 1981), the at times brutal outcome of sports contests in the Roman Empire would not be tolerated today (see Chapter 2). Karl Weinhold (1856, p. 297) also mentions that sports contests in Iceland were so serious in their consequences that they were outlawed in 1013. The history of American football provides another case—President Theodore Roosevelt made the football association develop better rules for violence control. Modern sports in their organizational setup and control can thus well be understood as having in a civilizing process provided better control of destructive outcomes of sports contests. At this level, however, we no longer deal with some material commodity called sport, we deal with a matter of social organization and control. In a way, modern sports, through its differentiated system of rules, controls, and emergent new forms of contests may have provided a major cultural accomplishment in the evolution of modern society. Most of our previous discussions and analyses cannot account for this, their simple form of causal thought is not appropriate for our problem and our expectations in general that sports as such materially provides accommodation and conflict resolution is wrong. Popularly speaking, it provides only a chance or challenge for accommodation—and the matter of consequences is yet another problem.

A Structural Interpretation of the Sports Contest

Before we address the problem of external consequences of a sports contest it is necessary to take a new look at the structure of the contest itself. In many theoretical attempts to explain conflict and sports a much too simplified model of sports and the sports contest prevails. Neither is the high variety of different sports disciplines being accounted for nor is there a deeper understanding of the structure of the sports contest, for example, as it is represented in the encounters of two parties or teams with one another. Many statements of the positive consequences of sporting events for social relations and those of higher intersystemic levels probably come from a surprising and yet correct observation, that as a rule sports contests go on properly, despite the fact that the opponents engage in some severe form of physical violence or aggression that would not be tolerated elsewhere.

Bernard Jeu (1973) has referred to this quality of modern sports as providing a counter-society. Sutton-Smith (1978) in referring to the games of children, and this author to sports in general (1970, 1981) have described this quality of conflict in a cooperative context as dialectical. In a different way, Georg Simmel (1908) has described the sports contest (Kampfspiel) as providing *Einheit im Kampf* (unity in struggle). There are many other interpretations accounting for *association* (Lüschen, 1970) or *communication* (Schelling, 1960) in sports contests and other social encounters. Even in war, as Kant acknowledged in his essay on eternal peace, there is some form of accommodation. The mutual understanding between competing parties in the sports contest is a systemic condition, only under which, to begin with, the contest can go on. Rules, organizational setup, and also the mutual agreements between opponents provide for such an association. In the end it is a matter of conditional structure—not necessarily individual feeling and motivation. Under the circumstances, one may well suggest that direct consequences for systems at large should not be expected. Indeed, their hostile state of affairs may well be a condition under which a sports contest cannot even be allowed. And there may be conditions external to sports, such as systems being reference groups for one another (Heinilä, 1966) or having severe strains in other areas, for example, the feuds between Protestant and Catholics in Glasgow, which may overburden the system of the sports contest or at least lead to incidents of violence.

In terms of consequences of sports contests for intersystemic relations external to sports only two may be expected with some likelihood: (1) the contest between two parties otherwise at odds with one another in international relations may take on a symbolic meaning and thus indirectly provide an impact. At the same time, there is a danger that a sporting event may even set up a violent clash or war as was the case in the "soccer war" between El Salvador and Honduras in 1969. (2) The sports contest may provide a model of accommodation and structural insights that can be helpful in intersystemic relations. The wide acceptance of the principle of fairness in ordinary life as a normative prerogative is an indication of such an impact. But one should observe again that this is meant, so far, mainly for interpersonal relations.

Some Methodological Observations and Structural Theory

As should be obvious by now, the chance for providing a comprehensive theory for the whole set of questions posed with regard to sports and conflict resolution on an intersystemic level is exceedingly difficult. In formal terms, the appeal to mainly commonsense notions and beliefs is to predict from a situative outcome, influenced by many variables, yet another outcome in the international context. If one were to use the common statement-type approach to theory, this already appears difficult for accounting for the outcome of a contest between two antagonists. The type of theoretical statement will need many qualifiers to meet the requirements of observability and testability. The result will be a fairly low-level generalization—not the type of theory many talk and dream about. The extension of such theoretical statements to the level of international relations appears almost impossible—and most of the previous commonsense claims have not even seriously tried that, using among others psychological concepts where systemic ones would have been needed. Under the circumstances one will have to ask whether the previous unsatisfactory type of research and theorizing will have to suffice, with the expectation that more detailed study and more careful design will enlarge our knowledge even on the systemic level within the contest itself. For the extension and testability of sports' function for intersystemic conflict one may not be so sure.

Beyond the statement approach to theory there is, however, through recent advances in epistemology, a new type of theorizing being advocated, which Stegmüller (1976) originally labelled the nonstatement approach and more recently renamed structural theory (1979). This should not be confused with what is commonly referred to as structuralism in the social sciences. Stegmüller has in mind that such theory is based on a type of insight that, after sufficient information one intuitively feels to be true. Advanced previously in mathematics and physics such a notion sounds almost like an invitation for renewed vagary in sociology and other social sciences. Yet, the arguments like those of Simmel and Jeu concerning the structure or form of the sports contest in terms of its unity in conflict appear to be such theoretical insight—they are based on a high level of informational input and yet they are difficult to break down into propositional statements and rigid testing. It may well be that through theoretical problems such as the unity in conflict of the sports contest further light can be shed onto such new methodology in social science theory. In the end it may also provide a chance to overcome the rigid formality and irrationality of the dialectical method, which at first sight and after referring to the structure of the sports contest as substantively dialectical, will quickly be advanced as a solution to our methodological problems.

Conclusion: Instead of a Comprehensive Theory Some Praxeological Advances for Sports Policy

In summary, our results may look meager in terms of our general expectations on sports and international understanding. They may also look meager in terms of a neat social science theory. Too much seems to be missing, there is not enough information, not enough research, and on top of that there are insurmountable methodological problems with structural theory to explain the unity of the sports contest itself. Actually, the result is not meager. The review of previous research and discussion may instigate further research and thought. The Simmelesque result of unity in conflict, of structural dialectic, can easily be extended to a notion of a basic structural disposition at least in ethnic societies with so-called dual organization (Lévi-Strauss, 1967, 1969). Moreover, while the result is inconclusive and rather cautious concerning sports' function for intersystemic and surely international relations, there is sufficient information, insight, and theoretical reasoning to advance some praxeological suggestions as a basis for future policy in sport. Some of it may not be so new, yet one hopes this discussion will have provided a more informed, and in the end, more rational approach. In this regard, it is also important to know what we cannot be sure about.

For the policy suggestions which follow it is assumed that we deal with conflict in the system of the sports contest only—at this time neither conflicts of an interpersonal nature nor of sports organizations are of interest to us. The former, as was discussed earlier, are actually very much in the center of analysis, the latter are so far almost totally overlooked (Matejko, 1975). For the sports contest as a form of conflict and for possible outcomes for relations between systems at large represented in such contest the following may be suggested as a basis for sports policies:

1. Sports contests are not uniform, and they provide a variety of structures that need to be handled differently, that is, a gymnastics contest has a different form and potential than a rugby match.

2. Even the most vigorous encounters need a consensus or, even better, an *association* between parties in order for such contests to go on. It is essential to understand such structural dispositions of association and support it through rules, values like fair play, and organizational contexts as much as possible. However, it would mean impeding the associative challenges of the sports contest were it strictly and rigidly ruled and policed by sanctions and quasilegal personnel.

3. The symbolic meaning of a contest between parties rivalling one another may take on added significance, that is, for those systems that are reference groups for one another, or for systems that are engaged in other forms of conflicting interest in economic matters or international power. It is essential for an appropriate policy to consider these contextual factors for the sports contest; a consequence may either be to (a) not allow a contest to go on at all if there is a danger of overburdening the sports contest in its structural disposition, or (b) carefully provide for controlling arrangements and thus make the ultimate use of such contests for a general if only symbolic accommodation. It is even possible, through special arrangements such as the use of the mass media, to increase the general significance of a sporting event. But even then one should not expect much beyond some symbolic significance. On the level of international relations the final arrangement will have to come from political moves.

4. There may be certain conditions under which either a positive or negative impact of sports on international relations is possible. This can go beyond the symbolic sphere under very special conditions. In purely formal terms, however, the association in the sports contest between competing parties may provide a structural model that could be useful in intersystemic relations. Because of the complex nature of the latter even such formal and theoretical use will be limited.

5. It is not unusual that sports organizations, despite the general claim of sports' impact on system relations at large, abandon their responsibility for such impacts in the wider range of the institution of sports. In particular, this holds for crowd behavior and its control at sporting events. Sports organizations have to recognize this.

6. It is paramount to understand that the sports contest is a system of conflict itself, that some sporting events clearly value violence and conflict. Under the circumstances a belief in sports' peaceful mission as a matter of course is dangerous. In its consequence it is destructive for the system of sports itself.

7. Even if the impact of sports on intersystemic conflict and relations is limited, as has been argued in reference to many exaggerated statements, some impact is a matter of reality and needs to be incorporated in appropriate organizational effort and a policy in sports that sees two major lines of action: strengthen the internal and external controls to bar as much negative impact as possible, and advance any potential positive impact to the highest possible level. Whether on the level of political relations the latter is to be instigated directly and in accord with the political powers or rather in a more functional way, is a matter of political systems, but possibly also one of the integrity of the system of sports.

Summary

A review of incidents of conflict and sports on an intersystemic level shows no clear pattern and the frequency of reports in the mass media is no reliable and valid indicator for either a positive or negative outcome of sports contests on international relations and peace. Theoretical explanations of sports' function for conflict resolution, either stating catharsis or conflict reinforcement, are insufficient despite the fact that a cross-cultural test of tribal societies clearly indicates a positive relationship of sports to war. Among others, evolutionary interpretations have to be brought in and may account for institutionalization and control of conflict in and through sports. Future interpretations also have to acknowledge the ambivalent and dialectical structure of sports and its contests, where violence is valued highly in many forms. Theoretical explanations in terms of a statement approach to theory will remain insufficient for trying to understand accommodation within a sports contest itself and for the relationship between systems at large. Structural or non-statement theory offers one possible approach. Even at this time of limited theoretical insight, conflicting results, and a general inability to forecast, the present level of knowledge and experience allow for a number of praxeological statements. These may be used in sports policy dealing with conflict, and conflict resolution.

Acknowledgment. This chapter is based on a paper presented at the International Congress, Sport and International Understanding, Helsinki, Finland, July 1982.

References

Dunning, E. The structural-functional properties of folk-games and modern sport. *Sportwissenschaft,* 1973, *3*, 215-232.
Dunning, E. The figurational dynamics of modern sport. *Sportwissenschaft,* 1979, *4*, 341-359.

Elias, N. The genesis of sport as a sociological problem. In E. Dunning (Ed.), *The sociology of sport*. London: Cass, 1971.

Elias, N. Sport and violence. *Actes Recherche Science Sociale*, 1976, *6*, 2-20.

Firth, R. A dart-match in Tikopia: The sociology of primitive sport. *Oceania*, 1930, *1*, 64-96.

Gluckman, M. Sport and conflict. In O. Grupe (Ed.), *Sport in the modern world*. Berlin: Springer, 1972.

Goldstein, J. H. (Ed.). *Sports, games, and play*. Hillsdale, N. J.: Erlbaum, 1979.

Heinilä, K. Notes on the intergroup conflicts in international sports. *International Review of Sport Sociology*, 1966, *1*, 30-40.

Jeu, B. La contre-société sportive et ses contradictions. *Esprit*, 1973, *10*, 391-416.

Kiviaho, P. The regional distribution of sport organizations as a function of political cleavages. *Sportwissenschaft*, 1974, *4*, 72-81.

Kotarbinski, T. *Praxeology*. London: Oxford University Press, 1963.

Lang, G. Der Ausbruch von Tumulten bei Sportveranstaltungen. In G. Lüschen & K. Weis (Eds.), *Die Soziologie des Sports*. Darmstadt: Luchterhand, 1976.

Lévi-Strauss, C. *Structural anthropology*. Garden City, N. Y.: Doubleday, 1967.

Lévi-Strauss, C. *The elementary structures of kinship*. Boston, 1969.

Lorenz, K. *Das sogenannte Böse*. Vienna: Borotha-Schöler, 1963.

Lüschen, G. Cooperation, association, and contest. *Journal of Conflict Resolution*, 1970, *14*, 21-34.

Lüschen, G. At the edge of human existence: Order and disorder in top athletics. In U. Simri (Ed.), *Proceedings of ICPER-Europe Congress*. Natanya: Wingate Institute, 1981.

Lüschen, G. Sport, conflict and conflict resolution. *International Social Science Journal*, 1982, *34*, 185-196.

Lüschen, G., & Sage, G. *Handbook of social science of sport*. Champaign, Ill.: Stipes, 1981.

Matejko, A. The diagnosis of conflict in sport. *Revue Internationale Sociologie*, 1975, *33*, 63-87.

McIntosh, P. The sociology of sport in the Ancient world. In G. Lüschen & G. Sage (Eds.), *Handbook of social science of sport*. Champaign, Ill.: Stipes, 1981.

Plack, A. *Der Mythos vom Aggressionstrieb*. Munich: Piper, 1973.

Sartre, J. P. *Critique of dialectical reason*. London: NLB, 1976.

Schelling, T. *The strategy of conflict*. Cambridge, Mass.: Harvard University Press, 1960.

Sherif, C. Intergroup conflict and competition. In O. Grupe (Ed.), *Sport in the modern world*. Berlin: Springer, 1972.

Sherif, M., & Sherif, C. *The robbers cave experiment*. Norman: University of Oklahoma Press, 1961.

Simmel, G. *Soziologie*. Berlin: Duncker & Humblot, 1908.

Sipes, R. War, sports, and aggression. *American Anthropologist*, 1973, *75*, 64-86.

Smith, M. Sport and collective violence. In D. Ball & J. Loy (Eds.), *Sport and social order*. Reading, Mass.: Addison-Wesley, 1975.

Sprenger, J. Zum Problem der Aggressionen im Sport. *Sportwissenschaft*, 1974, *4*, 231-257.

Stegmüller, W. *The structure and dynamics of theories*. New York: Springer, 1976.

Stegmüller, W. *The structuralist view of theories*. New York: Springer, 1979.

Sutton-Smith, B. *Die Dialektik des Spiels*. Schorndorf: Hofmann, 1978.

Weinhold, K. *Altnordisches Leben*. Berlin, 1856.

Weiszäcker, F. v. Interview on peace. WDR 3. June 30, 1982.

Chapter 10
Psychological Issues in Sports Aggression

Gordon W. Russell

Introduction

Sports offer an especially attractive research setting for those interested in increasing the generalizability of laboratory findings as well as the testing of predictions derived from various theories of human behavior. Two features with particular implications for aggression research are worth noting. In combative and some contact sports the aspiring athlete is taught basic skills in interpersonal aggression and lavishly rewarded when they are effectively applied in competition. In these sports interpersonal aggression is met with enthusiastic approval within the sport and a general tolerance on the part of society. Consequently, the arousal of such states as guilt, anxiety, and evaluation apprehension in laboratory subjects required to aggress against one another may not occur to the same degree in sports, providing the investigator with a somewhat unique set of research parameters. Few, if any comparable situations exist outside of wartime. Moreover, aggression research stands to profit from an additional set of *behavioral* measures. This important gain in triangulation may be achieved through the use of indices of "illegal" behavior, a class of aggression involving acts which violate the rules of a sport and which also satisfy conventional definitions of aggression. As noted elsewhere (Russell, 1981a), the researcher may find other important advantages and reasons to study aggression in the naturalistic context of sports.

Two topics from the sports aggression literature have been chosen for review. The first topic, *catharsis*, has been fairly extensively investigated in sports and builds upon a wealth of laboratory research. The effects of *outcome* on aggression is a minor topic by comparison, enjoying far less data from both the laboratory and sports settings. However, a pervasive belief in the cathartic value of sports and the obsession with winning shown by sportspeople suggests that these topics should have priority on the agenda of the sports aggression researcher. Throughout this review, links with traditional laboratory investigations will be established to emphasize the continuity and necessary interdependence between laboratory and field research. Even a casual inspection of articles in this area reveals that few writers have made more than passing reference to the theories predictive of their results; fewer have referenced or attempted to integrate their findings with comparable hypotheses tested in the social science laboratory. Suffice it to say the data of sports aggression cannot stand in isolation from those derived in controlled laboratory investigations nor, for that matter, from other extralaboratory situations.

Definitions

While "sports" will be broadly defined to encompass games and vigorous activities (e.g., darts, nail hammering), a somewhat narrower definition of "aggression" will be used in the selection of those studies bearing on the two topics under review. Numerous, often conflicting, definitions of aggression exist amidst considerable debate over the essential makeup of the behavior. While a review of that important debate is beyond the scope of the present paper, the reader is referred to Zillmann (1979, chap. 2) for an extended discussion of this continuing controversy. For present purposes the studies cited herein have been limited to those satisfying a general definition of aggression, for example, "behavior directed toward the goal of harming or injuring another living being who is motivated to avoid such treatment" (Baron, 1977). For the most part, the dependent variable will have been represented by measures of physical and verbal aggression and occasionally negative mood states, for example, anger.

The term "catharsis" will be used throughout to refer to reductions in peoples' aggressive behavior which occurs as a result of their either behaving aggressively or, merely observing others behave aggressively. Others (e.g., Quanty, 1976) have offered an expanded definition which includes a supposition that physiological arousal will also be reduced following an aggressive act or the observation of aggression. Although investigations of the physiological concomitants of sports aggression are uncommon, those few studies that did provide for measures of subjects' arousal will nevertheless be noted as they arise.

Chapter Plan

In the first section, the concept of catharsis will be traced forward from its initial appearance in the writings of Aristotle. In so doing, cathartic notions will be seen to occupy a central position in several of our most influential theories of behavior. The theorists themselves have attained a preeminence well beyond their respective disciplines, a fact which makes the pervasive acceptance of cathartic-like beliefs understandable. Thus, this brief sketch is intended more to draw attention to the deep entrenchment of catharsis in our everyday thinking through its links to influential figures than to providing a detailed review of its historical development (see reviews by Geen & Quanty, 1977; Zillmann, 1979).

Two following sections will be devoted to an examination of the evidence on catharsis, first, from the standpoint of athletes participating in aggressive or combative sports and secondly, the effects on spectators of witnessing such displays. Of course, spectators need not always be in the stands or on the terraces. Vastly greater numbers participate vicariously through the triumphs of modern technology, that is, radio, the silver screen, and television. Considerable interest and public controversy have arisen in recent years over the influences on viewers of media presentations, in particular the deleterious effects commonly attributed to violent movies and television programming. Therefore, the conclusions drawn by reviewers of research on media effects will be noted and extended to include studies specifically investigating the role of catharsis in media presentations of violent sports.

A concluding section of the chapter will examine the role of outcome in determining player and spectator aggression. Previous laboratory and field research will be reviewed as background to the presentation of original data derived from official ice hockey records. In summarizing the effects of outcome, several methodological refinements and suggestions for future research will be proposed.

Valves, Vents, and Drains: The Catharsis Hypothesis

> I don't see any violence in two players dropping their gloves and letting a little steam escape. I think that's a lot better than spearing somebody. I think it's an escape valve because you know yourself pressure builds up and there's no way to release it and if fighting is not allowed then another violent act will occur. (NHL player, circa 1977; cited in Smith, 1979)

As a societal assumption, catharsis is often cited as one of the obvious benefits of sports participation. (As part of an unpublished project, the author recently asked 525 students enrolled in introductory psychology courses several questions specifically tapping their belief in the cathartic value of sport. The percentages of males and females agreeing with the item: "Participating in combatant or aggressive sports is a good way for people to get rid of their aggressive urges?" did not differ. Overall, agreement was expressed by 63% of the subjects. The same question asked of 84 males in attendance at an ice hockey game produced 75% agreement.) The concept is found embedded in the sentiment that aggression is healthful or beneficial in relieving the individual of his or her pent-up hostility. Having expressed aggression, the likelihood that they will subsequently aggress is thereby diminished. This draining of aggressive impulses is presumed to occur either through the individual actually behaving aggressively or by merely watching others aggress. Thus, the football player should be less aggressive at the conclusion of the season than he was before the season began. The numerous opportunities he has been provided to discharge his aggressive impulses ensures, from a cathartic view, a more docile athlete in the post-season. Similarly, the baseball player assailing the umpire with verbal abuse for a close call at second base is supposedly getting the anger out of his system. By the same token, spectators in the stands witnessing the altercation at second are also presumed to be venting their aggression, a harmless—even prosocial—result of their attendance.

Origins of Catharsis

Before proceeding with an examination of that portion of the sports aggression literature having implications for catharsis, it is important to recognize the central role played by the concept in the formulations of those who have historically been concerned with questions relating to human aggression. The personal stature and influence of those who have argued the case for catharsis should be noted insofar as it offers a partial explanation for the currency of the concept.

Aristotle. The historical flow of ideas which has seen catharsis established as a dominant theme can be traced back at least as far as Aristotle (Berczeller, 1967). His insights into the Greek tragic theater prompted him to observe that members of the audience witnessing the display of "tragic" feelings (Goodman, 1964) would themselves be purged of these same emotions (e.g., fear, pity). Although Aristotle never specifically mentioned aggression, it has been commonly assumed, rightly or wrongly, that he would have viewed it in similar terms. It is noteworthy that Plato took the opposite view suggesting instead that rather than the audience being purged of the emotions they witnessed, they experience an increase in these emotions.

Freud. Catharsis has played a prominent and continuing role in the Freudian view. This influential viewpoint supposes that there is a continuous welling up of destructive impulses within the individual representing an outgrowth of the death instinct. Freud saw this condition as dooming mankind to a future not unlike its history, one plagued by repeated wars and terror. In a famous exchange of letters with Albert Einstein in 1932 (reproduced in Megargee & Hokanson, 1970) he held forth little hope for peace save the possibility of somehow creating a superordinate body to which all authority has been delegated for settling disputes among its constituent members. In speaking of the death instinct he observed: "if these forces are turned to destruction in the external world, the living creature will be relieved and the effect must be beneficial." Within this tradition, Anthony Storr (1968), a British psychotherapist, has written: "it is obvious that the encouragement of competition in all possible fields is likely to diminish the kind of hostility which leads to war rather than to increase it—rivalry between nations in sports can do nothing but good" (pp. 158-159).

Finally, in carrying the banner of catharsis to their readers, two psychiatrists, Procter and Eckerd (1976), provide us with a fanciful, if not simplistic, analogy of the presumed cathartic mechanism:

> People's emotions are similar to steam locomotives. If you build a fire in the boiler of a locomotive, keep raising the steam pressure and let it sit on the track, sooner or later something will blow. However, if you take it and spin the wheels and toot the whistle, the steam pressure can be kept at a safe level. Spectator sports give John Q. Citizen a socially acceptable way to lower his steam pressure by allowing him to spin his wheels and toot his whistle. (p. 83)

Certainly, we stand to realize a marvelous gain from spectatorship if "spinning one's wheels" and "tooting one's whistle" work in just that way. If not, then their concluding recommendation that mental patients be taken to sporting events would seem dubious at best.

Frustration-aggression hypothesis. The concept of catharsis subsequently appeared in the original formulations of the influential Yale group of theorists (Dollard, Doob, Miller, Mowrer, & Sears, 1939). Better known for their recognition of the role of frustration in producing aggression, a corollary was appended to their model by which they predicted a reduced likelihood of aggression following its expression. "The expression of any act of aggression," they wrote, "is a catharsis that reduces the instigation to all other acts of aggression" (Dollard et al., 1939, p. 53). As Quanty (1976, p. 100) has observed, Dollard and his colleagues simply gave formal expression to the Freudian position.

Ethology. The concept of catharsis has enjoyed a further resurgence in recent years through the writings of Nobel prize winners Konrad Lorenz and Nikolaas Tinbergen. Both are giants in the field of ethology, a European tradition of scientific inquiry based on the observation of subhuman species functioning in their natural habitats. While the influence of ethologists on scientists studying human behavior has been an important one, their impact on the thinking of the general public has been considerably stronger. The Lorenz (1966) volume *On Aggression* was a bestseller as were the works of several skillful popularizers in the ethologists' camp. What is especially intriguing in their argument is the plausible assertion that human behaviors contain representations of the patterns of behavior demonstrated to occur at the level of lower organisms, for example, aggression in defense of territory or aggression as a means of establishing dominance. These behavioral sequences or fixed action patterns of aggressive behavior are stereotypical, innately determined, and triggered in response to an appropriate environmental stimulus. The relevance of this viewpoint for catharsis lies in the assumption that aggressive energy is continuously being generated within the species member and seeks periodic release. Recommendations, then, that we occasionally relieve the mounting pressure by discharging aggressive energy through the performance of an aggressive act are well founded and obviously beneficial to the individual. Otherwise, dangerous levels may be reached and unleashed in devastating attacks on others. Given the inevitability of aggression, the task becomes one of directing that aggression into relatively safe channels. Competition is one such channel. The competition itself may take the form of debates, international competition for the conquest of space, or sports, each setting providing mankind with a safe outlet for aggression. Regarding sports, Lorenz (1966) has commented:

> While some early forms of sport, like the jousting of medieval knights, may have had an appreciable influence on sexual selection, the main function of sport today lies in the cathartic discharge of aggressive urge; besides that, of course, it is of the greatest importance in keeping people healthy. (p. 242)

Although the cathartic elements of the ethological view appear to have gained widespread recognition, it is less generally recognized that the two major figures in the field have found cause to change their opinions (Evans, 1974; Tinbergen, 1968). Indeed, Lorenz has been quoted as saying: "Nowadays, I have strong doubts whether watching aggressive behavior even in the guise of sport has any cathartic effect at all" (Evans, 1974, p. 93).

Player Aggression and Catharsis

One type of investigation which offers an indirect test of cathartic effects is that in which a comparison is made between groups of subjects who are involved in aggressive pursuits with others who are uninvolved. Cathartic predictions tested by static comparisons between sportsmen and nonsportsmen or between participants in contact versus noncontact sports assume that those involved in aggressive sports have many more opportunities than others to discharge their aggression. Hence, their scores would be predictably lower on aggression measures. Of course, the major threat to the internal validity of such comparisons is a selection factor. Any differences between such groups may have existed prior to their choosing a sport and not necessarily have arisen from their participation.

Static comparisons. A laboratory experiment by Zillmann, Johnson, and Day (1974) included a preliminary comparison of athletes involved in contact sports (football, wrestling), athletes in noncontact sports (swimming, tennis), and nonathletes. Subjects in the three categories did not differ on a behavioral measure (shock) of their aggression. Ostrow (1974), too, reported no preseason differences among two tennis squads and a noncompetitive control group. In a recent comparison (LeUnes & Nation, Note 1), U.S. football team members, students who formerly played in high school but discontinued their participation, and students in introductory psychology courses who had never "lettered" in a sport, were indistinguishable on a measure of anger. However, in an earlier comparison with physical education (PE) students, football players were found to score higher on an inventory measure of direct aggression (Patterson, 1974). Athletes were similarly found to score higher than nonathletes (Thirer, 1976).

Results consistent with a cathartic prediction have been reported in several studies. Using a Thematic Apperception Test (TAT) measure of aggression, college boxers were found to score lower than cross-country runners, wrestlers, or a control group (Husman, 1955). It should be noted that the boxers experienced more guilt than subjects in the control group. This finding was similar to that obtained by Atkins, Hilton, Neigher, and Bahr (Note 2) in which provoked police officers who chose boxing as an activity scored lower on TAT aggression than officers choosing other activities, for example, a verbal interchange. As in the Husman (1955) study, boxers again scored higher on guilt than subjects in the comparison groups. As noted by Quanty (1976), subjects who experience high levels of guilt have been found to be less aggressive than others (Knott, Lasater, & Shuman, 1974) raising the possibility that the induction of guilt rather than a cathartic response may have produced the lower aggression.

Before-after comparisons. A decidedly more rigorous test of catharsis is provided by research designs in which one of two equivalent groups of subjects—ideally, randomly assigned—are provided with opportunities to aggress. The result of their aggressive behavior, in contrast to subjects in a nonaggressive control condition, should reveal a subsequent lowering of their aggression if a cathartic prediction is to find support.

Ostrow (1974) provided a test of catharsis over a full season of tennis using two intercollegiate squads and noncompetitive control subjects. Comparisons between pre- and postseason hostility scores revealed no differences except in the case of an inactive squad, that is, players who either failed to make the team or participated minimally. These men showed an increase in aggression over the season which, as Ostrow notes, could have arisen just as easily from the frustration and resentment associated with their failing to make the team as from their participation in tennis. Ryan (1970) had subjects in a vigorous activity condition pound a rubber mallet in contrast to inactive control subjects. No differences in hostility were observed between the groups when they were subsequently provided an opportunity to shock a confederate.

In an interesting field study, Patterson (1974) administered a hostility inventory to high school football players and PE students both before and at the conclusion of the football season. The PE students evidenced no change over the season whereas the football players were significantly more hostile in the postseason. In his study of college athletes, Husman (1955) reported a marginal increase in the aggression of wrestlers over a season of competition.

Verbal aggression is a further means by which athletes and spectators in some sports can express their anger. In certain sports, for example, baseball, verbal attacks are seen as normative, traditional behavior. A test of catharsis using a dependent measure of verbal aggression was reported by Hornberger (1959). Interestingly, subjects engaged in a vigorous activity, that is, hammering nails, subsequently displayed more verbal aggression than controls. Evidence of the effects of verbal aggression itself on subsequent behavior has been provided by Loew (1967). College students trained to merely speak aggressive words aloud later were more aggressive to a (confederate) peer than control group students reciting neutral words. Far from producing cathartic effects, vigorous aggression-like behavior can seemingly increase verbal aggression. Indeed, simply uttering aggressive words may be a sufficient instigation to physical aggression.

An interesting exception to the above trend is provided in a study by Kidd and Walton (1966) who assessed the therapeutic value of dart throwing by young boys diagnosed as aggressive. The youngsters were provided with opportunities to throw darts at photos of the people who were significant in their lives. The authors reported a decrease in hostility toward authority figures and peers (a mere 7% of the target choices) following four weekly sessions; hostility towards parents (58%), siblings (25%), and teachers (10%) remained inexplicably unchanged.

Archival studies. As a complementary investigative technique, archival studies of sports aggression offer the advantage of an increase in triangulation of measurement. Although the approach is not without its shortcomings, its use in sports appears to escape the two major sources of bias, selective deposit and selective survival (Webb, Campbell, Schwartz, Sechrest, & Grove, 1981).

The cathartic view would predict that the greatest amount of interpersonal aggression would occur early in an aggressive sport, thereafter diminishing in frequency and intensity. However, a series of archival studies comparing period to period aggression in ice hockey reveals just the opposite trend. The results of five investigations (see Russell, 1981a) and more recently Harrell (1981), provide a consensus that interpersonal aggression increases during games. Similarly, repeated meetings between rivalrous teams are not accompanied by a reduction in interteam hostility. Rather, a positive relationship has been reported (Russell, 1983) between aggression and the number of times any two teams have met previously during the hockey season.

Continuing in the tradition of archival studies, anthropologist Richard Sipes (1973) has examined the historical record noting both the extent to which combatant sports were present in past societies and the degree of their involvement in conflicts, for example, war, revolution, and so forth. Once again, support for a cathartic prediction was not forthcoming. Rather, a correlational analysis revealed a positive relationship between the two variables. Thus from an anthropological perspective, this signal investigation suggests that far from producing catharsis, combatant sports have been closely allied with inter- and intrasocietal aggression over much of mankind's recorded history.

A footnote. All this is not to suggest that the trend of increased aggression apparent above is an inevitable outcome of participation in even combatant sports. Providing a nonviolent philosophical context in which athletes acquire and display aggressive skills may eliminate or reverse the general tendency towards increased aggression. Nosanchuk (1981) has studied the influence of the passive and peaceful philosophy which accompanies training in karate. Even though devotees of the martial arts learn and practice lethal skills in traditional *dojos*, Nosanchuk's data indicate that students become less aggressive with increased training. This study suggests a valuable line of research exploring the effects of this and other peaceful teachings imparted to athletes involved in contact and/or combatant sports.

To summarize, studies of the effects of engaging in aggressive activities prompt a conclusion that such participation either produces no change or, more often, results in an enhancement of the athletes' aggression.

Spectators' Aggression

A consideration of the effects on spectators of observing aggression on the field of play treats the second part of our original definition. In an ebullient defense of football spectatorship, Brill (1929) argues the case for cartharsis:

> On the other hand, through the operation of the psychological laws of identification and catharsis, the thoroughgoing fan is distinctly benefitted mentally, physically and morally by spectator-participation in his favorite sport. And his wife might find him a much less pleasant animal to have around the house, when he was there, if he did not absent himself from time to time to let off the accumulated steam of ancient instincts. (p. 430)

In further extolling the benefits of (male) spectatorship he notes:

> He will purge himself of impulses which too dammed up would lead to private broils and public disorders. He will achieve exaltation, vicarious but real. He will be a better individual, a better citizen, a better husband and father. (p. 434)

Observing aggression. Two studies using a TAT measure of aggression have produced offsetting results. While Kingsmore (1970) found support for a cathartic position among fans viewing basketball and professional wrestling, Turner (1970) reported an increase in the hostility of spectators watching basketball and an amateur wrestling card. More recently, Sloan (1979) reported that partisan Notre Dame crowds seeing their football and basketball teams suffer defeat were more angry following such games than before. Sloan also reported that females attending Notre Dames' annual Bengal Bouts, an amateur fight card, became increasingly hostile over the course of the evening while males evidenced no change. University of Arizona basketball crowds also exhibited increasing hostility during individual league games (Leuck, Krahenbuhl, & Odenkirk, 1979).

A field experiment deserving of high marks is that conducted by Jeffrey Goldstein and Robert Arms (1971) on the occasion of the Army-Navy football game played annually in Philadelphia. Their research design is worthy of close scrutiny insofar as it conjoined the cathartic and enhancement hypotheses, that is, in effect provided for either outcome. Inasmuch as spectators witnessed a competition, the relative merits of two major theories, both predicting enhancement, could also be assessed. Briefly, the frustration-aggression hypothesis (e.g., Berkowitz, 1969) predicts that *only* those fans rooting for the eventual losers in the contest would show an increase in aggression. They alone would be thwarted in their quest for a victory. Social learning theory (e.g., Bandura, 1973) predicts a general increase in spectator hostility resulting from an overall weakening in the strength of inhibitions against the expression of aggression. Thus, both Army and Navy fans would be expected to show increased hostility. Conversely, cathartic viewpoints would not distinguish between the loyalties of fans in predicting an overall reduction in hostility for those in attendance.

The procedures used by Goldstein and Arms (1971) involved having trained undergraduate student experimenters intercept men on a random basis (every Nth male) as they made their way into the stadium before the game. They were asked to complete a short version of the Buss-Durkee (Buss & Durkee, 1957) hostility inventory, answer several biographical items, for example, age, and indicate which team they were supporting. After the game the experimenters intercepted another random sample of males following the same procedure. An equally competitive, but nonaggressive intercollegiate gymnastics meet served as a control event. Here again, the same procedure was followed.

Their results revealed a significant increase in hostility from before to after the football game while no changes occurred at the gymnastics meet. Interestingly, fans of both Army (winners) and Navy (losers) showed increased hostility from the pre- to postgame stages. This result supports the disinhibition explanation proposed by Bandura (1973) to account for the general effects of heightened hostility arising from the observation of aggression. Exposure to the aggression of others seemingly acts to weaken one's internal mechanisms controlling the expression of similar behavior. Of course, the results by no means negate the frustration-aggression formulation; they merely suggest that a disinhibitory process more adequately accounts for the underlying dynamics of increased hostility in this particular setting.

Several rival interpretations remained, however, to challenge Goldstein and Arms'

(1971) conclusions. Foremost among the alternate explanations for their results were differences in fans and in the norms governing the behavior of spectators at the two events. Other explanations include the likelihood that many of the men were intoxicated at the football game and became increasingly so as the game wore on, an unlikely state of affairs at the gymnastics meet. An increase in hostility would indeed be predicted, especially for those intoxicated fans who felt threatened in their situation (Taylor, Gammon, & Capasso, 1976). Mann (1974) has suggested that because Army trounced the Navy team 27 to 0, the increase in hostility might have arisen from spectators' witnessing a dull, lopsided contest. One might also question whether the student experimenters were able to follow the random interception procedures throughout. Did they unwittingly pass over the more ominous-looking males during the pregame phase and, with a gain in confidence, follow the procedures to the letter during the postgame stage?

These and other rival explanations for the Goldstein and Arms results prompted a systematic replication by Arms, Russell, and Sandilands (1979). They preserved the overall design of the original investigation, but with several important modifications. Ice hockey was substituted for football; in addition, professional wrestling was included to represent a stylized or fictional form of aggression. A provincial swimming competition served as the control event. Rather than approaching dyed-in-the-wool fans, they used students enrolled in introductory psychology courses as subjects. University students offered the advantage of being a known entity (they were sober among other things) and allowed their random assignment to an event and, to either the pre- or postevent conditions of the design. Three hostility measures were administered to roughly equal numbers of males and females in a spare dressing room before their particular event began, with the procedure being repeated after the event for others assigned to that condition. In addition to the Buss-Durkee (Buss & Durkee, 1957) scales and a punishment index (Goldstein, Rosnow, Raday, Silverman, & Gaskell, 1975), the short form of the Nowlis (1965) Mood Adjective Check List (MACL) was also administered. Inasmuch as a number of dimensions of mood are tapped by the MACL the investigator is allowed the means to explore other covarying mood changes arising from the spectator experience. The results again failed to offer support for the cathartic position. Where significant changes occurred, they were in the direction of increased hostility after watching the realistic (hockey) and stylized (wrestling) forms of aggression. The highly competitive but nonaggressive swim meet produced no change in the hostility of subjects.

The results of this field investigation provide greater confidence that the increased spectator hostility observed at the Army-Navy game arose from the aggression taking place on the field of play and not from other extraneous factors. The random selection and assignment of students to pre- and postevent conditions negates a subject selection bias that could have intruded in the Goldstein and Arms experiment. By the same token, differences between football and gymnastics fans seems an unlikely explanation for their findings. The suggestion that an increase in fan hostility arose from their witnessing a mismatch (Mann, 1974) also seems less plausible. While the hockey game was won handily (11 to 1) by the home team, the outcome of the final tag team match on the wrestling card was in doubt until the dying minutes.

In an extension of these studies, Russell (1981b) attempted to track changes in spectator aggression (and arousal) in more detail over the course of an especially violent hockey game by using additional data points. The common practice of taking only pre- and postevent measures may mask curvilinearity, including a cathartic effect, in the underlying relationships. Intermediate data points at the end of the first and second periods should reveal any curvilinearity and provide a clearer picture of spectators' emotional responses. Furthermore, a same-sport control game was used to provide greater control over intersport differences (e.g., norms, venue, pace, etc.). A second hockey game with an aggressive penalty total well below the average for the league served this purpose.

Analysis of MACL scores (Nowlis, 1965) revealed that the shape of the aggression and arousal functions at the violent game was indeed curvilinear, that is, an inverted-U curve. Levels of aggression and arousal increased from pregame states and peaked at the conclusion of the second period in which most of the game's violence erupted. Thereafter, aggression and arousal subsided. Otherwise, spectators' aggression at the relatively nonviolent comparison game remained at a constant level throughout, although their arousal function was again curvilinear.

More recently, Harrell (1981) has examined the role of individual differences in determining the response of spectators to athletic aggression. Males attending 14 World Hockey Association games completed a short form of the Buss-Durkee hostility inventory either before the games or at the conclusion of the first or second periods. Subjects who were frequently exposed to hockey, that is, those who indicated a tolerance for aggression, showed an increase in verbal hostility. Conversely, those who were intolerant of fighting showed a reduction in hostility. Perhaps because it would be difficult to make a differential case for cathartic effects, Harrell (1981) chose to interpret his findings in cognitive terms.

Summary. Thus, extending the question of the effects of observing aggression to sports audiences has produced a consistent pattern of findings. People watching athletes aggress are either unaffected or they become more aggressive. The suggestion has also been made (Russell, 1981b) that the effects may actually be somewhat stronger than traditional before-after studies would indicate. If arousal and aggression functions are curvilinear and centered over a concentration of player violence, then both states would be expected to subside gradually with the cessation of violence. Under conditions where fans do not ruminate over a bad call or dwell on some earlier injustice, some evidence (Zillmann & Bryant, 1974) suggests that arousal and hostility may return to a base level fairly quickly, perhaps in a matter of minutes. Thus, if most of the violence occurs during the first period of a hockey game, then its effects on the audience may have largely dissipated by the end of the contest when postgame measures are administered. Therefore, the immediate effects of witnessing sports aggression are likely *understated*, especially where interpersonal aggression occurs early in a contest.

Other mood states. In describing the Arms et al. (1979) study reference was made to their having explored the impact of aggressive displays on moods other than aggression. In keeping with one interpretation of Aristotle's original intent (Goodman, 1964), catharsis may occur with the display of a range of "tragic" moods. One would predict, therefore, that negative mood states—to the extent they can be equated with "tragic"—should become increasingly positive in spectators as they witness their display.

There is a common assumption that sports events are occasions when people sharing the same enthusiasms are brought closer together in a spirit of friendship and goodwill. This view has been articulated by Mehrabian (1976) in applying his arousal model to spectator behavior in sports arenas, as follows:

> The congregation of large numbers of highly aroused, uninhibited people who share similar interests and attitudes is also conducive to socializing; it may lead to the development of new friendships or the renewal or intensification of old ones.

Continuing in the same vein:

> In the generally pleasant setting, then, gregariousness is further enhanced. (p. 284)

In contrast to the foregoing, the Arms et al. (1979) study revealed instead a marked deterioration in the quality of interpersonal relationships, not just at the two aggressive sports but also at the swim meet. Analyses of mood changes indicated that subjects became generally less socially affectionate (e.g., forgiving, warmhearted) and less surgent (e.g., carefree, playful) during the events. While the anxiety of spectators remained constant, fatigue was seen to increase slightly. These results and those of a replication (Russell, 1981b) strongly imply that (aggressive) sports events are not rich social occasions fostering harmony and love for our fellow man. Hostility notwithstanding, most moods appear to be unaffected by the observation of aggression on the field of play. Where changes do occur, a preliminary conclusion would suggest that they generally become more negative. However, it should be emphasized that except for related investigations of spectators' enjoyment (Zillmann, Bryant, & Sapolsky, 1979), few studies have treated the topic in a sports context.

Catharsis Through the Sports Media

The question of the media's role in social violence has many facets, including the influence of role models, social contagion, and the values and attitudes that are promoted. However, the present discussion is intended to treat the issue from the perspective of sports and confine itself to the topic at hand, catharsis.

Industry spokesmen and others can often be found defending violent programming stating that evidence of harmful effects is inconclusive, or that screen violence provides viewers with a means of vicariously venting their hostilities. Writers concerned with media violence typically seek to bolster their case with tallies of the average number of shootings, stabbings, rapes, and punchouts as a function of some period of viewing. The villains singled out are invariably cartoons, police, crime, and war shows; rarely is there mention of sports programming. However, it is important to recognize that some of the most heavily televised sports (e.g., boxing, football, hockey) are just those in which viewers will see acts of interpersonal mayhem on a scale which rivals that seen elsewhere in the media, at least by a frequency, if not an intensity criterion.

Laboratory investigations. Whether by coincidence or design, sports have served as a source of violent stimulus materials in numerous investigations. The procedures used by Berkowitz in a series of experiments investigating the role of aggressive cues (e.g., Berkowitz, 1964, 1970; Berkowitz & Alioto, 1973) involved angered subjects being shown a movie film clip of a brutal fight scene from *The Champion*. Their subsequent aggression, when compared to control subjects shown an equally exciting but nonaggressive movie segment (a track meet), typically revealed heightened aggression. The intentions observers attribute to those filmed in competition have also been shown to influence their subsequent aggression (Berkowitz & Alioto, 1973). Angered subjects told that the athletes in a football or boxing film were seeking revenge for previous insults later were more aggressive than subjects told that they were professionals simply doing their job. Hartmann (1969) conducted a particularly interesting experiment in which aroused and nonaroused subjects viewed a two-person basketball game which deteriorated into a fight. Subjects saw either of two versions of the fight: one focusing on the aggressor's attacks, the other on the victim's verbal and gestural pain cues. Control subjects viewed cooperative play throughout. Consistent with findings in this research tradition, aroused subjects were more aggressive than controls following exposure to both fight versions. Although the pain cues version resulted in aroused and unaroused subjects exhibiting more aggression than their respective control groups, expressions of pain enhanced aggression in aroused subjects and reduced it in unaroused subjects. The extensive use of scenes of sports violence in laboratory investigations of aggression has provided a solid empirical base from which to generalize and draw conclusions about the specific effects of observing sports violence.

Despite the importance of (anger) arousal as a condition for aggression (Rule & Nesdale, 1976), a number of laboratory studies has investigated the effects of filmed sports violence without specifically inducing arousal in the subjects. Nevertheless, as tests of cathartic effects, their results are illuminating. Actual fight sequences in hockey (Celozzi, 1977; Eastwood, 1974), football (Lennon & Hatfield, 1980), and a basketball game in which fans joined their team in an attack on the visiting squad (Thirer, 1976) were shown to groups of subjects. The more natural group setting with unprovoked subjects watching a somewhat longer film provides a valuable link with comparable situations in the real world. Findings from these studies are consistent with the controlled experiments noted above in showing either no effects (Eastwood, 1974; Thirer, 1976) or an increase in subjects' hostility from pre- to postfilm conditions (Celozzi, 1977; Lennon & Hatfield, 1980).

Field investigations. While the social experimental laboratory affords opportunities to investigate the catharsis hypothesis under carefully controlled circumstances, the gain in control may be somewhat offset by a number of delimiting factors. Several persistent questions related to the artificiality of the research setting, the use of brief film clips, and the representation of aggression have been raised by critics reluctant to generalize to everyday situations (Baron, 1977, Chap. 3). The results of recent field studies have generally been consistent with those arising from laboratory investigations and should dispel the reservations of even the most ardent critics. Several examples will suffice to highlight this tradition and also to provide a sample of the results obtained in tests of a catharsis hypothesis under the real-life conditions of extended exposure to film and television violence.

A recent field study (Goranson, Note 3) assessed the effects on amateur hockey players of aggression displayed in nationally televised games involving the professional team in their area. Despite various analyses, generally nonsignificant relationships resulted between the level of televised aggression and the aggression of the youngsters in league play shortly thereafter. Had a cathartic prediction been made, it would have failed for support. However, a positive relationship between a preference for televised contact sports and the aggression of grade 3 and 13 girls has been reported by Lefkowitz, Eron, Walder, and Huesmann (1977). A similar link failed to materialize with young boys.

The long-term effects of television were examined in a 2-year, longitudinal field study (Joy, Kimball, & Zabrack, Note 4) made possible when television was introduced in a small British Columbia community given the pseudonym "Notel." Two nearby towns, equivalent in all major socioeconomic aspects, were chosen for comparison with Notel. One community ("Unitel") had been receiving only the national CBC signal, while the other ("Multitel") also received the major U.S. networks. While CBC programming content includes numerous sports features, there is peer-mandated pressure for Canadian boys to view, and be knowledgable about, televised games of the National Hockey League and the Canadian Football League. The battery of aggression measures used in this investigation included peer and teacher ratings, and ratings by trained observers of verbal and physical aggression on school playgrounds. In contrast to the control communities, the children of Notel showed increases in physical and, especially, verbal aggression following the introduction of television.

Stylized aggression. A special case for the occurrence of catharsis stemming from exposure to stylized aggression has been persuasively argued by Noble (1973). Aggression which is fictional, or a spoof, would qualify as a stylized display. The suggestion is not without merit insofar as Kingsmore (1970) has reported a pre- to postevent decline in extrapunitive aggression among spectators watching a professional wrestling card. However, it will be recalled that Arms et al. (1979) found that while the hostility of male spectators remained constant at a wrestling match, that of females increased somewhat during the course of the evening. Interestingly, supplemental data indicated that their student subjects almost unanimously saw the wrestling card as a farce or sham aggression, whereas it may be assumed that many of Kingsmore's (1970) wrestling fans viewed the matches as authentic. Thus, where the theatrical aspects of the sport were most apparent, there was an absence of cathartic effects.

Laboratory experiments on the question of stylized aggression have produced a consistent pattern of results. Berkowitz and Alioto (1973) provided male subjects with either of two introductions to a World War II film depicting the invasion of a Japanese-held island by the U.S. Marines. One introduction informed subjects that they would see a documentary of actual battle footage whereas others were told the movie was a Hollywood reenactment. While aggression increased with both introductions, among previously angered subjects more aggression was displayed by those provided a realistic introduction than those whose introduction to the scene stressed its Hollywood origins. Noble (1973) similarly found that British youngsters played more destructively following exposure to realistically rather than stylistically filmed aggression. However, other investigators (e.g., Worchel, Hardy, & Hurley, 1976) have reported that while both types elicited more aggression than a neutral control film, realistic and stylized displays were found to be equally effective. Thus, while the relative effectiveness of stylized and realistic aggression may be open to debate, it appears that a special case for stylized aggression producing catharsis is unsupported by research.

Summary. The foregoing represents an overview of the literature involving tests of cathartic predictions in a sports setting. Having extended the question to studies involving both players and spectators, one must agree with Goranson (Note 5) who, with respect to vicarious aggression, concluded: "I think that this is one of the rare occasions in behavioural research where an unqualified conclusion is warranted. The observation of violence does not reduce aggressiveness" (p. 12). Quite apart from the intuitive appeal and general acceptance of catharsis, support from research conducted in the social-experimental laboratory (Berkowitz, 1970; Geen & Quanty, 1977; Quanty, 1976), and in the present specialized setting of sports has simply not been forthcoming. This has been the case with respect to those who merely watch aggressive sports and, one could add, those athletes involved in aggressive contests. Specific tests of catharsis in sports media presentations have again produced results consistent with the conclusions of an earlier review of the effects of media violence (Goranson, 1970), that is, "Observed violence serves to facilitate the expression of aggression, rather than to reduce aggression by 'draining off aggressive energy'" (p. 28). Overall, the weight of evidence suggests either no effects or, more often, that an increase in aggression results from aggressive behavior or the observation of aggression. Sports do not constitute a unique set of circumstances in which catharsis is somehow favored.

Outcome

Introduction

Because of the structure of sports and the presence of certain strongly held values, our understanding of some research issues may be furthered more than others. For example, a media-induced change in emphasis from the elements of participation or process, to winning (Goldstein & Bredemeier, 1977), while it marks a setback in the wholesome development of sports, nevertheless provides a research setting in which outcome is featured as a highly salient variable. The intense interest of the sports world in the outcome of competition may provide the researcher with a natural laboratory in which outcome can be more effectively investigated than elsewhere.

While sports competitions ostensibly offer a straightforward means of assessing outcome, that is, winning versus losing, it is far from clear that this particular procedure is an entirely valid representation of the variable. As suggested elsewhere (Russell, 1981b) outcome may be subjectively determined by competitors and spectators alike at points in the competition which may or may not coincide with the expiry of official playing time. Thus, the outcome of a mismatch or rout may be a foregone conclusion to virtually everyone in attendance early on in a contest. Effects assessed at the conclusion of such a contest and attributed to outcome may have arisen instead from the experience of waiting out the final whistle. Indeed, the impact of outcome in such matches may have largely dissipated before it can be assessed by measures taken at the conclusion of the event.

The structure of sports activities and media emphasis ensures that there is usually one individual or team who can be identified as the winner of a competition; all others are cast in the role of losers suffering varying degrees of defeat. The link presumed to exist between such negative outcomes and aggression is expressed in Berkowitz's observation that: "The contest may have been a fair one, and the loser may know he is supposed to be a good sport, but he still is thwarted. . . . Aggressive tendencies are frequently the result" (Berkowitz, 1962, p. 178).

Even a cursory review of the literature on outcome reveals that the goal of a common definition of the concept has proven illusive. What follows is a preliminary framework for organizing the results of empirical investigations and for distinguishing among several views and operational definitions of outcome.

Interim outcomes. Sports officialdom and media people engage in an almost daily monitoring of the progress of individuals and teams pursuing victory in competition. Updated summaries of league standings are published regularly so that some teams find themselves relegated to a losing position before the season is barely underway. These early returns resemble an outcome insofar as they produce consequences not unlike those which occur at the end of a losing season: attendance declines, coaches may be fired, players are traded. It is suggested therefore, that effects attributable to outcome may be evident *during* as well as at the official conclusion of competition be it during a game, a week of competition, or a season's play.

If intermediate summaries do take on many of the characteristics of the final outcome for athletes, then interim standings will produce frustrations for all save those in first place (Berkowitz, 1962, 1973). Those for whom victory just eludes their grasp would be the most severely thwarted and consequently would be expected to exhibit the greatest amount of aggression. Those placed more distantly in a competition are minimally frustrated and would be expected to show only marginal increases in aggression (Dollard et al., 1939).

Support for this predicted relationship between the magnitude of frustration and resulting aggression has been provided by Mary Harris (1974). In an imaginative field investigation, she arranged for her confederates to barge into queues ahead of people at various points in lines which had formed at grocery stores and ticket windows. As was predicted, those closest to the front reacted more aggressively towards the interloper; those further back in the queue expressed less hostility towards someone cutting into line ahead of them. A similar relationship has been reported in ice hockey where teams strive from the start of the season to gain and hold first place in the league standings. Those teams whose best efforts have produced a second place standing and who thereby are severely thwarted draw the greatest number of aggressive penalties. Teams in each successive position thereafter show a decline in interpersonal aggression (Russell & Drewry, 1976). Thus, within league play, those whose hopes are being most cruelly dashed become involved in the greatest number of altercations.

Dichotomized outcome. The most popular, certainly the easiest, means of operationalizing outcome is to treat the data as a dichotomy, that is, win/loss. However, studies in this tradition have produced conflicting results overall. In two studies of European soccer (Lefebvre & Passer, 1974; Volkamer, 1971) members of losing sides committed more aggressive fouls than did winners. Results also consistent with a frustration-aggression prediction were reported by Bass (1962) who found that manager-subjects who lost in a competitive laboratory situation were more aggressive than those who had defeated them. Ryan (1970) noted a similar result insofar as losers in a nail hammering competition were more aggressive than winners.

At least an equal number of studies has reported either no differences or that winners exhibit more aggression than losers. Children involved in competition were subsequently more aggressive in a free play situation than their noncompetitive controls (Christy, Gelfand, & Hartmann, 1971). However, effects attributable to winning or losing were indistinguishable from one another. Epstein and Taylor (1967) also found no differences in the aggression of winning and losing laboratory subjects as did Wankel (Note 6) in an analysis of hockey team records. However, three investigations, one in hockey (Cullen & Cullen, 1975), another in handball (Albrecht, 1979), and a third conducted in a social-experimental laboratory (Borden & Taylor, 1976) found winners to be more aggressive than losers.

Score differential. Some investigators have chosen to take the margin of victory into account in representing outcome. In his analysis of hockey records, Wankel (Note 6) reported a positive correlation between the final score differential and game aggression. However, Volkamer (1971) reported a negative relationship between soccer aggression and the difference in goals. Neither investigator made mention of curvilinearity in the underlying data points nor did they analyze the aggression of winners and losers separately along the continuum of score differences.

A Study

Procedure. In an attempt to extend this earlier work, an analysis of all aggression occurring in the Western Hockey League (WHL) for the entire 1978-1979 season (N = 430 games) was undertaken. Outcome was calculated for *each* team at each of 11 points (a tie, ± 5 or more goals) representing their final game score vis-à-vis that of their opponent. The aggression measure was the total minutes in penalties awarded a team for all rule violations of an aggressive nature. Nonaggressive infractions, for example, playing with a broken stick, were screened from the calculations. As recent work (Russell, 1983) has shown that the correlation between tripping and all other aggressive penalties approaches unity, tripping was included in the game totals for each team.

Results and discussion. The principal results are presented in Fig. 10-1. A 2 (winners vs. losers) × 6 (score differential) mixed analysis of variance with repeated measures on the first factor with game nested under the second factor resulted in a significant main effect only for levels of score differential ($F = 3.31, df = 5/42, p = .006$). Neither the main effect of winners nor its interaction with the score differential was significant (F's < 1). A trend analysis revealed a significant cubic component across the win/loss score continuum. Other trend components were nonsignificant.

The means of aggressive penalty minutes differed significantly as a function of teams' final score differences. Also, the score effect for aggression had a significant cubic component. Thus, a U-function best represents the relationship between the final game score differential and interpersonal aggression. Teams winning handily and those defeated by lopsided scores exhibited the highest levels of aggression. Contrary to a frustration-aggression prediction, those teams most severely thwarted in their quest for a victory, that is, those narrowly losing by one or two goals engaged in the least amount of aggression.

A high degree of symmetry is also evident in Fig. 10-1, a result consistent with a correlation of .44 previously reported between the aggression of teams pitted against each other in games over a season of play (Russell & Drewry, 1976). One explanation advanced to account for the dynamics underlying such norms would suggest

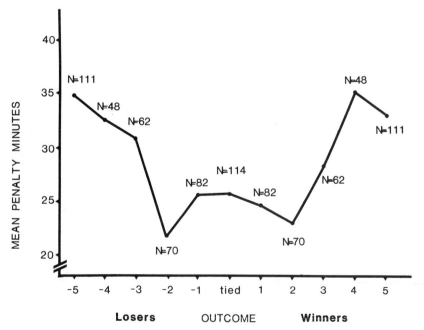

Fig. 10-1. Relationship between game outcome and aggression in ice hockey.

that the victim of a successful attack experiences a loss of self-esteem (Feshbach, 1970). However, an equally successful retaliation can act to restore the loss and indeed, provide gratification.

The present results were foreshadowed by Wankel's (Note 6) analysis of intercollegiate hockey games in Ontario. Although a comparison of winning and losing teams failed to reveal differences in player aggression, the inclusion of tied matches in a further analysis resulted in highly significant differences. The players drew far fewer aggressive penalties in games ending in a tie than they did in contests they ultimately won or lost. The present curvilinear relationship is also highly similar to a previous analysis of player aggression occurring as a function of the existing score *during* games (Russell & Drewry, 1976). Here again, the least amount of interpersonal aggression was seen to occur when the score in a game was very close. Of course, the score during a game is not unrelated to the final score. Indeed, one explanation offered for the earlier findings of a U-shaped function (Russell & Drewry, 1976; Wankel, Note 6) is equally suited to the present result. Such an explanation would allow that conscious tactical considerations may simply override any effects predicted to arise from players' frustrations with having lost by a narrow margin. When a match is close it is generally regarded as an inopportune time to incur a penalty. Thus, players embroiled in a close match may quite deliberately inhibit their impulses to aggress in the interests of a team victory. In this case the penalty record may belie an underlying state of hostility.

Alternatively, it can be suggested that players defeated in close scoring games can maintain a measure of dignity secure in the knowledge that with more effort, a little luck, or unbiased officiating, they could have won. Certainly, they would win in a rematch! However, rationalizations are only convincing for the narrow loss and offer little comfort to players soundly defeated by a wide margin. For them, something akin to acute embarrassment or humiliation may be felt. Whether they then act to restore self-esteem or in retaliation for insult, there is nevertheless strong provocation for aggression. Thus, a crushing defeat occurring in the generally hostile atmosphere of contact sports greatly increases the likelihood of interpersonal aggression being initiated by the vanquished. However, at no time are the victors exempted from their continuing obligation to meet aggression with aggression.

A caveat. Further research in nonsports settings and with sports other than hockey is necessary to determine if the U-shaped relationship of outcome to aggression is specific to competitive situations in which penalties for aggression adversely affect the performance of a player or team. If outcome proves to be confounded with performance then results such as those presented herein and elsewhere (e.g., Russell & Drewry, 1976) are necessarily restricted to hockey and similar sports or settings. However, the caveat applies principally to player aggression within games where outcome is defined by means of the final score. In contrast, investigations of the effects of outcome on spectators are unaffected by possible confounding with performance.

Spectators and outcome. While outcome has been identified as a major predictor of spectators' enjoyment of sporting events (Zillmann et al., 1979), analyses of its role in spectator hostility have produced mixed results. Spectators at World Hockey

Association games expressed less anger over the prospect of their team's defeat as a loss grew increasingly imminent (Harrell, 1981). As the percentage of games in which their favorite team led or was tied dropped from 40% at the end of the first period to 32% after the second period, their reported anger over the impending defeat declined from pregame levels. This reduction in anger occurred despite an overall increase in fighting from the first to second periods.

While University of Arizona basketball fans became increasingly hostile over the course of games, their heightened hostility was unrelated to either the outcome or the closeness of contests (Leuck et al., 1979). A similar result occurred in the Goldstein and Arms (1971) football study whereby the fans of both the winning Army and the losing Navy teams showed increases in hostility. Replications of this study (Arms et al., 1979; Russell, 1981b) involving hockey fans again revealed heightened hostility at games won handily by the home team. Moreover, fans at professional wrestling showed a similar increase al though their favorites in a final tag team match did not emerge triumphant until the dying seconds of the contest (Arms et al., 1979).

Sloan (1979) however, has reported results generally consistent with a frustration-aggression position. Loyal Notre Dame football and basketball fans were found to be more angry following losses; wins produced no change on this dimension. Wins by the Notre Dame basketball team resulted in increased happiness or satisfaction while fans witnessing football victories became increasingly benevolent. Losses in these sports produced decreases in both moods.

Summary. Research designs in which outcome has been operationalized simply as win versus loss have produced conflicting results. Considerable information is lost by this dichotomizing procedure and insights into a fairly complex relationship (at least with aggression) are thereby obscured. The same may be said of representing outcome as the final score differential, a practice which combines the possibly different reactions of winning and losing competitors. The inclusion of additional data points reflecting the margin of victory or defeat of each team revealed a U-shaped relationship between outcome and aggression. However, it remains to be determined if the result demonstrated to occur in hockey is sport-specific. Alternately, a cognitive approach to representing outcome was proposed whereby outcome is not equated with the expiration of official playing time. Rather, it is a probablistic judgment by individual players or observers that the eventual winner of a contest has essentially been determined although playing time may still remain.

Conclusions

In the foregoing, I have sought to organize and evaluate the issues of catharsis and outcome as they have been investigated within the sports aggression literature. Notwithstanding a considerable diversity in the quality of those studies selected for inclusion in the review, they provide scant evidence in support of a catharsis hypothesis. Rather, the weight of evidence is entirely consistent with previous reviews of the nonsports literature, that is, while participants or observers of aggression may sometimes be unaffected, more often they will show an increase in their aggressive behavior. While the frustration-aggression hypothesis predicts an increase in aggression following losses, tests conducted in competitive sports have produced mixed results. Support for the hypothesis has been forthcoming principally where the investigator represents outcome as league standings during the season. Otherwise, win/loss representations of outcome have failed to produce a supportive pattern of findings either among participants or the observers of aggressive competitions. Finally, investigations of outcome in which the aggression of competing teams is analyzed separately with additional data points reveal a U-shaped relationship centered on a tied score. Although the relationship appears stable in ice hockey, its generality remains to be determined.

Acknowledgments. The author wishes to thank John R. Vokey for his assistance with the analysis. Thanks also to Ed Chynoweth, Commissioner of the Western Hockey League.

Reference Notes

1. LeUnes, A., & Nation, J. R. *Saturday's Heroes: A psychological portrait of college football players.* Unpublished manuscript, Texas A & M University, 1981.
2. Atkins, A., Hilton, I., Neigher, W., & Bahr, A. *Anger, fight, fantasy, and catharsis.* Paper presented at the meeting of the American Psychological Association, Honolulu, 1972.
3. Goranson, R. E. *The impact of televised hockey violence* (Report No. 1). The LaMarsh Research Programme, Toronto: York University, 1982.
4. Joy, L. A., Kimball, M. M., & Zabrack, M. L. *Television exposure and children's aggressive behavior.* Paper presented at the meeting of the Canadian Psychological Association, Vancouver, 1977.
5. Goranson, R. E. *Sports violence and the catharsis hypothesis.* Paper presented at the meeting of the Canadian Society for Psychomotor Learning and Sport Psychology, Toronto, 1978.
6. Wankel, L. M. *An examination of illegal aggression in intercollegiate hockey.* Paper presented at the meeting of the Canadian Society for Psychomotor Learning and Sport Psychology, Ottawa, 1973.

References

Albrecht, D. Zur sportartspezifischen aggression im wettkampfspiel. *Sportwissenschaft,* 1979, *9,* 78-91.
Arms, R. L., Russell, G. W., & Sandilands, M. L. Effects of viewing aggressive sports on the hostility of spectators. *Social Psychology Quarterly,* 1979, *42,* 275-279.
Bandura, A. *Aggression: A social learning analysis.* Englewood Cliffs, N. J.: Prentice Hall, 1973.
Baron, R. A. *Human aggression.* New York: Plenum Press, 1977.
Bass, B. M. Mood changes in a management training laboratory. *Journal of Applied Psychology,* 1962, *46,* 361-364.
Berczeller, E. The "aesthetic feelings" and Aristotle's *catharsis* theory. *Journal of Psychology,* 1967, *65,* 261-267.

Berkowitz, L. *Aggression: A social psychological analysis.* New York: McGraw-Hill, 1962.

Berkowitz, L. The effects of observing violence. *Scientific American,* 1964, *210,* 35-41.

Berkowitz, L. (Ed.). *Roots of aggression.* New York: Atherton Press, 1969.

Berkowitz, L. Experimental investigations of hostility catharsis. *Journal of Consulting and Clinical Psychology,* 1970, *35,* 1-7.

Berkowitz, L. Sports, competition, and aggression. *Physical Educator,* 1973, *30,* 59-61.

Berkowitz, L., & Alioto, J. T. The meaning of an observed event as a determinant of its aggressive consequences. *Journal of Personality and Social Psychology,* 1973, *28,* 206-217.

Borden, R. J., & Taylor, S. P. Pennies for pain: A note on instrumental aggression toward a pacifist by vanquished, victorious, and evenly matched opponents. *Victimology,* 1976, *1,* 154-157.

Brill, A. A. The way of the fan. *North American Review,* 1929, *226,* 400-434.

Buss, A. H., & Durkee, A. An inventory for assessing different kinds of hostility. *Journal of Consulting Psychology,* 1957, *21,* 343-349.

Celozzi, M. J. *The stimulating versus cathartic effects of viewing televised violence in ice hockey and the relationship on subsequent levels of aggression and hostility.* Unpublished doctoral dissertation, University of Southern Mississippi, 1977.

Christy, P. R., Gelfand, D., & Hartmann, D. P. Effects of competition-induced frustration on two classes of modeled behavior. *Developmental Psychology,* 1971, *5,* 104-111.

Cullen, J. B., & Cullen, F. T. The structural and contextural conditions of group norm violation: Some implications from the game of ice hockey. *International Review of Sport Sociology,* 1975, *2,* 69-78.

Dollard, J., Doob, L., Miller, N., Mowrer, O. H., & Sears, R. R. *Frustration and aggression.* New Haven, Conn.: Yale University Press, 1939.

Eastwood, J. M. The effects of viewing a film of professional hockey on aggression. *Medicine and Science in Sports,* 1974, *6,* 158-163.

Epstein, S., & Taylor, S. P. Instigation to aggression as a function of degree of defeat and perceived aggressive intent of the opponent. *Journal of Personality,* 1967, *35,* 265-289.

Evans, R. I. A conversation with Konrad Lorenz about aggression, homosexuality, pornography, and the need for a new ethic. *Psychology Today,* 1974, *8,* 82-93.

Feshbach, S. Aggression. In P. H. Mussen (Ed.), *Carmichael's manual of child psychology* (Vol. 2). New York: Wiley, 1970.

Geen, R. G., & Quanty, M. B. The catharsis of aggression: An evaluation of a hypothesis. In L. Berkowitz (Ed.), *Advances in experimental social psychology* (Vol. 10). New York: Academic Press, 1977.

Goldstein, J. H., & Arms, R. L. Effects of observing athletic contests on hostility. *Sociometry,* 1971, *34,* 83-90.

Goldstein, J. H., & Bredemeier, B. J. Sports and socialization: Some basic issues. *Journal of Communication,* 1977, *27,* 154-159.

Goldstein, J. H., Rosnow, R. L., Raday, T., Silverman, I., & Gaskell, G. D. Punitiveness in response to films varying in content: A cross-national field study of aggression. *European Journal of Social Psychology,* 1975, *5,* 149-165.

Goodman, P. Letter to the editor. *Scientific American,* 1964, *210,* 8.

Goranson, R. E. Media violence and aggressive behavior: A review of experimental research. In L. Berkowitz (Ed.), *Advances in experimental social psychology* (Vol. 5). New York: Academic Press, 1970.

Harrell, W. A. Verbal aggressiveness in spectators at professional hockey games: The effects of tolerance of violence and amount of exposure to hockey. *Human Relations,* 1981, *34,* 643-655.

Harris, M. B. Mediators between frustration and aggression in a field experiment. *Journal of Experimental Social Psychology,* 1974, *10,* 561-571.

Hartmann, D. P. Influence of symbolically modeled aggression and pain cues on aggressive behavior. *Journal of Personality and Social Psychology,* 1969, *11,* 280-288.

Hornberger, R. H. The differential reduction of aggressive responses as a function of interpolated activities. *American Psychologist,* 1959, *14,* 354.

Husman, B. F. Aggression in boxers and wrestlers as measured by projective techniques. *Research Quarterly,* 1955, *26,* 421-425.

Kidd, A. H., & Walton, N. Y. Dart throwing as a method of reducing extrapunitive aggression. *Psychological Reports,* 1966, *19,* 88-90.

Kingsmore, J. M. The effect of professional wrestling and a professional basketball contest upon the aggressive tendencies of spectators. In G. S. Kenyon (Ed.), *Contemporary psychology of sport.* Chicago: Athletic Institute, 1970.

Knott, P. D., Lasater, L., & Shuman, R. Aggression-guilt and conditionability for aggressiveness. *Journal of Personality,* 1974, *42,* 332-344.

Lefebvre, L. M., & Passer, M. W. The effects of game location and importance on aggression in team sport. *International Journal of Sport Psychology,* 1974, *5,* 102-110.

Lefkowitz, M. M., Eron, L. D., Walder, L. O., & Huesmann, L. R. *Growing up to be violent.* New York: Pergamon Press, 1977.

Lennon, J. X., & Hatfield, F. C. The effects of crowding and observation of athletic events on spectator tendency toward aggressive behavior. *Journal of Sport Behavior,* 1980, *3,* 61-67.

Leuck, M. R., Krahenbuhl, G. S., & Odenkirk, J. E. Assessment of spectator aggression at intercollegiate basketball contests. *Review of Sport and Leisure,* 1979, *4,* 40-52.

Loew, C. A. Acquisition of a hostile attitude and its relationship to aggressive behavior. *Journal of Personality and Social Psychology,* 1967, *5,* 335-377.

Lorenz, K. *On aggression.* New York: Harcourt, Brace & World, 1966.

Mann, L. On being a sore loser: How fans react to their team's failure. *Australian Journal of Psychology,* 1974, *26,* 37-47.

Megargee, E. I., & Hokanson, J. E. (Eds.). *The dynamics of aggression.* New York: Harper & Row, 1970.

Mehrabian, A. *Public places, and private spaces: Psychology of work, play and living environments.* New York: Fitzhenry & Whiteside, 1976.

Noble, G. Effects of different forms of filmed aggression on children's constructive and destructive play. *Journal of Personality and Social Psychology,* 1973, *26,* 54-59.

Nosanchuk, T. A. The way of the warrior: The effects of traditional martial arts training on aggressiveness. *Human Relations,* 1981, *34,* 435-444.

Nowlis, V. Research with the Mood Adjective Check List. In S. S. Tompkins & C. Izard (Eds.), *Affect, cognition, and personality.* New York: Springer, 1965.

Ostrow, A. The aggressive tendencies of male intercollegiate tennis team players as measured by selected psychological tests. *New Zealand Journal of Health, Physical Education, and Recreation,* 1974, *6,* 19-21.

Patterson, A. Hostility catharsis: A naturalistic quasi-experiment. *Personality and Social Psychology Bulletin,* 1974, *1,* 195-197.

Proctor, R. C., & Eckerd, W. M. "Toot-toot" or spectator sports: Psychological and therapeutic implications. *American Journal of Sports Medicine,* 1976, *4,* 78-83.

Quanty, M. B. Aggression catharsis: Experimental investigations and implications. In R. G. Geen & E. C. O'Neal (Eds.), *Perspectives on aggression.* New York: Academic Press, 1976.

Rule, B. G., & Nesdale, A. R. Emotional arousal and aggressive behavior. *Psychological Bulletin,* 1976, *83,* 851-863.

Russell, G. W. Aggression in sport. In P. F. Brain & D. Benton (Eds.), *Multidisciplinary approaches to aggression research.* Amsterdam: Elsevier/North-Holland Biomedical Press, 1981. (a)

Russell, G. W. Spectator moods at an aggressive sports event. *Journal of Sport Psychology,* 1981, *3,* 217-227. (b)

Russell, G. W. Crowd size and density in relation to athletic aggression and performance. *Social Behavior and Personality,* 1983, *11,* 1.

Russell, G. W., & Drewry, B. R. Crowd size and competitive aspects of aggression in ice hockey: An archival study. *Human Relations,* 1976, *29,* 723-735.

Ryan, E. D. The cathartic effect of vigorous motor activity on aggressive behavior. *Research Quarterly,* 1970, *41,* 542-551.

Sipes, R. G. War, sports and aggression: An empirical test of two rival theories. *American Anthropologist,* 1973, *75,* 64-86.

Sloan, L. R. The function and impact of sports for fans: A review of theory and contemporary research. In J. H. Goldstein (Ed.), *Sports, games, and play.* Hillsdale, N. J.: Erlbaum, 1979.

Smith, M. D. Social determinants of violence in hockey: A review. *Canadian Journal of Applied Sport Sciences,* 1979, *4,* 76-82.

Storr, A. *Human aggression.* New York: Antheneum, 1968.

Taylor, S. P. Gammon, C. B., & Capasso, D. R. Aggression as a function of the interaction of alcohol and threat. *Journal of Personality and Social Psychology,* 1976, *34,* 938-941.

Thirer, J. *Changes in aggression of various classifications of athletes and nonathletes as influenced by type of film viewed.* Unpublished doctoral dissertation, The Florida State University, 1976.

Tinbergen, N. On war and peace in animals and man. *Science,* 1968, *160,* 1411-1418.

Turner, E. T. The effects of viewing college football, basketball and wrestling on the elicited aggressive responses of male spectators. *Medicine and Science in Sports*, 1970, *2*, 100-105.

Volkamer, M. Zurur aggressivitat in konkumenz-orientierten sozialen. *Sportwissenschaft*, 1971, *1*, 68-76.

Webb, E. J., Campbell, D. T., Schwartz, R. D., Sechrest, L., & Grove, J. B. *Nonreactive measures in the social sciences*. Boston: Houghton Mifflin, 1981.

Worchel, S., Hardy, T. W., & Hurley, R. The effects of commercial interruption of violent and nonviolent films on viewers' subsequent aggression. *Journal of Experimental Social Psychology*, 1976, *12*, 220-232.

Zillmann, D. *Hostility and aggression*. Hillsdale, N. J.: Erlbaum, 1979.

Zillmann, D., & Bryant, J. Effects of residual excitation on the emotional response to provocation and delayed aggressive behavior. *Journal of Personality and Social Psychology*, 1974, *30*, 782-791.

Zillmann, D., Bryant, J., & Sapolsky, B. S. The enjoyment of watching sport contests. In J. H. Goldstein (Ed.), *Sports, games, and play*. Hillsdale, N. J.: Erlbaum, 1979.

Zillmann, D., Johnson, R. C., & Day, K. D. Provoked and unprovoked aggressiveness in athletes. *Journal of Research in Personality*, 1974, *8*, 139-152.

Chapter 11

Olympic Games Participation and Warfare

Robert Keefer, Jeffrey H. Goldstein, and David Kasiarz

Introduction

> The aims of the Olympic Movement are to promote the development of
> those fine physical and moral qualities which are the basis of amateur
> sport and to bring together the athletes of the world in a great quadrennial
> festival of sports thereby creating international respect and goodwill and
> thus helping to construct a better and more peaceful world. (Killian &
> Rodda, 1976, p. 258)

These words from the "Fundamental Principles" of the Olympic Rules and Regulations are largely attributed to the progenitor of the modern Olympic Games, Baron
Pierre de Coubertin, a wealthy French educator who almost single-handedly revived
the ancient Games in the late 19th century. As the quote indicates, the Olympic
Games were then and are today viewed as a source of peace in the world. Part of
this favorable judgment derives from Coubertin's original thesis that by meeting
others from around the world, young men would grow more tolerant, and friend-
ships and international respect would arise that would help stem the tide of war in
the world.

Coubertin's reasons for reinstating the Olympic Games were certainly more complex than simple altruism; however, he claimed no motives other than those in the
Fundamental Principles (although additional motives have been attributed to him
by others; e.g., Espy, 1979; Lowe, Kanin, & Strenk, 1978, pp. 110-117; Mandell,
1976). He believed that sports would benefit young men physically and mentally
(and only young men, it might be pointed out), that amateurism was essential, and
that the Olympic Games could ultimately promote world peace (Coubertin, 1896).
Furthermore, Coubertin (and the rules of the International Olympic Committee,
IOC) clearly stated that politics should not be a factor in the Games, or in sports in
general. For example, under the Fundamental Principles one reads "The Games are
contests between individuals and not between countries or areas" (Killian & Rodda,
1976, p. 258).

This last point is belied by the history of the modern Games. From their very
inception, the Games have been steeped in politics, however much they aim for
neutrality (Espy, 1979; Kyrolainen & Varis, 1981; Lowe, Kanin, & Strenk, 1978;

Sipes, 1973). Though decrying nationalism in the Games, Coubertin himself pointed out the pride involved in winning an event for one's country (Coubertin, 1896). Books have been written on the political aspects of the Olympic Games, including *The Nazi Olympics* (Mandell, 1971), and of the exclusion of Germany and Japan from the 1948 Games, and of Rhodesia from the Mexico City Games of 1968 (Cheffers, 1972; Espy, 1979). Other examples include the problem of "two Germanies" after World War II, the admission of the Soviet Union to the Games, the exclusion of Taiwan from the Montreal Games in 1976, the demonstrations by black American athletes in the Mexico City Games, the murder of Israeli athletes in Munich by terrorists, and other such incidents. This, of course, ignores the multitude of political intrigues and maneuvers behind the scenes between Olympiads. Despite continued calls for a removal of politics from the games (for example, the suggestion by the President of the IOC that only the Olympic banner be raised at the Games, rather than the flag of each nation, Brundage, 1960), politics remain at the very heart of the Games (Espy, 1979; Milshteyn & Molchanov, 1976).

A more influential view supporting the idea that Olympic competition would result in less international conflict is what Sipes (1973) called the "drive discharge" model, and which is more commonly known among aggression researchers as the catharsis model. In this view, aggression is seen to be a drive in all individuals that culminates in war, and funneling this drive into bellicose sports will make war less likely. Many go beyond this statement to suggest that merely viewing sports is sufficient to reduce this natural inclination to aggress. For example, Proctor and Eckard (1976) state that emotions build in people like steam in a steam engine and that spectator sports give the average citizen a way to "lower his steam pressure by allowing him to spin his wheels and toot his whistle."

In the cathartic model, which serves as a justification for the Olympic Games, individuals—athletes as well as spectators and fans—are assumed to experience a purgation of their aggressive drives through competitive athletics (Ardrey, 1966; Freud, 1948; Lorenz, 1966; see also Chapters 9 and 10). Storr (1968), for example, has stated that "rivalry between nations in sports can do nothing but good" (pp. 132-133). This is the prevailing popular view of competitive athletics, and of the Olympic Games, in particular. The number of distinguished philosophers, biologists, psychiatrists, and others who have subscribed to this position is impressive. And while there is no reason that they cannot all be wrong, it is interesting to note that they often arrived at their positions through the consideration of different sorts of evidence (Goldstein, 1982a). It should be noted, however, that there is only slight empirical support for this position (e.g., Kingsmore, 1970; Nosanchuk, 1979). Despite the relative lack of evidence in support of the sports-catharsis model, we should indicate that nearly all the systematic research on the aggressive effects of sports has been so limited as to time and place—nearly all of it conducted in Western countries since 1970—as to sample only a limited and unrepresentative portion of the phenomenon.

There is, of course, an opposing view of the modern Olympic Games. Rather than fostering international understanding and serving as a cathartic outlet for hostility and aggression, the Olympic Games might foster a sense of nationalism and militarism, and even international conflict. According to this perspective, sports, and aggressive or body contact sports in particular, increase hostility and aggression among both athletes and fans (Goldstein, 1982b; Sipes, 1973; see Chapter 10). The bases for this point of view derive from social learning theory (Bandura, 1973), disinhibition (Goldstein, Davis, & Herman, 1975), deindividuation theory (e.g., Zimbardo, 1969), and the effects of sports on autonomic arousal, which in turn influences aggressive behavior (Russell, 1981; Zillmann, Bryant, & Sapolsky, 1979). Although no research has examined these theoretical models in terms of the Olympic Games, there is a growing number of studies on the relationship between sports participation or observation and aggressive behavior. The vast majority of such studies report that observers and athletes tend to become more aggressive as a result of witnessing or taking part in body-contact sports (Arms, Russell, & Sandilands, 1979; Goldstein & Arms, 1971; Harrell, 1981; Smith, 1974; see also Marsh, Rosser, & Harré, 1978), and may even become more aggressive during the course of non-contact sports, as well (Leuk, Krahenbuhl, & Odenkirk, 1979). Furthermore, there is evidence to suggest that sports, as presented in the mass media, tend to emphasize politically conservative values, which in turn may be related to nationalistic attitudes (Goldstein & Bredemeier, 1977; Prisuta, 1979; see also Michener, 1976).

Sipes (1973) conducted a cross-cultural study of the relationship between a nation's frequency of warfare and presence of combative sports, which he defined as involving body contact, the real or symbolic gaining of playing field territory, or "patently war-like activity." Of the 20 societies studied—10 war-like and 10 pacific— 9 of the 10 war-like societies engaged in combative sports as recreation, but only 2 of the 10 non-war-like societies did so.

Sipes also examined the relationship between militarism and sports in the United States from 1920 to 1970. The percentage of the adult male population in the armed forces was used as a measure of military activity, and the number of hunting licenses issued as a measure of combative sports participation. Betting on horse races was the measure of participation in noncombative sports. Sipes also examined spectator attendance at National League baseball and NFL football games. He notes of his analyses that "the two more combative sports, football and hunting, show an overall rise during World War II and the Korean Conflict. So does betting. The less combative spectator sport, baseball, shows distinct drops during both combat periods. . . . The behavior definitely does not follow the predictions of the drive discharge model" (p. 79).

To date, there have been few studies of the relationship between national characteristics and Olympic participation. Ball (1972) was interested only in correlates of national success in the Olympic Games, and not in participation. Kyrolainen and Varis (1981) present only theoretical conceptions of sports and international conflict. The implications of a study linking participation in the Olympic Games to war are clear; if Coubertin, the IOC, and others (e.g., Proctor & Eckard, 1976; Storr, 1968) are correct, participation in the Games should be negatively correlated with participation in warfare. This would follow from the fact that a great deal of aggression would be released both in the participation and witnessing of the Olympic Games. If, however, participation in the Olympic Games and participation in warfare are found to be positively correlated, as we would expect on the basis of existing empirical evidence, support would be lent to the contention that international athletic competition fosters conflict or that the two stem from a common set of factors, such as basic values.

The purpose of the present research is to provide a preliminary examination of the relationship between Olympic Games participation and warfare. The argument is that Olympic participation is often entered into and discussed in a nationalistic, ideological, and even quasimilitary context. Therefore, Olympic Games participation may give rise to increased nationalism which, in turn, gives rise to heightened militarism. A recent example of increased nationalism followed the U.S. hockey team defeat of the team from the Soviet Union in the 1980 Winter Olympic Games. A second hypothesis is that, given a positive relationship between Olympic Games participation and war, warfare will be more closely related to participation in body-contact sports than noncontact sports. This follows from Sipes' (1973) work showing that combative sports are associated with war-like cultures and noncombative sports predominate in peaceful cultures (see also Roberts & Sutton-Smith, 1962).

A Test of the Hypotheses

Two sets of data were used: Olympic data supplied by the IOC and data on warfare from the Correlates of War project compiled by Singer and Small (1974; Small & Singer, 1982). The period of study runs from the inception of the modern Olympic Games in 1896 to the last year covered by the war data set employed in our research, 1965, for a total period of 69 years. Only countries that had existed as independent

Table 11-1. Countries Included in the Sample

Afghanistan	Finland	Norway
Albania	France	Panama
Argentina	Greece	Paraguay
Australia	Guatemala	Peru
Belgium	Haiti	Poland
Bolivia	Holland	Portugal
Brazil	Honduras	Rumania
Bulgaria	Hungary	Salvador
Canada	Iran	South Africa
Chile	Ireland	Spain
China	Italy	Sweden[a]
Columbia	Japan	Switzerland
Costa Rica	Liberia	Thailand
Cuba	Luxembourg	Turkey
Czechoslovakia	Mexico	United States of America[a]
Denmark	Mongolia	Uruguay
Dominican Republic	Morocco	USSR
Ecuador	Nepal	Venezuela
England	New Zealand	Yemen
Ethiopia	Nicaragua	Yugoslavia

[a]Eliminated from the final regression analyses; see text.

Table 11-2. Classification of Olympic Sports

Contact sports	Noncontact sports
Basketball	Archery
Boxing	Athletics
Fencing	Canoeing
Football	Cycling
Hockey	Equestrian events
Judo	Gymnastics
Wrestling	Handball
	Pentathlon
	Rowing
	Shooting
	Swimming
	Volleyball
	Weightlifting
	Yachting

nations for at least 40 years during the study period (1896-1965) were included in the analyses. This qualification was imposed to reduce Type I error, as countries with extremely brief histories would have had little chance for participation in either war or the Olympic Games. Sixty countries met this criterion (see Table 11-1). The 40-year criterion represents 59% of the study period. Singer and Small's (1974) criteria for existence as an independent nation were used.

War data were taken from a compilation prepared by Singer and Small (1974; Small & Singer, 1982) and available on computer tape. The variable used as an overall measure of war participation for a country was the total number of months that country had spent at war during the study period. This is a more sensitive measure of war involvement than either the gross number of wars in this period or the number of battle deaths, which is partially a function of population.

Olympic data were obtained from the *Encyclopedia of the National Olympic Committees* (1979-1980). The number of athletes sent to the Olympics by a country during the study period was used as the measure of Olympic participation. Also examined were the number of Olympic sports that had been entered. Olympic sports should be distinguished from Olympic events: an Olympic sport is a category, such as gymnastics or swimming, that consists of various events, such as the rings or the 100-meter relay. The sports were also separated into "contact" and "noncontact" sports by having independent judges rate the 21 sports included in the modern Games (as of 1964). Seven were considered to be contact sports and fourteen to be noncontact sports (see Table 11-2).

A multiple regression analysis was performed to determine the relationship between the war variables and the Olympic variables. The "forward" regression method was used for the final analysis employing SPSS computer program, version 8.3.

A country's population is related both to its participation in the Olympics and to warfare, and in preliminary analyses, population density was positively correlated with both total months at war ($r = .35, p < .004$) and total number of athletes sent to the Games ($r = .36$, $p < .003$). Therefore, both of these variables were partialled out of the regression equation. Population and population density figures were obtained from the *Statistical Yearbook* of the United Nations for 1965. Relative population density and size were relatively stable throughout the study period and so only population data from this particular year were used.

Population data were positively skewed, and to normalize the population distribution, a log transformation of population was performed (Cohen & Cohen, 1975, pp. 242-250). The assumptions underlying the use of multiple regression require that the normal probability plot for standardized residuals (a plot of the expected normal values against the standardized residuals, also known as a "*Q-Q* plot") be colinear, that is, that there be no "outliers" on the plot (Daniel & Wood, 1980, pp. 25-26). A preliminary analysis for outliers was performed using the BMDP program for multiple regression. Two outliers were discovered and eliminated from the final analyses, bringing the total number of countries available for analysis to 58 (see Table 11-1). This data set, including the transformations, was used in the primary analyses.

The primary multiple regression analysis testing the first hypothesis was designed to determine if the number of athletes a country had sent to the Olympic Games during the period 1896 to 1965 could be predicted from the number of months that country had spent at war, after partialling out the effects of population and population density. Two additional multiple regressions were performed to check the assumption that number of months at war would be a more sensitive, and therefore more accurate, predictor than number of wars or number of battle deaths incurred by a country. Regression analyses testing the second hypothesis were designed to determine if the number of Olympic contact sports would be better predicted by the number of months at war than the number of Olympic noncontact sports.[1]

Results

The multiple regression equation for the first hypothesis (predicting the number of athletes attending the Olympic Games from the total number of months spent at war, holding population variables constant) is

$$\hat{Y}^* = (-.017)x_p^* + (.367)x_d^* + (.546)x_w^* \quad (r^2 = .173, p < .001).$$

As demonstrated in the analysis of regression, this equation successfully predicts

---

[1] Standardized multiple regressions will be reported in the form

$$\hat{Y}^* = b_p^* x_p^* + b_d^* x_d^* + b_w^* x_w^*,$$

where Y^* is the standardized predicted value, b_i^* is the standardized regression weight, and x_i^* is the standardized predictor value. The b_p^* values designate the standardized regression weight for the population values. The b_d^* values designate the standardized regression weights for the population density values. The b_w^* values designate the regression weights for the total months at war values. The change in the squared multiple correlation, r_c^2, due to the b_w^* value and its significance will be reported with the equation.

Table 11-3. Relationship Between Warfare and Contact Sports

Frequency of war	Number of contact sports entered	
	Below median	Above median
Below median (0, 1)	24	12
Above median (≥ 2)	6	18

Note: χ^2 corrected = 8.40, *df* 1, *p* < .01.

the number of athletes attending the Olympic Games ($F = 23.2, df\ 3, 54, p < .001$; $r^2 = .563$), thus supporting the first hypothesis.

Total number of wars predicted the number of athletes at the Olympic Games nearly as well as the total months at war ($F = 21.2, df\ 3, 54, p < .001; r_c^2 = 541$). Battle deaths did not significantly predict the total number of athletes.

The regression equation predicting noncontact sports is

$$\hat{Y}^* = (-.002)x_p^* + (.381)x_d^* + (.378)x_w^* \quad (r^2 = .083, p < .01).$$

For predicting contact sports the multiple regression equation is

$$\hat{Y}^* = (-.003)x_p^* + (.350)x_d^* + (.368)x_w^* \quad (r^2 = .078, p < .02).$$

Both equations significantly predict the intended values, and both have positive weights for the primary predictor, number of months at war. Thus, because there is no differential predictive ability between noncontact and body-contact sports, the second hypothesis is not supported.

Several additional analyses were performed. A chi square using median splits on the number of contact sports and gross number of wars was computed for all 60 countries in the original sample. Table 11-3 indicates, as do the regression analyses, that there is a positive relationship between warfare and participation in body-contact sports. Likewise, for number of wars and number of Olympic athletes, the relationship was significantly positive ($\chi^2 = 11.73, p < .001$), thus corroborating the regression analysis.

Discussion

The data from this study are consistent with earlier research on the effects of sports on aggression, but extend them to international sports and international conflict. The total months at war variable successfully predicted a significant percentage of the Olympic Games participation variance. The hypothesis that total months at war would predict contact sports better than noncontact sports was not supported. We should note that Sipes did find such a relationship for the United States over a period of 50 years. However, there are several important differences between the two studies that might account for the difference in findings: We used data from 58 countries rather than from a single country; we had a less sensitive measure of sports participation than did Sipes; and in the modern Olympic Games there are about twice as many noncontact sports as contact sports, thus perhaps making the former more easily predicted than the latter.

There are a number of important issues surrounding this research that should be identified. In particular, the study examines a number of personal variables, such as number of athletes, and relates them to suprapersonal variables, such as the incidence of wars between nations. We recognize that in some sense the war data represent a variety of structural variables within countries and between countries and can therefore not be predicted entirely from personal variables. However, the fact that we are able to account for a significant proportion of the variance associated with Olympic Games participation by war data suggests that, despite the complexities involved in this relationship, nonetheless the two covary. We have begun to explore some of the more complex and subtle aspects of this relationship. Attitudes toward the Olympic Games may be a crucial variable modifying this relationship, and we are attempting to operationalize it by examining official IOC communications about forthcoming Olympics and by content-analyzing newspaper editorials about the Games. In the literature on social learning and frustration and aggression, reinforcement is often seen as a crucial variable. We are also examining reinforcement for aggression in the form of medals won for body-contact sports and their relationship to war data. Finally, we have treated in this preliminary study all data simultaneously. In subsequent research using these data sets, we intend to examine temporal changes in war data as a function of Olympic Games participation. We will examine temporal lags in an attempt to treat the relationship between warfare and athletics as a dynamic process.

Our research, combined with previous research on sports and violence, suggests that at the present time Olympic Games participation does not reduce international conflict in the way so often predicted. We would not presume that the relationship between warfare and athletic competition is necessarily and inevitably a statistically positive one, however. As psychologists we know that the perception of an event, rather than the objective event, is often the more important determinant of behavior. This is certainly true of sports, as demonstrated by Hastorf and Cantril (1954) in their classic study of perceiving rule infractions at a college football game. It should come as no surprise, then, to learn that the attitudes of spectators determine not only how an event is perceived, but what effects it has on behavior (Mann, 1974). If spectators believe that opponents in an athletic contest dislike one another, they tend to enjoy the game more, but also believe that the players' actions themselves are more hostile and competitive than if they believe the opponents to be friends (Zillmann et al., 1979). If fans believe that boxers are deliberately trying to injure one another, rather than merely acting professionally and trying to win a bout, they are more aggressive when provoked afterwards (Berkowitz & Alioto, 1973).

In this regard, a study by Harrell (1981) is most revealing. Active hockey fans who were tolerant of aggression (measured in response to the question,"In your opinion, should fighting be allowed to go unpenalized because it is an important part of the game?" Nearly half of those interviewed said "yes.") were more hostile after the first and second periods of a professional hockey game than fans who were intolerant of aggression.

Conclusions

While the present study found a positive relationship between participation in the Olympic Games and in warfare, it neither implies a causal nor an inevitable relationship between these two types of activity. The results of our study are consistent with the great majority of empirical studies on the relationship between sports participation or spectatorship and violence of various types. But we know, too, that such studies have been severely restricted by time and location: all of them being conducted in the past 10-15 years in industrial societies. Furthermore, we also have discovered that there are a number of variables that attenuate the relationship between sports and violence. These include the perceived attitude of the competitors, the spectators' attitudes toward sports violence, and the amount of provocation of the potential aggressor. In the case of the modern Olympic Games, such moderator variables may manifest themselves in several ways. Attitudes toward the Olympic Games may be influenced by news and press releases of the IOC, the presentation and coverage of the Olympics in mass media, and both official government statements on the Olympics and individuals' own experiences with competitive athletics.

If sports competition is presented to athletes and fans in such a way as to emphasize ideological, hostile, or combative aspects of sports, then they may continue to have the effects of fostering nationlism and fueling militarism. On the other hand, if the cooperative and prosocial aspects of sports are emphasized, they will undoubtedly come to foster greater cooperation (Berg, 1978; Goldstein, 1982b). It is not inconceivable that the long-discussed cathartic effects of competitive athletics are possible. Indeed, we have recently argued that in many situations, both athletes and fans report having experienced just such effects (Goldstein, 1982b). The Olympic ideal referred to by Coubertin is not beyond our grasp. It may only require a change in the way international athletic competition is conceived and presented, rather than any change in the competition itself.

Acknowledgments. This research was supported in part by a BioMedical Research Support Grant from Temple University. The authors are indebted to Leona Aiken for her assistance in matters statistical.

The war data utilized in this research were made available in part by the Social Science Data Library, Temple University, whose assistance is gratefully acknowledged. The data were originally collected by J. David Singer and Melvin Small and were made available by the Inter-University Consortium for Political Research.

References

Ardrey, R. *The territorial imperative.* New York: Atheneum, 1966.

Arms, R. L., Russell, G. W., & Sandilands, M. L. Effects on the hostility of spectators of viewing aggressive sports. *Social Psychology Quarterly,* 1979, *42*, 275-279.

Ball, D. W. Olympic games competition: Structural correlates of national success. *International Journal of Comparative Sociology,* 1972, *13,* 186-200.

Bandura, A. *Aggression: A social learning analysis.* Englewood Cliffs, N.J.: Prentice-Hall, 1973.

Berg, B. Helping behavior on the gridiron: It helps if you're winning. *Psychological Reports*, 1978, *42*, 531-534.

Berkowitz, L., & Alioto, J. T. The meaning of an observed event as a determinant of its aggressive consequences. *Journal of Personality and Social Psychology*, 1973, *28*, 206-217.

Brundage, A. Brundage urges use of one flag. *New York Times*, February 14, 1960.

Cheffers, J. *A wilderness of spite: Rhodesia denied.* New York: Vantage, 1972.

Cohen, J., & Cohen, P. *Applied multiple regression/correlation analysis for the behavioral sciences.* Hillsdale, N.J.: Erlbaum, 1975.

Coubertin, P. de The Olympic Games of 1896. *The Century Magazine*, 1896, *53*(1), 39-53.

Daniel, C., & Wood, F. S. *Fitting equations to data.* New York: Wiley, 1980.

Espy, R. *The politics of the olympic games.* Berkeley: University of California Press, 1979.

Freud, S. *Beyond the pleasure principle.* London: Hogarth, 1948.

Goldstein, J. H. Violence in sports. Paper presented at Biennial Meeting of the International Society for Research on Aggression. Mexico City, August 1982. (a)

Goldstein, J. H. Sports violence. *National Forum*, 1982, *62*(1), 9-11. (b)

Goldstein, J. H., & Arms, R. L. Effects of observing athletic contests on hostility. *Sociometry*, 1971, *34*, 83-90.

Goldstein, J. H., & Bredemeier, B. J. Sports and socialization: Some basic issues. *Journal of Communication*, 1977, *27*, 154-159.

Goldstein, J. H., Davis, R. W., & Herman, D. Escalation of aggression: Experimental studies. *Journal of Personality and Social Psychology*, 1975, *31*, 162-170.

Harrell, W. A. Verbal aggressiveness in spectators at professional hockey games: The effects of tolerance of violence and amount of exposure to hockey. *Human Relations*, 1981, *34*, 643-655.

Hastorf, A. H., & Cantril, H. They saw a game: A case study. *Journal of Abnormal and Social Psychology*, 1954, *49*, 129-134.

Killian, L., & Rodda, J. *The olympic games.* New York: Macmillan, 1976.

Kingsmore, J. M. The effect of a professional wrestling and a professional basketball contest upon the aggressive tendencies of spectators. In G. S. Kenyon (Ed.), *Contemporary psychology of sport.* Chicago: Athletic Institute, 1970.

Kyrolainen, H., & Varis, T. Approaches to the study of sports in international relations. *Current Research on Peace and Violence*, 1981, *4*(1), 55-88.

Leuck, M. R., Krahenbuhl, G. S., & Odenkirk, J. E. Assessment of spectator aggression at intercollegiate basketball contests. *Review of Sport and Leisure*, 1979, *4*, 40-52.

Lorenz, K. *On aggression.* New York: Harcourt, Brace & World, 1966.

Lowe, B., Kanin, D. B., & Strenk, A. *Sport and international relations.* Champaign, Ill.: Sipes, 1978.

Mandell, R. D. *The Nazi olympics.* New York: Macmillan, 1971.

Mandell, R. D. *The first modern olympics.* Berkeley: University of California Press, 1976.

Mann, L. On being a sore loser: How fans react to their team's failure. *Australian Journal of Psychology*, 1974, *26*, 37-47.

Marsh, P., Rosser, E., & Harré, R. *The rules of disorder.* London: Routledge & Kegan Paul, 1978.

Michener, J. A. *Sports in America.* New York: Random House, 1976.

Milshteyn, O. A., & Molchanov, S. V. The shaping of public opinion regarding sport by the mass media as a factor promoting international understanding. *International Review of Sport Sociology,* 1976, *3,* 71-84.

Nosanchuk, T. A. *The way of the warrior: The effects of traditional martial arts training on aggressiveness.* Department of Sociology and Anthropology, Carleton University, Ottawa, Working paper 79-10, 1979.

Prisuta, R. H. Televised sports and political values. *Journal of Communication,* 1979, *29*(1), 94-102.

Proctor, R. C., & Eckard, W. M. "Toot-toot" or spectator sports: Psychological and therapeutic implications. *American Journal of Sports Medicine,* 1976, *4*(2), 78-83.

Roberts, J. M., & Sutton-Smith, B. Child training and game involvement. *Ethnology,* 1962, *1,* 166-185.

Russell, G. W. Spectator moods at an aggressive sports event. *Journal of Sport Psychology,* 1981, *3,* 217-227.

Singer, J. D., & Small, M. *The wages of war,* 1816-1965. Ann Arbor: Inter-University Consortium for Political Research, 1974.

Sipes, R. G. War, sports and aggression: An empirical test of two rival theories. *American Anthropologist,* 1973, *75,* 64-86.

Small, M., & Singer, J. D. *Resort to arms.* Beverly Hills: Sage, 1982.

Smith, M. D. Significant others' influence on the assaultive behaviour of young hockey players. *International Review of Sport Sociology,* 1974, *3/4,* 217-227.

Statistical Yearbook. New York: United Nations, 1965.

Storr, A. *Human aggression.* New York: Atheneum, 1968.

Zillmann, D., Bryant, J., & Sapolsky, B. S. The enjoyment of watching sport contests. In J. H. Goldstein (Ed.), *Sports, games, and play.* Hillsdale, N.J.: Erlbaum, 1979.

Zimbardo, P. G. The human choice: Individuation, reason and order vs. deindividuation, impulse and chaos. In W. Arnold & D. Levine (Eds.), *Nebraska symposium on motivation.* Vol. 17. Lincoln: University of Nebraska Press, 1969.

Chapter 12

Sports Violence and the Media

Jennings Bryant and Dolf Zillmann

With all my heart do I admire
Athletes who sweat for fun or hire,
Who take the field in gaudy pomp
And maim each other as they romp;
My limp and bashful spirit feeds
On other people's heroic deeds.
(Ogden Nash, 1937/1980, p. 408)

Although the notion that spectators enjoy violence in sports seems to be a truism in contemporary society, it has received scant scholarly attention. In this chapter we consider the nature and consequences of sports violence; present popular notions, formal proposals, and empirical evidence for the enhancement of spectators' enjoyment of sports contests through aggressive play; and examine ways in which the media exploit sports violence.

The Presence and Nature of Sports Violence

A glance at selected headlines from the popular press indicates the extent to which violence is a dominant feature of contemporary sports:

BALL GAMES OR BRAWL GAMES?
BUD GRANT WANTS END TO VIOLENCE
BLOOD, SWEAT AND FEARS: ARE THE REFS STOPPING
GOOD FIGHTS TOO SOON?
WATCHING OUT FOR THE HIT MAN
HIT MEN
TAKE THE BODY!
YES, YOU CAN CALL HIM THE ASSASSIN
BLOW THE WHISTLE ON DIRTY HOCKEY
PLAYING FOR BLOOD

Such extensive violence is not without its consequences, accidental and intentional, dysfunctional as well as potentially useful. One blatantly dysfunctional and debatably accidental consequence of sports violence is the maiming and even death of its athlete victims, such as the paralysis of NFL wide receiver Darryl Stingley via a literally bone-crushing tackle ("A Crippled Player," 1981). In spite of improvement in protective equipment for athletes involved in contact sports, elimination of or even substantial reduction in serious injury appears unlikely (Friedman, 1981). Players are frequently encouraged to make their interpersonal aggression as destructive as possible (Fox, 1980). And, "if a player gets hit properly, he's going to get hurt, and there's nothing you can do about it" (Crowder, quoted in Tomasik, 1982). Although it is difficult to determine the role of excessive force in injuries to college and professional athletes (cf. Friedman, 1981), one NFL public information specialist recently estimated, probably conservatively, that more than 75% of all serious injuries to professional football players result from "interpersonal contact" (NFL Public Information Office, 1982).

That gratuitous, destructive violence is frequently intentional and is even demanded by those who coach and manage sports is clear. Consider the case of former National Hockey League player, 6'4", 220-pound Paul Mulvey. A routine fight had broken out on the ice between a player from Mulvey's team, the Los Angeles Kings, and an opponent from the Vancouver Canucks. Mulvey was seated on the bench. Don Perry, coach of the Kings, turned to Mulvey and told him to go join the fracas, "and don't dance." Perry had demanded aggression from Mulvey, had ordered him to hit someone. "He wanted him to play the 'goon'—hockey language for an enforcer, a heavy, a hit man" (Schaap, 1982, p. 4). What makes the story newsworthy is that Mulvey refused. "I'm not going to be a designated assassin," Mulvey said. "He decided he was not going to hit people without provocation, and when he made that simple decision, he suddenly and unsuspectingly became a symbol—a man who had taken a stand against the biggest curse of professional hockey, against senseless violence" (Schaap, p. 5). For Mulvey's courage and integrity, he was immediately shipped to the minor leagues. "Perry was furious. He ordered Mulvey off the team, ordered him not to come to practice anymore, declared him a nonperson."

Other sports are also riddled with violence, whether played by professionals, collegians, schoolboys, or peewees. Hockey, basketball, football, soccer, rugby, boxing, and wrestling, among others, all have rules and penalty systems to control excessive violence, but success in each sport depends somewhat on physical intimidation and the infliction of pain. In an article entitled "The Team that People Just Love to Hate," which examines the violence of the National Hockey League's Philadelphia Flyers, the relationship between penalties for violent play and intimidation is clearly articulated: "The Flyers' whole strategy is based on the fact that everything won't be called, and that all of their intimidation is going to leave an effect" (Brooks, 1980, p. 34). Even baseball, almost universally classified as a noncontact sport, celebrates the intimidation potential of violence. After all, the first player inducted into baseball's Hall of Fame was Ty Cobb, who has been described as "the most violent, . . . thoroughly maladjusted personality to pass across American sports" (Stump, 1980, p. 326). A recent article entitled "Watching Out for the Hit Man" reinforces this view; it was subtitled, "Despite macho disclaimers, there *is* a fear factor in baseball" (Robinson, 1981, p. 32). "Intimidation is the name of the game today" (Friedman, 1981, p. 43). Thus, according to sports writers and analysts, violence is a predominant feature in contemporary sports, and it is an important factor in victory.

Why does the public *tolerate* such extensive violence in its favorite spectator sports? Or is that the wrong question? Better, perhaps, why do people *desire,* why do they *demand* so much violence in their spectator sports?

Does Aggression Increase Spectators' Enjoyment of Sports?

Popular Notions of the Appeal of Violence

In spectator sports, as in other forms of mass entertainment, it is apparently accepted as a truism that the American public enjoys witnessing violence. As one critic has asserted, "There is a human preoccupation with watching violence. We are drawn to it irresistibly" (Pearce, quoted in Gunther, 1976, p. 10). Vince Lombardi has been even more specific in delineating the relationship between violence in one sport—professional football—and that sport's appeal: It "is a violent sport. That's why the crowds love it" (Michener, 1976, p. 520).

Considerations of the appeal of violence in sports permeate the popular press. For instance, it has been argued that "pro hockey seems bent on replacing skill and finesse with savagery and violence—under the guise of giving the public what it wants" (Surface, 1976, p. 31). In discussing "the spearing, slashing, high-sticking and fighting incidents that follow the [Philadelphia] Flyers across the length and breadth of the NHL schedule like a very bad cold" (Brooks, 1980, p. 34), their General Manager Keith Allen, has been quite specific about the team's motivation for violence and brawling: " 'We put more fannies in the seats than any team in the league,' he says. 'Not even the Montreal Canadiens outdraw us' " (Brooks, 1980, p. 35).

Perhaps the most graphic popular notion of the appeal of violence is expressed in two recent Tank McNamara cartoons. The first cartoon features daredevil Feeble McWeevil, who is depicted sitting despondently while a second character, apparently his manager or promoter, urges him to begin his death-defying motorcycle leap. The captions read:

> *Promoter*: "What's your problem? See those stands? Fifty thousand people are paying to see you jump over those 14 cars."
> *McWeevil*: "Those people aren't paying to see me jump over 14 cars. They're paying to see me jump over 13 cars."

The second cartoon takes the position that spectators really watch violent sports to see someone get killed. In this strip, two unidentified mechanics discuss a televised sports "spectacular" as they work under an automobile:

> *Mechanic 1*: "Did you see the 'Heavy' Beer 'Tournament of Lunatics' on 'Trashsports Spectacular'?"
> *Mechanic 2*: "Aww, they fake everything. Those stunts aren't really dangerous."

Mechanic 1: "This looked pretty dangerous. This guy jumped a cement truck over a vat of burning gasoline into a tank filled with barracudas. How could you tell that it was faked?"
Mechanic 2: "Did he get killed?"
Mechanic 1: "Nah."
Mechanic 2: "Then it was faked. Shoot, I used to watch those thrill shows on TV, but I got disgusted with 'em. Nobody never gets killed."

The same sentiment is poetically presented in this selection from William D. Barney's *The Rasslers* (1980):

> Only one thing is genuine in all
> the sweat—the Watching Faces who have willed
> one hope, one prayer.
>   Please God, don't let them stall.
> Let someone get hurt good. Maybe get killed. (p. 403)

Images of the contemporary spectator's desire for sports violence are all rather pale, however, when compared with William Harrison's vision of the future of sports. He proclaims in *Roller Ball Murder* (1974/1980) that the quest for the ultimate thrill in sports will lead to a future where the goal is mutilation and murder:

> The statistical nuances of Roller Ball Murder entertain the multitudes as much as any other aspect of the game. The greatest number of points scored in a single game: 81. The highest velocity of a ball when actually caught by a runner: 176 mph. Highest number of players put out of action in a single game by a single skater: 13—world's record by yours truly. Most deaths in a single contest: 9—Rome vs. Chicago, December 4. 2012. (p. 12)

Theories of the Enjoyment of Aggression in Sports

A number of rationales can be offered to explain why violence in sports should facilitate the spectator's enjoyment (cf. Bryant, Comisky, & Zillmann, 1981). By far the most common theory is that the active or vicarious participation in sports competition produces *catharsis,* that is, a purgation from pent-up feelings of hostility. This view has been popularized by Lorenz (1963). His discussion of sports as ritualized aggression has recently been summarized in theoretical terms: "If, following Lorenz, one were to assume (a) that destructive energy spontaneously builds up in the organism, (b) that the performance of aggressive acts reduces such energy to tolerable levels, a process which is pleasantly experienced, (c) that the performance of competitive actions also serves this pleasing outlet function, and (d) that even merely witnessing competitive actions serves this function, one seems to have accounted for the popularity of sports—doing and viewing" (Zillmann, Bryant, & Sapolsky, 1979, p. 310). In line with this reasoning, the more ferocious the violence in sports contests, the greater the opportunity for reducing destructive energy in the spectator through vicarious participation, and the greater the pleasure that should result from the experience of relief. Actually, the catharsis proposal is associated with numerous conceptual difficulties, and it is challenged by a wealth of nonsupportive empirical evidence from recent research on human aggression (Geen & Quanty, 1977; Zillmann, 1979). These difficulties notwithstanding, it is clear that this rationale is widely accepted in society.

As a second rationale, Hobbes, Nietzsche, Spencer, and many others, but especially Adler (1927), have claimed that humans are consistently striving to enhance self-esteem and power by *asserting dominance* over others. According to this view, the will to power and the desire for interpersonal dominance are among the strongest motivating factors in human existence. Cheska (1968/1981) considers this concept of power and dominance to be objectified in modern sports. The ultimate degree of power she has labeled "direct control." " The control may be *direct* as dominance by physical qualities, manipulation, or confinement of others by players in the athletic arena" (p. 371). If it can be assumed that the football fan vicariously shares with the fullback in slamming through the would-be tackler on offense or with the linebacker in sacking the quarterback on defense, or that the basketball spectator empathizes with the "power forward" setting up the slam pick and taking the opponent out of the play, then sports spectatorship offers a legitimate way of "asserting dominance" over others in a rather graphic form. In this instance, violence may serve to indicate or emphasize the degree of dominance. It could be expected that the more decisive the dominance (within the rules of the game), the greater the pleasure for the viewer—at least for the spectator who fits the Adlerian scheme of motivation and who is capable of sharing power vicariously. This view is often expressed in terms of "identifying with the hero" (a sports hero or a heroic team, in this case). For example, Cheska argues that "control may be associated as identification and involvement of spectators with participating athletes in the enactment of the power process" (p. 371). Although such reasoning appears to be common sense, it is conceptually troublesome and empirically unfounded (cf. Zillmann, 1980).

A final rationale also focuses upon competition. It has long been argued that conflict and competition are key elements in the *enjoyment of drama*. As an example, consider the popular catch phrase "The human drama of athletic competition." Along these lines, it has recently been asserted that vigorous and vicious play, particularly when mutual injury and pain are likely, is the most archaic index of high competitiveness. Rough and aggressive play is seen to stand for human conflict at its peak, and intense conflict is the heart and soul of high drama (Zillmann et al., 1979). As Novak (1976) has said, "the most satisfying element in sports is spirit. Other elements being equal, the more spirited team will win: the one that hits the hardest, drives itself the most" (p. 149). This reasoning suggests that increased interpersonal aggression in sports serves to prove to the viewer that the protagonists are "giving it all they've got." Vigor and aggression serve to prove that the players "mean business." Therefore aggression has utility not for its own sake, but because it is the ultimate proof that the athletes are giving their all to the contest. This intensification of the struggle raises the stakes by increasing the likelihood of serious injury in the ferocious conflict.

Sportive action in which the stakes are exceptionally high has been labeled "deep play" (Bentham, 1802/1931). This phenomenon has been examined from an anthropological perspective by Geertz (1976), who considers the intense cockfights of Bali as a type of deep play conducted solely for spectators. Balinese cockfights apparently serve simultaneously as favorite sport and popular drama. "In the cock-fight, man and beast, good and evil, ego and id, and creative power of aroused mas-culinity and the destructive power of loosened animality fuse in a bloody drama of hatred, cruelty, violence, and death" (p. 658). Geertz's description of the fight emphasizes the vigor and intensity of the violent conflict of deep play: "The cocks fly almost immediately at one another in a wing-beating, head-thrusting, leg-kicking explosion of animal fury so pure, so absolute, and in its own way so beautiful, as to be almost abstract, a Platonic concept of hate" (p. 659).

Whether the contestants are animal, as in the cockfight, man versus animal, as in the bullfight, or man, it appears that the increases in the intensity of the action or the size of the stakes produce deeper play, higher drama. Cheska (1968/1981, p. 376) has claimed that "the elements of drama—participants, ritual, plot, production, symbolism, social message—are all brilliantly choreographed in the sports spectacu-lar." Since an examination of the mechanisms involved in the appreciation of drama is beyond the scope of this paper (cf. Zillmann, 1980), it must presently suffice to say that however it works, drama entertains, and aggression and conflict are proven effective elements in the creation of high drama.

The latter rationale can be utilized to counter the popular notion that sports fans consider serious injury and fatal accidents the ultimate thrill, or if not that, a desirable "bonus," an extra treat. Such a negative or "low" view of human nature is unnecessary, although it may provide a sensationalistic posture from which to stimulate the curious to read beyond a bold headline such as: THEY PLAY FOR BLOOD. It is just as plausible that sports fans may be attracted to "thrill sports"—where death or serious injury, though improbable, are imminent possibilities—not for the lust for blood per se, but because the contestants' willingness to risk serious injury and death creates the type of intensity necessary for the maximal enjoyment of the dramatic event. It is likely that only under unusual conditions in which the spectators fear or hate the victim or potential victim—such as depicted in the "red-neck" stock car race spectators' hatred for the "nigger" Wendell Scott, portrayed by Richard Pryor in the movie *Greased Lightning*—will people really enjoy seeing the destruction of the sports contestant. Such dispositional factors are also an important ingredient of other forms of entertainment (e.g., Zillmann, 1980; Zill-mann & Cantor, 1976).

Evidence for the Appeal of Sports Violence

In spite of the pervasiveness of the claim that violence in sports has considerable entertainment value, and regardless of the coherent and the contrived rationales that have been proposed to account for it, pertinent empirical evidence is scarce. Only three investigations have directly assessed the appeal of sports violence for spectators.

In an investigation of the appeal of rough-and-tumble play in televised profes-sional football (Bryant et al., 1981), play from numerous NFL games were selected and pretested to create a variation in the degree of roughness/violence of plays (low, intermediate, high). Plays were matched on a number of stimulus dimensions other than degree of violence in order to reduce extraneous, potentially contaminating influences. Male and female viewers rated their enjoyment of each play. As can be seen from an examination of Fig. 12-1, enjoyment of the plays was found to increase with the degree of roughness and violence. However, this relationship was significant for male viewers only. It was not reliable for females. Although there were no appreciable gender differences in the appreciation of plays featuring low and intermediate levels of violence, highly violent plays were significantly more enjoyed by males than by females. The findings suggest that a high degree of aggressiveness is an important ingredient of the enjoyment of sports contests, at least for male viewers.

Evidence from a study by Comisky, Bryant, and Zillmann (1977) further substantiates the claim that enjoyment of sports contests is facilitated by roughness, enthusiasm, and violence of play. Examples of what appeared to be extremely rough play and normal play were selected from a professional ice hockey game, and specific video and audio properties were ascertained in a pretest. The pretest revealed a fortuitous occurrence: For one segment in which extremely rough or violent play was visually presented, the broadcast commentary was rather bland, with the announcers letting the abundant action serve as its own entertainment. In contrast, during a segment in which minimally rough or violent play was visually presented, the announcer and color commentator filled the audio track with descriptions of rough and tough ice hockey, with the action threatening to turn into a brawl at any minute. This situation permitted tests of, first, broadcast commentary's effects on viewers' perceptions of the roughness of action, and, secondly, of perceptions of sports violence on the overall appreciation of play.

In a quasiexperimental design, spectators viewed one of the two segments in one of two presentation modes, with versus without commentary, and rated their appreciation of the segment and how rough or violent they perceived the action to be.

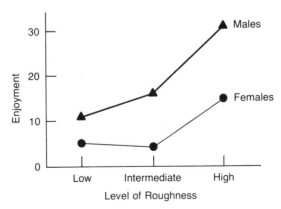

Fig. 12-1. Viewers' enjoyment of plays of televised professional football as a function of degree of roughness and violence involved. For males (triangles), violent play resulted in significantly greater enjoyment than play associated with lower levels of roughness. The corresponding trend in women's (circles) enjoyment of violent play was not significant, however. (Adapted from Bryant, Comisky, & Zillmann, 1981.)

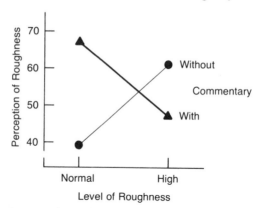

Fig. 12-2. Viewers' perceptions of roughness of play in professional ice hockey as a function of broadcast commentary. Viewers in the no commentary condition (circles) correctly perceived the depicted rough play as rough—that is, as rougher than normal play. In contrast, viewers in the commentary condition (triangles) perceived the normal play that was associated with commentary stressing roughness and idleness as rougher than the actually rough play that was associated with commentary ignoring roughness. Enjoyment of play proved to be a function of perceived roughness. (Adapted from Comisky, Bryant, & Zillmann, 1977.)

As Fig. 12-2 shows, the presence of the commentary altered perceptions of roughness of play critically: In the normal–action condition, the commentary stressing roughness of action made the play seem rough, even rougher than the depicted rough play. In the rough-action condition, in contrast, the commentary ignoring roughness made rough play appear less rough and more normal. Thus, there can be no doubt that commentary can alter perceptions of play.

More important for the present discussion, ratings of entertainment value followed the degree to which play was *perceived* to be rough. The condition perceived to be the most entertaining was that featuring normal play which the commentary presented as rough, the condition which had been rated as the roughest by the viewers. Visually depicted rough play presented without the commentary which ignored roughness received intermediate appreciation ratings; it had also received intermediate ratings of perceived roughness. And normal play without commentary and visually rough play with commentary ignoring roughness received similarly low ratings of appreciation. Clearly, then, perceived roughness and violence can contribute to viewers' enjoyment of sports contests.

The third, related investigation (Bryant, Brown, Comisky, & Zillmann, 1982) featured neither actual nor perceived violence nor roughness; it dealt with perceived hostility or hatred between opponent athletes, with the affective relationships altered by commentary. The commentary of a televised tennis match was altered so that it appeared to spectators that the two players either loved, hated, or had no particular affective disposition toward each other. Once again, commentary proved to be an effective means of altering spectators' perceptions: Compared with presenting the players as the best of friends or not specifying their affective relationships, reporting that the opponents were bitter enemies made the play appear to be more hostile, tense, and intense. Moreover, as is indicated in Fig. 12-3, spectators who thought the opponents were hated foes, rather than good friends or neutral opponents, reported significantly greater enjoyment from watching the match than did the viewers in the other condition. Not only did hatred, and the concomitant increase in perceived hostility, intensity, and competitiveness, contribute substantially to enjoyment, other indices of entertainment—ratings of excitement, involvement, and interest—were also significantly higher in the condition featuring enmity than in the conditions of amity or unspecified affect.

Taken together, these three studies clearly indicate that athletes' interpersonal aggression and hostility contribute to spectators' enjoyment of sports contests. The truism appears to be correct: At least within certain limits, sports spectators do love aggression. The limits are unclear, however. Does sports enjoyment thrive on fierce competitiveness? Or need the competition entail blood and gore, incapacitation and mutilation, even death—as some sports writers and analysts apparently believe? Research findings are incomplete. They stop at fisticuffs in ice hockey; that is, at violent actions that typically cause bruises and occasionally result in injuries such as loss of an eye, but that nonetheless are treated as part of the game by most sports commentators. Brawls thus sanctioned that do *not* result in injury apparently enhance the enjoyment of the sports event (Comisky et al., 1977)—but would bloody brawls, and brawls that produce cripples? It takes a low view of human nature, indeed, to suggest that they would. Notwithstanding speculations, research fails us at this point. The effect of injurious play in sports on spectators' enjoyment is simply not known at present.

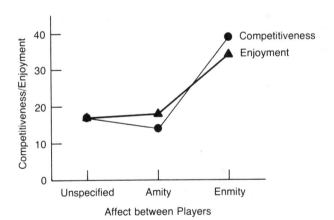

Fig. 12-3. Viewers' enjoyment of identical play in tennis as a function of perceived affect between the players. Through commentary, respondents were led to believe that the players were the best of friends or the worst of enemies. No personal relationship was indicated in a control. Perceptions of competitiveness of players and play (circles) was greatly enhanced in the enmity condition. Enjoyment (triangles) followed the illusion of greater competitive intensity. (Adapted from Bryant, Brown, Comisky, & Zillmann, 1982.)

Media Exploitation of Sports Violence

Evidence for the Exploitation of Violence

Prior to addressing the question of how media exploit sports violence, the question "Do they?" must be addressed. It should be rather obvious that they do. The fact that sports journalists widely believe that sports fans love violence has already been established. Given a capitalistic media system that maximizes profits by increasing the size of its audience, it almost goes without saying that violence—should it function as an audience attraction—will be exploited. The justification for this exploitation is ready-made: "We're only giving the public what it wants."

An extreme example of media exploitation of violence occurred in a recent televised presentation of a rugby match on one of the sports cable networks. An informal analysis of the video portion of the 1-hour coverage of the edited match revealed numerous close-up camera shots of injuries resulting in blood. Several of these presentations were preceded or followed immediately by close-ups of banners or bumper stickers of some variant of the popular theme, "Give Blood, Play Rugby." Numerous additional unrelated shots of such banners or stickers were interspersed throughout coverage of the match.

A systematic analysis of televised sports coverage has been conducted by Bryant et al., (1977), who analyzed the commentary of six televised professional football games from the 1976 season. Each sentence of the sportscast was classified as descriptive, dramatic, or humorous, and dramatic sentences were further categorized by type of conflict (e.g., interpersonal, team), motif (e.g., competition, physical competence, pity), and other categories of interest. Approximately 27% of the sentences were found to serve the "drama of competition," supporting the contention that the contemporary sportscaster has assumed the role of complementing the drama on the field and of generating involvement and excitement for the televised spectator—becoming "dramatist" and "cheerleader." Howard Cosell, in discussing the commentators' role in popularizing televised football, has put it rather well: "ABC will not be like the others. We'll be Number 1 because we make football entertaining" (Novak, 1976, p. 276). Whether the others have not actually become more like ABC will be discussed shortly.

When dramatic commentary was analyzed by type of conflict, intrapersonal conflict emerged as the most common type (47%), followed by team conflict (36%) and interpersonal conflict (16%). The investigators note surprise that sports dramatists made so little use of interpersonal conflict, which is the mainstay of television drama. For the present discussion, perhaps the most important statistic is the proportion of commentary devoted to conflict of any type: 14% of all commentary.

The study by Bryant et al. (1977) is limited to one sport, professional football, and the information from the 1976 telecasts may be dated. Additionally, the study did not contain a specific category for references to roughness or violence of play, and it dealt only with the auditory channel. The latter is important, as the announcerless NFL telecast by NBC in December of 1980 indicates that the video channel may contain a great deal of dramatization and emphasis of roughness and violence (Davis, Bryant, & Brown, 1981). To compensate for these shortcomings, Bryant and Zillmann (1982 a, 1982 b) conducted content analyses of the audio and video portions of six telecasts from the 1981 NFL season and of three telecasts of the 1981 NHL games. Preliminary analyses of the data from these investigations reveal several trends in sports coverage and provide additional information on visual coverage of NFL contests and of visual coverage and commentary of NHL games.

For NFL coverage, (a) the 1981 NFL telecasts contain a larger proportion of dramatic commentary (35%) than the 1976 telecasts (27%). This represents a 30% increase in 5 years. (b) Coverage by all three networks featured increases in the proportion of dramatic commentary in the recent season (ABC: from 30% to 37%; CBS: from 28% to 35%; NBC: from 22% to 33%). The substantial increases in dramatic commentary by CBS (25%) and NBC (50%), along with the somewhat smaller increase by drama leader, ABC (20%), indicate that all of the major networks are trying to "make football entertaining." (c) The relative proportion of commentary devoted to interpersonal (player vs. player) conflict had increased from 1976 to 1981 on all three networks. As percent of dramatic commentary, ABC: from 22 to 25; CBS: from 10 to 18; NBC: from 19 to 23. In general, statements regarding team conflict had also increased slightly, while those devoted to intrapersonal conflict had decreased. (d) Positive comments (value judgments) about exceptionally rough play which did not result in penalties or injury (4% of dramatic commentary on networks combined) exceeded negative comments about the same kind of play (<1% of dramatic commentary on networks combined) by 5 to 1. When penalties but not injury resulted from exceptionally rough play, positive and negative comments were approximately equal (< 1% of dramatic commentary for each). When injury or injury-plus-penalty resulted, negative comments exceeded positive by 3 to 1 (< 1% of dramatic commentary conbined). All in all, exceptionally rough or violent play which did not result in immediately dysfunctional consequences was strongly supported by the announcers, especially by the color commentators (e.g., "Now that's the way to make a halfback think twice before hitting that hole again"). (e) Analysis of the video channel was even more revealing. Overall, more than 35% of camera coverage was devoted to dramatic embellishment of descriptive play coverage. (f) The time length of postwhistle camera coverage (e.g., camera lingering on victim or perpetrator of violence as he returned to huddle) of plays judged to be exceptionally rough was nearly twice that of exceptionally mild plays. More than twice as many instant replays were presented of rough than mild plays. Moreover, longer average sideline camera coverage was devoted to injured players or to players who had made vicious tackles than to players who had just otherwise made spectacular plays not associated with exceptional roughness (excluding scoring plays).

Analysis of the NHL telecasts is less complete; however, many similar patterns have emerged. (a) For example, 31% of the NHL commentary has been classified as dramatic, as have 22% of the camera shots (video portion of the telecasts). (b) Interpersonal conflict is emphasized much more frequently in NHL coverage than in NFL coverage (34% vs. 22% of dramatic commentary). (c) In spite of a purported deemphasis of coverage of fights or brawls, the average fisticuff during a NHL telecast received 34 seconds of camera coverage and four sentences of commentary.

Overall, these recent analyses of sportscasts indicate that drama in sports telecasts is not limited to coverage of professional football, nor is the dramatization restricted to the audio track. Professional hockey is similarly dramatized, and more than one-fourth of all camera coverage adds histrionics to the play. It seems clear that sportscasts are becoming even more "entertainment, not sports" (cf. Novak, 1976, p. 276). Moreover, emphasizing roughness and violence has become an important part of the way television codifies sports/entertainment coverage.

Ways in Which Media Exploit Violence

Coverage of violent play. The mass media exploit and potentially foster violence in sports in a number of ways, all of course in the name of better serving the entertainment needs of sports fans. The emphasis of violence by extensive coverage of rough and violent play has been discussed already. Most significantly, rough play is given more air time than normal play, and rough, violent play not resulting in dysfunctional consequences is praised more than criticized. Although this emphasis of violence may be unfortunate from a social-learning or a social-welfare perspective, the previously discussed empirical evidence suggests that it is a most appropriate strategy for the creation of effective drama.

There are certainly other, alternative ways of guaranteeing highly intense, competitive play to the spectator. For example, emphasizing that the "winner takes all" of the gate should also prove to the audience that the competing parties will maximize their efforts, especially if the "purse" is impressively large. In most sports events covered by the media, however, the loser's share has become so large (beyond the personal financial expectations of most sports fans), that this technique may have lost its appeal. Championships and records may similarly be seen as assuring supreme effort by players. However, the promotional techniques concerning such events are only applicable to a small portion of sports competition, usually towards the end of a sports season. In contrast, violence—as readily available proof of competitive intensity and fighting spirit—is conveniently present and its depiction and evaluation can be easily manipulated.

Sports journalists have also employed techniques which go beyond mere coverage to exploit sports violence. The entertainment value, the audience appeal, and any social effects of these techniques are almost completely untested, however. One of the exploitive techniques in question is the writing or the producing of *features* about sports violence and violent athletes; another is the incorporation of violent incidents of serious (even fatal) consequences from past events into the *promotion* of upcoming events.

Features. Feature articles or documentaries about sports and sports figures are the "bread and butter" of numerous sports publications and electronic sports magazine programs. An informal survey of recent issues of such print publications revealed considerable attention to sports violence. For example, in one year *Sport* published eight feature articles concerned with some aspect of sports violence; *Sports Illustrated* included four such articles in a year. Even publications which do not focus on sports explore and/or exploit sports violence. For example, in one 12-month period, *TV Guide* included three features on sports violence, two of which were only marginally related to television.

Obviously one can not conclude "exploitation" from mere coverage. The coverage alternatively can be interpreted as an exhibition of professional concern with sports violence and as a first step toward reforming the games. A closer look at specific examples is suggestive of exploitation, however. For instance, and although there is room for argument, it has frequently been suggested that during the late 1970s, the two premier "cheap-shot" artist, "hit men" in the NFL were Jack Tatum and Doug Plank. During a 10-month period, *Sport* carried a feature story on each. The sensationalistic titles were "Plank and the Joy of Hitting" (Schulian, 1979) and "Yes, You Can Call Him the Assassin" (Fox, 1980). Or, consider a particular theme, say "Intimidation": For football, see "Hit Men: Twelve Guys You Wouldn't Want to Meet in a Well-Lit Stadium" (Steiner, 1981); for baseball, there's "Nobody Intimidates My Team" (Shaw, 1978). Basketball has "I Don't Want Anybody in My Territory" (Bell, 1978). Hockey tops them all. It features an article "ranking NHL players on the basis of their pugilistic abilities" ("Fergy's Favorites," 1981). At least all of these articles deal with sports teams or figures. The capital exploiter is a *Parade* article entitled "Christie Brinkley's Violence" with a subhead "How a superstar model finds fulfillment at ringside" (Scott, 1982). The latter article specifically links violence with drama via the caption, "I want to capture the human drama written on the faces" under a photograph of a beaten and battered boxer. There can be no doubt, then, that many sports features exploit violence. This exploitation is straightforward, for the most part. Occasionally, however, concern about sports violence is voiced; but it remains unclear whether concern is the real issue or whether the expression of concern lends itself to selling copies.

Just as it did in the days of "yellow journalism," violence in feature stories still sells newspapers, magazines, and books. To illustrate the marketing potential of feature-length mayhem, Jack Tatum, the free safety who made a quadriplegic of Darryl Stingley, capitalized on his notoriety with a best-seller entitled *They Call Me Assassin* (Fox, 1980). The sports press labeled the book "Tatum's self righteous defense of violence" ("Sinner, Judge Thyself," 1980). The violence formula apparently works as well in features as it does in coverage.

Promotions. One of the major television programming changes of the past decade has been in self-promotion. The rapid evolution of "promos" or promotional spots is generally considered to be a programming innovation of Fred Silverman when he was programming chief at ABC. " 'Grabbers' are the Silverman trademark" (Hobson, 1977). Sex and violence are frequent ingredients of these grabbers. Since sports has more of the latter than the former, sports promotions frequently exploit violence, including accidental death. For example, following the watery death of the Atlas Van Lines driver in unlimited hydrofoil racing in 1981, the 1982 races were almost universally promoted on television with a 10-20 second clip of this sensational disaster. Other thrill sports such as automobile racing are similarly advertised.

What is the purpose of this promotion based on maiming and death? Is it pure pandering? Does the audience really attend sporting events hoping to see an athlete trapped in twisted steel, engulfed in flames? As was suggested earlier, such a fatalistic posture is unnecessary. It is equally if not more plausible that the fiery crash serves an an "establishing shot." It signals or indicates that the upcoming sports event has tremendous risk for its participants, rather than promising death. The fatal accident serves as proof that the contestants are willing to risk their all in the contest. Just as greater intensity—as indicated by increased interpersonal aggression—apparently enhances enjoyment of sports and, when included in promotional materials, should enhance anticipation of enjoyment of a sporting event, increasing spectators' perception of the magnitude of risk that the participant is willing to take should increase anticipated pleasure. In other words, displaying violence and death in promotional material is expected to enhance spectators' anticipation of enjoyment of the event because they have *tangible evidence* that intense conflict and risk are likely.

Evidence from related research suggests at least three limiting conditions to these propositions relating to effective promotion. First, the intensity of the conflict, as indexed by the degree of aggression or hostility, should not exceed the spectator's considerations of propriety. Research on humor appreciation has indicated that whenever an audience member's boundaries of moral judgment or of propriety are breeched, mirth will diminish (Bryant, 1977, Zillmann & Bryant, 1974). There is no reason to expect that similar judgmental processes are absent when spectators are considering whether to attend, view, or listen to a sporting event. Secondly, and closely related to the first limiting condition, substantial individual differences can be expected in the degree of violence or risk that will attract spectators. Bryant (1978) found that viewers' level of sensation-seeking (Zuckerman, 1971) critically affected their enjoyment of suspenseful drama, for example. (From a marketing perspective, this may not be a serious limiting condition in promotion of sporting events. Most viewers who are appalled at and repelled by violence or extreme risk are probably not the primary nor even a major audience for contact or thrill sports anyway.) The third limiting condition is that the potential spectators' perceptions of the sport protagonists' risk must not exceed the limit beyond which the player is seen as having a reasonable chance for survival. In investigating optimal levels of outcome uncertainty in suspenseful drama, Comisky and Bryant (1982) found that viewers' experienced suspense was maximal when the hero's chances of survival were extremely slim but still credible. In line with pertinent theory (Zillmann, 1980), conditions of total subjective certainty that the hero would or would not survive yielded diminished suspense. On the other hand, increases in suspense consistently have been found to yield increased viewer enjoyment, so long as the resolution of the suspense is effective (Zillmann, Hay, & Bryant, 1975; Zillmann, 1980).

All in all, and granted that research evidence on the subject is scarce and somewhat eclectic, sports violence seems to be an effective means of attracting and entertaining the sports spectator. And the media seem to have discovered at least three ways in which they can exploit the appeal of violence: coverage of sports events, sports features, and promotions of upcoming sporting events.

Where Will It All End?

The research findings concerning the effects of roughness, viciousness, and violence in sports on the spectators interest in and enjoyment of the event, scarce and incomplete as they may be, are consistent in their projection: Rough play, presumably because it attests to fierce competitiveness in a most basic way, fosters interest and facilitates enjoyment. The exploitation of such play, wherever and whenever it exists, by the media (together with the sports commentators' and sports analysts' seemingly untiring efforts at converting common play into rough play by insinuating intense rivalry, animosity, hostility, and outright hatred among opponents) appears to reflect a good grasp of the spectators' likes and an implicit best-seller formula for sports. The research findings certainly do not challenge the sports programmers' assumptions that have led to a greater and greater emphasis of viciousness and violence in sports events earmarked for mass consumption.

Will it blow over? A look at other media events suggests that it will not. In drama (especially the suspense and horror variety), violence has reached new heights. Its depiction is more vivid and more graphic than ever, and specific acts of violence have become more bizarre than ever. Martin Scorsese's comment that "There seems to be a roller-coaster effect. Violence just keeps increasing" (quoted in Farber, 1979) applies to sports as well as to drama. Such escalation of violence in the media has recently been attributed to excitatory habituation (Zillmann, 1982). Massive exposure to arousing events apparently transforms even stimuli that initially produced extreme reactions into mild and rather innocuous ones (Zillman & Bryant, 1982). To the extent that the enjoyment of drama and of sports thrives on excitement and this excitement is due, in part, to roughness and violence, such material needs to become stronger and stronger to get the job of furnishing excitement done. Could it be that sports fans have grown callous toward roughness—as movie buffs seem to have grown callous toward graphic maimings and spectacular killings? If so, one should expect a new, increased acceptance of sports violence. Bad bruises, minor nontransitory injuries, and occasionally the kind that cripples for life might become common elements of exciting sports events. The so-called "obscene" salaries that the stars of popular sports currently receive might actually pave the way toward a greater acceptance of violence in sports. The spectators need not be ill at ease as they see players go down in pain. In their perception, these players are more than adequately compensated for risking their necks once in a while. Are we, then, regressing toward more violence in sports—toward gladiator-like combat? A look at sports in the mass media would seem to suggest that we are. But only time will tell.

References

A crippled player tackles a new life. *Newsweek*, December 21, 1981, p. 9.

Adler, A. *Practice and theory of individual psychology*. New York: Harcourt, Brace, & World, 1927

Barney, W. D. The rasslers. In T. Dodge (Ed.), *A literature of sports*. Lexington, Mass.: D. C. Heath, 1980.

Bell, M. I don't want anybody in my territory. *Sport*, 1978, pp. 14-22.

Bentham, J. *The theory of legislation*. International Library of Psychology, London: Kegan Paul, 1931. (Originally published, 1802.)

Brooks, L. The team that people just love to hate. *Sports Illustrated*, November 17, 1980, pp. 34-35.

Bryant, J. Degree of hostility in squelches as a factor in humour appreciation. In A. J. Chapman & H. C. Foot (Eds.), *It's a funny thing, humour.* Oxford: Pergamon Press, 1977.

Bryant, J. *The effect of sensation seeking on enjoyment of the climax and resolution of suspenseful drama.* Paper presented at the meeting of the Popular Culture Association, Cincinnati, Ohio, May 1978.

Bryant, J., Brown, D., Comisky, P. W., & Zillmann, D. Sports and spectators: Commentary and appreciation. *Journal of Communication*, 1982, *32*(1), 109-119.

Bryant, J., Comisky, P., & Zillmann, D. Drama in sports commentary. *Journal of Communication,* 1977, *27*(3), 140-149.

Bryant, J., Comisky, P., & Zillmann, D. The appeal of rough-and-tumble play in televised professional football. *Communication Quarterly,* 1981, *29*, 256-262.

Bryant, J., & Zillmann, D. *Drama in sports commentary: An update on NFL telecasts.* Unpublished data, 1982. (a)

Bryant, J., & Zillmann, D. *Dramatic audio-visual codes in NHL telecasts.* Unpublished data, 1982. (b)

Cheska, A. T. Sports spectacular: The social ritual of power. In M. Hart & S. Birrell (Eds.), *Sport in the sociocultural process.* Dubuque, Iowa: Wm. C. Brown, 1981. (Originally published, 1968.)

Comisky, P., & Bryant, J. Factors involved in generating suspense. *Human Communication Research,* 1982, *9*, 49-58.

Comisky, P., Bryant, J., & Zillmann, D. Commentary as a substitute for action. *Journal of Communication,* 1977, *27*(3), 150-153.

Davis, L. K., Bryant, J., & Brown, D. *Comprehensive analysis of NBC no-announce telecast, December 20, 1980.* Contract report to News and Social Research Division, National Broadcasting Company, 1981.

Farber, S. The bloody movies: Why violence sells. In A. Wells (Ed.), *Mass media and society* (3rd ed.). Palo Alto, Calif. Mayfield, 1979.

Fergies favorites. *Sports Illustrated,* April 13, 1981, p. 10.

Fox, L. Yes, you can call him the assassin. *Sport,* August 1980, pp. 21-23.

Friedman, D. *Don't* use you head! *TV Guide,* November 7, 1981, pp. 43-45.

Geen, R. G., & Quanty, M. B. The catharsis of aggression: An evaluation of a hypothesis. In L. Berkowitz (Ed.), *Advances in experimental social psychology* (vol. 10). New York: Academic Press, 1977.

Geertz, C. Deep play: A description of the Balinese cockfight. In J. S. Bruner, A. Jolly, & K. Sylva (Eds.), *Play—Its role in development and evolution.* New York: Basic Books, 1976.

Gunther, M. All that TV violence: Why do we love/hate it? *TV Guide,* November 6, 1976, pp. 6-10.

Harrison, W. Roller ball murder. In T. Dodge (Ed.), *A literature of sports.* Lexington, Mass.: D. C. Heath, 1980. (Originally published, 1974.)

Hobson, D. ABC's quarter million dollar man performs heroics too. *TV Guide,* May 7, 1977, pp. 2-8.

Lorenz, K. *Das Sogenannte Bose; Zur Naturgeschichte der Aggression.* Wien: Borotha-Schaelar, 1963.

Michener, J. A. *Sports in America.* Greenwich, Conn.: Fawcett Crest, 1976.

Nash, O. Confessions of a born spectator. In R. Dodge (Ed.), *A literature of sports.* Lexington, Mass.: D. C. Heath, 1980. (Originally published, 1937.)

NFL Public Information Office. Telephone call, October 5, 1982.

Novak, M. *The joy of sports.* New York: Basic Books, 1976.

Robinson, R. Watching out for the hit man. *TV Guide,* May 9, 1981, p. 32.

Schaap, D. The man who would not fight. *Parade,* May 9, 1982, pp. 4-5, 7.

Schulian, J. Plank and joy of hitting. *Sport,* October 1979, pp. 73-78.

Scott, M. Christie Brinkley's violence. *Parade,* September 26, 1982, pp. 12, 15.

Shaw, D. Nobody intimidates my team. *Sport,* January 1978, pp. 44-47.

Sinner, judge thyself. *Sport,* April 1980, p. 19.

Steiner, S. Hit men. *Sport,* October 1981, pp. 20-27.

Stump A. Fight to live. In T. Dodge (Ed.), *A literature of sports.* Lexington, Mass.: D. C. Heath, 1980.

Surface, B. Turn off the Mayhem! *Reader's Digest,* March 1976, pp. 31-41.

Tomasik, M. UE injuries hurt trainer, too. *Evansville Press,* October 1, 1982, p. 22.

Zillmann, D. *Hostility and aggression.* Hillsdale, N.J.: Erlbaum, 1979.

Zillmann, D. Anatomy of suspense. In P. H. Tannenbaum (Ed.), *The entertainment functions of television.* Hillsdale, N.J.: Erlbaum, 1980.

Zillmann, D. Television viewing and arousal. In D. Pearl, L. Bouthilet, & J. Lazar (Eds.), *Television and behavior: Ten years of scientific progress and implications for the Eighties.* Rockville, Md.: NIMH, 1982.

Zillmann, D. & Bryant, J. Retaliatory equity as a factor in humor appreciation. *Journal of Experimental Social Psychology,* 1974, *10,* 480-488.

Zillmann, D., & Bryant, J. Effects of massive exposure to pornography. In N. M. Malamuth & E. Donnerstein (Eds.), *Pornography and sexual aggression.* New York: Academic Press, 1982.

Zillmann, D., Bryant, J., & Sapolsky, B. S. The enjoyment of watching sports contests. In J. H. Goldstein (Ed.), *Sports, games and play.* Hillsdale, N.J.: Erlbaum, 1979.

Zillmann, D., & Cantor, J. R. A disposition theory of humor and mirth. In A. J. Chapman & H. C. Foot (Eds.), *Humour and laughter: Theory, research and applications.* London: John Wiley, 1976.

Zillmann, D., Hay, T. A., & Bryant, J. The effect of suspense and its resolution on the appreciation of dramatic presentations. *Journal of Research in Personality,* 1975, *9,* 307-323.

Zuckerman, M. Dimensions of sensation seeking. *Journal of Consulting and Clinical Psychology,* 1971, *36,* 45-52.

Author Index

Adler, A.   199, 209
Albrecht, D.   173, 177
Alioto, J. T.   169, 170, 178, 190, 192
Alves, W. M.   86, 106
Ardrey, R.   184, 191
Arendt, H.   47, 48, 55, 77
Arms, R. L.   89, 108, 165, 166, 167, 168, 170, 176, 177, 178, 185, 191, 192
Aronfreed, J.   51, 77
Aronson, E.   116, 126
Atkins, A.   162, 177
Audi, R.   44, 77
Auguet, R.   12, 18

Backes, P.   111, 128
Backhaus, W.   11, 18
Bahr, A.   162, 177
Bailey, V.   21, 29
Ball, D. W.   185, 191
Balsdon, J. P.   9, 10, 15, 18
Bandura, A.   51, 77, 78, 165, 177, 185, 191
Barker, R. G.   117, 124
Barney, W. D.   198, 209
Baron, R. A.   89, 106, 170, 177
Base, C. W.   97, 108
Bass, B. M.   173, 177
Bell, M.   207, 209
Bell, P. A.   89, 106
Bellah, R.   53, 79
Bentham, J.   199, 209
Berczeller, E.   160, 177

Berg, B.   191, 192
Berk, R. E.   97, 108
Berkowitz, L.   48, 57, 78, 86, 107, 116, 124, 165, 169, 170, 171, 172, 178, 190, 192
Berscheid, E.   86, 109
Betts, J. R.   35, 44
Black, R.   24, 29
Block, J.   67, 79
Bollinger, T.   16, 18
Borden, R. J.   173, 178
Bornewasser, M.   115, 118, 119, 124, 126
Bott, E.   144, 145
Bouton, J.   96, 107
Bowes, J.   26, 29
Bradley, G. W.   89, 107
Bredemeier, B. J.   3, 48, 73, 77, 78, 171, 178, 185, 192
Brickman, P.   85, 89, 95, 96, 98, 100, 101, 102, 103, 104, 106, 107
Brill, A. A.   164, 178
Briscoe, M. E.   116, 125
Brooks, L.   196, 197, 209
Brown, D.   202, 203, 204, 210
Brown, M.   67, 75, 80
Brown, R.   49, 78
Brown, R. C.   117, 125, 128
Brundage, A.   7, 184, 192
Bryant, J.   2, 3, 89, 107, 167, 168, 181, 185, 193, 198, 200, 201, 202, 203, 204, 208, 209, 210, 211
Buchanan, R. W.   89, 107

Burnstein, E.   117, 124
Buss, A. H.   73, 78, 116, 118, 125, 165, 166, 178
Buss, A. R.   116, 125
Butler, D.   118, 127

Cameron, A.   15, 16, 17, 18
Campbell, D. T.   163, 181
Cantor, J. R.   200, 211
Cantril, H.   93, 94, 108, 190, 192
Capasso, D. R.   166, 180
Caplan, A. H.   41, 44
Caputo, C.   118, 127
Carew, R.   145
Caroll, R.   22, 29
Carpenter, B.   117, 125
Cavanaugh, B. M.   88, 107
Celozzi, M. J.   169, 178
Cheffers, J.   184, 192
Cheska, A. T.   199, 200, 210
Christy, P. R.   173, 178
Clayton, W.   26
Coakley, J.   49, 78
Cohen, J.   188, 192
Cohen, P.   188, 192
Cohn, L.   64
Combs-Schilling, E.   104, 108
Comisky, P.   107, 198, 201, 202, 203, 208, 210
Cosell, H.   1
Coubertin, P. de.   7, 18, 183, 184, 185, 192
Crosby, F.   86, 107
Cullen, F. T.   173, 178
Cullen, J. B.   173, 178
Cunningham, H.   21, 29
Curzon, L. H.   21, 29

DaGloria, J.   114, 115, 118, 125
Damon, W.   67, 68, 69, 70, 71, 78, 79
Dangerfield, G.   29
Daniel, C.   188, 192
Darley, J. M.   117, 125
Davis, J. A.   86, 107
Davis, L. K.   204, 210
Davis, P.   35, 44
Davis, R. W.   185, 192
Day, K. D.   162, 181
Dengerink, H. A.   116, 125

Denney, R.   133, 146
DeRidder, P.   114, 115, 118, 125
Dio Cassius   12, 18
Dobbs, B.   24, 25, 30
Dodge, K.   66, 78
Dollard, J.   55, 78, 86, 107, 161, 172, 178
Donnerstein, E.   89, 107
Doob, L. W.   55, 78, 86, 107, 161, 178
Dremen, S.   78
Drewry, B. R.   173, 174, 175, 180
Dunning, E.   2, 3, 133, 145, 146, 154
Durkee, A.   73, 78, 165, 166, 178
Durkheim, E.   130, 135
Dyck, R. J.   116, 125

Eastwood, J. M.   169, 178
Ebbersberger, H.   123, 125
Eckerd, W. M.   160, 180, 184, 185, 193
Edwards, C.   23, 25, 30
Edwards, J. D.   99, 107
Eglash, A.   102, 107
Eitzen, D. S.   4, 87, 107
Elias, N.   129, 130, 132, 133, 135, 140, 146, 150, 155
Epstein, S.   173, 178
Eron, L. D.   170, 179
Espy, R.   183, 184, 192
Evans, R. I.   161, 178
Eysenck, H. J.   129, 146

Fairfax-Blakeborough, J.   21, 30
Farber, S.   209, 210
Feger, H.   114, 125
Feldman, K.   67, 75, 80
Felson, R. B.   114, 118, 125
Ferguson, T.   116, 125
Feshbach, S.   55, 78, 175, 178
Festinger, L.   66, 78
Fischler, S.   92, 93, 97, 98, 107
Flakne, G. W.   41, 44
Forer, L.   102, 107
Forgas, J. P.   125
Forsyth, D. R.   118, 125
Fox, L.   196, 210
Fox, R.   130, 146
Frame, C.   66, 78
Francis, C.   22, 24, 30
Fraser, C.   115, 128

Freedman, J. L.   89, 107
Freud, S.   51, 55, 78, 160, 184, 192
Friedlander, L.   9, 12, 18
Friedman, D.   196, 210
Fry, M.   102, 107

Gabler, H.   111, 125
Gaes, G. G.   114, 128
Gammon, C. B.   89, 109, 166, 180
Gandy, J.   102, 107
Gardner, R.   131, 146
Gaskell, G. D.   89, 96, 108, 166, 179
Geen, R. G.   158, 171, 178, 199, 210
Geertz, C.   199, 200, 210
Gelfand, D.   173, 178
Gerson, R.   67, 68, 69, 70, 71, 79
Gilligan, C.   57, 58, 60, 71, 79, 80
Gluckman, M.   147, 155
Goldstein, J. H.   2, 3, 4, 47, 57, 79, 89,
    108, 149, 155, 165, 166, 171, 176,
    178, 179, 184, 185, 191, 192
Goodman, P.   160, 167, 179
Goranson, R. E.   170, 171, 177, 179
Gouldner, A. W.   117, 125
Grant, M.   9, 10, 11, 18
Graves, H.   29, 30
Green, G.   24, 30
Greendorfer, S.   79
Greenwell, J.   116, 125
Grescoe, P.   38, 44
Gristina, A. D.   37, 44
Gross, B.   111, 128
Grove, J. B.   163, 181
Guilland, R.   16, 18
Gunther, M.   197, 210
Gurr, T. R.   86, 108
Guttmann, A.   1, 3, 7, 17, 18

Haan, N.   53, 58, 65, 66, 67, 71, 72, 73,
    75, 79
Hallowell, I.   38, 41, 44
Hamilton, D.   118
Hamilton, V. L.   97, 108
Hardy, S.   15, 18
Hardy, T. W.   171, 181
Harré, R.   2, 22, 30, 130, 143, 146, 185,
    193
Harrell, W. A.   164, 167, 176, 179, 185,
    190, 192

Harris, H. A.   14, 18
Harris, M. B.   172, 179
Harrison, W.   198, 210
Hart, D. P.   129, 146
Hart, H.   79
Hartmann, D. P.   169, 173, 178, 179
Hartshorne, H.   67, 79
Harvey, J. H.   125, 126
Hastorf, A. H.   93, 94, 108, 190, 192
Hatfield, F. C.   169, 179
Hawkins, C.   96, 108
Hay, T. A.   208, 211
Hechter, W.   33, 44
Heider, F.   116, 126
Heider, K.   131, 146
Heingartner, A.   67, 75, 80
Heinilä, K.   150, 151, 155
Henze, A.   11, 18
Herman, D.   185, 192
Hickey, J.   71, 80
Hilton, I.   162, 177
Hobbes, T.   199
Hobson, D.   207, 210
Hoenle, A.   11, 18
Hokanson, J. E.   160, 179
Holstein, C.   75, 79
Horace   11, 18
Horai, J.   118, 126
Hornberger, R. H.   163, 179
Horrow, R. B.   35, 38, 39, 40, 44, 63, 79
Huesmann, L. R.   170, 179
Huizinga, J.   66, 79, 133, 146
Hunt, E. G.   29, 30
Hurley, R.   171, 181
Husman, B. F.   162, 163, 179
Hutchinson, J.   22, 30

Ickes, W. J.   116, 125, 126
Ingham, R.   22, 30

Jacobs, B.   105, 108
Jeu, B.   151, 152, 155
Johnson, R. C.   162, 181
Jones, C.   116, 126
Jones, E. E.   118, 126
Joseph, J. M.   115, 117, 126, 127
Joy, L. A.   170, 177
Jung, D.   111, 128
Juvenal   11, 12, 18

Kane, T. R.   115, 117, 126, 127
Kanin, D. B.   183, 192
Kasiarz, D.   3
Kauffman, M.   71, 80
Keates, T.   22, 23, 30
Keefer, R.   3
Kelley, H. H.   118, 127
Kidd, A. H.   163, 179
Killian, L.   183, 192
Kimball, M. M.   170, 177
Kinderman, H.   14, 18
Kingsmore, J. M.   165, 170, 179, 184,
      192
Knott, P. D.   162, 179
Kohlberg, L.   53, 57, 58, 60, 67, 71, 73,
      75, 79, 80
Krahenbuhl, G. S.   165, 179, 185, 192
Kramer, R.   75, 80
Kroll, W.   77, 80
Kuhlman, W.   39, 40, 41, 44, 108
Kushner, B.   36, 45, 81, 96, 109
Kyrolainen, H.   183, 185, 192

Laflin, J.   81
Lagerspetz, K. M. J.   115, 117, 126
Lang, G. E.   87, 88, 89, 99, 100, 108
Lasater, L.   162, 179
Lefebvre, L. M.   173, 179
Lefkowitz, M. M.   170, 179
Legant, P.   118, 127
Lehman, D. R.   3
Lennon, J. X.   169, 179
Leuck, M. R.   165, 176, 179, 185, 192
LeUnes, A.   162, 177
Levine, P.   49, 80
Levi-Strauss, C.   153, 155
Levy, A. S.   89, 107
Lewis, J. M.   87, 91, 92, 108
Leyens, J. P.   114
Lickona, T.   80
Lindskold, S.   117, 128
Linneweber, V.   117, 118, 119, 124,
      126
Lipsky, R.   108
Loew, C. A.   163, 179
Lorenz, K.   80, 143, 149, 150, 155, 161,
      179, 184, 192, 198, 210
Löschper, V.   115, 118, 119, 124, 126
Lovell, J.   29, 30

Lowe, B.   183, 192
Lüschen, G.   3, 4, 151, 155

Maguire, J.   145
Malamuth, N. M.   116, 126
Malka, J.   123, 125
Mallick, S. K.   115, 126
Mandell, R. D.   183, 184, 192
Mann, L.   23, 30, 87, 88, 89, 90, 94, 99,
      100, 108, 166, 179, 190, 192
Maracek, J.   118, 127
Mark, M. M.   3, 106, 108
Marsh, P.   2, 22, 30, 129, 130, 143, 146,
      185, 193
Marshall, D.   37
Mason, A.   21, 27, 30
Matejko, A.   153, 155
Mather, F. C.   28, 30
May, M.   67, 79
May, R.   55, 58, 67, 80
McApa, M.   116, 126
McCandless, B. R.   115, 126
McClelland, D.   58, 80
McDonald, F. J.   78
McGregor, W.   27, 30
McIntosh, P.   77, 80, 88, 99, 108, 150,
      155
McIntyre, T. D.   129, 146
Meacham, S.   29, 30
Megargee, E. I.   160, 179
Mehrabian, A.   168, 179
Melnick, M. J.   129, 146
Meshbesher, R. I.   38, 41, 44
Michener, J. A.   84, 108, 185, 193, 197,
      210
Milgram, S.   75, 80
Miller, N. E.   55, 78, 86, 107, 161, 178
Milshteyn, O. A.   184, 193
Mischel, W.   51, 80
Molchanov, S. V.   184, 193
Moore, B.   51, 80
Mowrer, O. H.   55, 78, 86, 107, 161,
      178
Mummendey, A.   3, 115, 117, 118, 119,
      124, 126
Mummendey, H. D.   3
Murphy, P.   145

Nader, L.   104, 108

Nation, J. R.   162, 177
Needham, E.   27, 30
Neigher, W.   162, 177
Nesdale, A. R.   116, 126, 127, 169, 180
Newtson, D.   126
Nias, K. D.   129, 146
Nicastro, J.   37, 44
Nickel, T. W.   116, 126
Nietzsche, F.   199
Nisbett, R. E.   118, 126, 127
Noble, G.   170, 171, 180
Nosanchuk, T. A.   164, 180, 184, 193
Novak, M.   199, 204, 206, 214
Novation   13, 18
Nowlis, V.   166, 167, 180
Nucci, L.   61, 64, 65, 80

Odenkirk, J. E.   165, 179, 185, 192
Ord, R.   22, 30
Orvis, B. R.   118, 127
Ostrow, A.   162, 163, 180
Ovid   12, 18
Owen, G.   132, 133, 146

Park, R.   77, 80
Parker, H. J.   144, 146
Passer, M. W.   173, 179
Pastore, N.   87, 108, 127
Patterson, A.   162, 163, 180
Pearce, P.   23, 30
Peart, J. H.   21
Pearton, R.   89, 96, 108
Pepitone, A.   117, 127
Petronius   18
Philo, H. M.   36, 44
Piaget, J.   52, 80
Pisor, K.   116, 127
Plack, A.   149, 155
Pligt, J. v. d.   116, 118, 127
Pohler, R.   123, 125
Price, J.   89, 107
Price, R.   21, 30
Prisuta, R. H.   185, 193
Proctor, R. C.   160, 180, 184, 185, 193

Quanty, M. B.   158, 161, 162, 171, 178, 180, 199, 210

Rabinow, P.   53, 79

Raday, T.   166, 179
Rawls, J.   53, 80
Regan, D. T.   118, 127
Reitan, H. T.   116, 127
Rest, J.   73, 80
Richardson, C.   21, 30
Richter, D.   21, 29, 30
Riesman, D.   133, 146
Riess, M.   115, 127, 128
Rivera, A. N.   114, 117, 127, 128
Robert, L.   9, 14, 18
Roberts, J. M.   186, 193
Robinson, R.   196, 211
Rodda, J.   183, 192
Rosenfeld, P.   115, 127
Rosnow, R. L.   166, 179
Rosser, E.   2, 22, 30, 130, 143, 146, 185, 193
Rossi, P. H.   86, 97, 106, 108
Rothman, G.   75, 76, 80
Rovere, G. D.   37, 44
Rule, B. G.   116, 125, 126, 127, 169, 180
Runfola, R. T.   42, 44
Russell, G. W.   3, 157, 164, 166, 167, 168, 172, 173, 174, 175, 176, 177, 180, 185, 191, 193
Ryan, E. D.   163, 173, 180
Ryan, K.   85, 107
Rytina, S.   97, 108

Salvian   13, 19
Sandilands, M. L.   166, 177, 185, 191
Sapolsky, B. S.   168, 181, 185, 193, 198, 211
Schaap, D.   196, 211
Schafer, S.   102, 105, 108
Scharf, P.   71, 80
Schelling, T.   151, 158
Schmidt, W.   111, 127
Schott, F.   115, 127
Schrodt, B.   13, 19
Schuck, J.   116, 127
Schulian, J.   207, 211
Schulz, H.-J.   111, 125
Schwartz, G. S.   115, 127
Schwartz, R. D.   163, 181
Schwartz, S.   67, 75, 80
Scott, J.   81
Scott, M.   207, 211

Sears, R. R.   55, 78, 86, 107, 161, 178
Sechrest, L.   163, 181
Selg, H.   127
Sellin, J. T.   97, 108
Seneca   12, 19
Shaver, K. G.   81
Shaw, D.   207, 211
Shaw, M. E.   116, 127
Sheard, K.   133, 146
Shearman, M.   21, 30
Sherif, C.   149, 155
Sherif, M.   114, 127, 149, 155
Shields, D.   73, 77
Shumaker, S. A.   117, 128
Shuman, R.   162, 179
Silva, J.   48, 57, 81, 88, 107
Silverman, I.   166, 179
Simmel, G.   151, 152, 155
Simmons, C. H.   108
Singer, B. D.   57, 81
Singer, J. D.   186, 187, 193
Sipes, R.   149, 150, 155, 164, 180, 184,
     185, 186, 190, 193
Sloan, L. R.   165, 176, 180
Small, M.   186, 187, 193
Smith, G. O.   27, 30
Smith, K. J.   102, 108
Smith, M. B.   67, 79
Smith, M. D.   3, 22, 26, 30, 36, 37, 38,
     45, 57, 81, 87, 89, 90, 91, 95, 96,
     109, 155, 159, 180, 185, 193
Smits, T.   87, 91, 109
Spencer, E.   21, 30, 199
Stagg, A. A.   36, 45
Stapleton, R. E.   117, 127
Stegmüller, W.   152, 156
Steiner, S.   207, 211
Stine, G.   36, 44
Stokols, D.   117, 128
Stone, G.   66, 81
Storms, M. D.   118, 128
Storr, A.   160, 180, 184, 185, 193
Strenk, A.   183, 192
Stroud, J.   75, 79
Stump, A.   196, 211
Suetonius   10, 19
Sullivan, W.   53, 79
Surface, B.   197, 211
Sutton-Smith, B.   151, 156, 186, 193

Tacitus   14, 19
Tajfel, H.   114, 115, 117, 128
Tandy, R.   81
Tatum, J.   36, 45, 81, 96, 109
Taylor, I. R.   22, 30
Taylor, S. P.   89, 109, 166, 173, 178,
     180
Tedeschi, J. T.   114, 115, 116, 117, 118,
     125, 126, 127, 128
Tertullian   13, 19
Thirer, J.   162, 169, 180
Tiger, L.   130, 146
Tinbergen, N.   161, 180
Tischler, S.   21, 22, 27, 31
Tomasik, M.   196, 211
Torg, J. S.   103, 109
Totten, J.   118, 127
Trivizas, E.   22, 31
Tucker, D.   89, 109
Tumolesi, P. S.   10, 19
Turiel, E.   61, 62, 63, 64, 65, 75, 76, 80,
     81
Turner, E. T.   165, 181

Underwood, J.   36, 45, 50, 64, 81

Vamplew, W.   1, 3, 21, 22, 24, 27, 31
Varis, T.   183, 185, 192
Verspohl, F. J.   14, 19
Ville, G.   13, 19
Volkamer, M.   112, 128, 173, 181

Wacke, A.   10, 19
Waite, E.   97, 108
Walder, L. O.   170, 179
Walster, E.   86, 109
Walster, G. W.   86, 109
Walton, N. Y.   163, 179
Wankel, L. M.   173, 175, 177
Watson, A. F. T.   25, 31
Webb, E. J.   163, 181
Webb, H.   81
Weber, M.   130
Weber, R.   111, 125
Weinhold, K.   150, 156
Weinstein, N. D.   117, 128
Weis, K.   111, 128, 129, 146
Weissman, W.   12, 19
Weizsäcker, V. v.   147, 156

Westman, M.   115, 117, 126
Whittaker, C. R.   16, 19
Williams, J.   145
Willis, P.   144, 146
Wilmott, P.   144, 146
Wilson, D.   89, 107
Wolfgang, M. E.   97, 108
Wood, F. S.   188, 192
Worchel, P.   117, 125
Worchel, S.   171, 181
Wortman, C. B.   85, 107
Wright, H. F.   124

Yeager, R. C.   4, 5
Yiannakis, A.   129, 146
Young, M.   144, 146
Young, P. M.   26, 31

Zabrack, M. L.   170, 177
Zillmann, D.   2, 3, 89, 107, 158, 162,
     167, 168, 175, 181, 185, 190, 193,
     198, 199, 200, 201, 202, 203, 205,
     208, 209, 210, 211
Zimbardo, P. G.   89, 109, 185, 193
Zuckerman, M.   116, 118, 128, 208, 211

Subject Index

Achievement 141
Aggression 85, 116, 117, 185; *see also*
   Sports violence; Violence
  among athletes 185
  as social interaction 113–119
  attribution of 66, 114, 115–118, 123
  before vs. after sports
    participation 163
  cognitive dissonance and 66
  constructive vs. destructive 48
  definition of 48, 55, 115–117, 158
  drama and 168, 199–200
  escalation of 114, 139, 208–209
  frustration and 55, 86, 100, 190
  guilt and 162
  inhibition of 175
  instrumental 48, 96, 97–99
  judgment of 3, 116
  masculinity norms and 138–145
  modeling and 170–171
  moral reasoning and 66–77
  observation of 164–171
  outcome and 171–177
  reactive vs. hostile 48
  reduction of 4, 117, 150
  "sham" 170–171
  socialization of 139, 141
  spectators and 185
  temporal factors in 96, 114, 115, 117,
    121, 123, 164, 190
  tolerance of 190, 191
  verbal 163
  violence and 47

Alcohol 26, 27
Amateurism 189
Anger, *see* Arousal; Frustration
Arenas 10, 22, 26, 89
Arousal 90, 168, 169, 185
Assertion
  vs. aggression 48
Athletes
  attitudes toward aggression 40, 50,
    57, 191
  catharsis among 162–164
  interpersonal aggression 203
  level of aggression 73–75
  professional 10
  professionalism of 22
  slaves and debtors as 11
  social status 11, 14
  vs. fans 38, 85
  vs. non-athletes 162
Attitudes
  sex differences 58
  toward violence 190, 191
Attribution 2, 94
  of aggression 114–117, 123
  of responsibility 116, 118
  to justify aggression 66
Aztecs 9

Baseball 39, 98, 185, 196
Basketball 39, 176
Betting, *see* Gambling
Body contact sports 34, 162–164, 185
  culture and 186

Body contact sports *(cont.)*
  on mass media 186, 191
  warfare and 186
Bonding 130, 135–145
  in medieval Europe 137, 143, 145
  segmental vs. functional 135–138,
    142
Boxing 1, 33, 35, 131, 141, 190
Brutality in sports 35–44; *see also*
    Sports violence

Catharsis 15, 112, 149, 157–177, 184,
    188–189
  contact vs. noncontact
    sports 162–164
  definition 158
  description of 159, 184, 198
  ethology and 161
  history of concept 159–161
  mass media and 169–171
  Olympic games and 148, 185–191
  ritual aggression and 170–171
  social learning theory vs. 3
  spectator sports and 22, 37, 147,
    149, 160, 164–171
Chariot races 9, 14–17
Civilizing process 129–130, 131, 135,
    140, 145, 150
  rugby and 132–134
Cockfighting 200
Cognitive development 51–55
  and moral reasoning 67–68
Cognitive dissonance 66
Colosseum 10
Communication and perceived
    injustice 94
Competition 104, 112, 134, 139, 141,
    190, 198
  game outcome and 171–177
  sports violence and 206
Conflict 113, 114, 147, 154
  of interest 114
  of value 114
  resolution of 147, 148, 149
  sports and 100–101, 147–154
Confrontation as crowd disorder 24
Contact sports and catharsis 162–164
  vs. noncontact sports 189

Cooperation in sport 151, 191
Crime 38, 99, 105
Criminal justice system 99, 100, 102,
    105
Criminal violence 38–44
Crowd
  density 28
  size 9, 21
Crowd control 22–23
  methods of 24–28
  police and 27
  segregation of crowd 25–26
Crowd disorder, *see also* Spectator
    violence
  commercialism and 22
  decline of 22
  perceived injustice and 90
  types of 23–24, 87–88

Dani of New Guinea 131
Defensive attribution, *see* Attribution
Deindividuation 89, 90, 185
Delay of gratification 141
Deterrence, *see* Penalties
Deviance 95, 100, 101
Display
  definition 66
Division of labor 140, 141
Dominance 161
  sports violence and 199
Drive discharge, *see* Catharsis

Ego defense 65, 93, 94
Emotion and violence 28
Equity, *see* Justice; Perceived injustice
Equity-based penalties 90
Escalation 114, 139, 208–209
Ethology 161
Expressive riot 24

Fans
  dispositional factors 200
  explanations for sports violence 88
  identification with teams 22
  politics and 16–18
Football (American) 35–36, 84, 94,
    101, 165, 176, 185, 200–201,
    204–205

Football (European), *see* Soccer
Football compared to gladiatorial
   games   7
Frustration
   and aggression   55, 86, 100, 161, 172,
   190
   crowd disorders and   23
Functional bonding   135, 136–143
   competition and   139
   rational violence and   139–142
Funeral games   9

Gambling   25, 26–27, 185
German Football
   Confederation   119–124
Gladiatorial games   7–19
Guilt and aggression   162
Gymnastics   165

Handball   173
Hockey, *see* Ice hockey
Horse racing   21–31, 83–84, 95, 185
   gambling and   27
Hostility   89, 163, 165, 176, 185
Hunting   185

Ice hockey   37–38, 42–44, 84, 88, 96,
   98, 99, 159, 163–164, 166, 167,
   173–175, 186, 190, 196–197,
   201–202, 205–206
Identification   199
Injury, *see* Sports violence
Instinct, aggression as   55
Instrumental aggression   48, 96–99,
   112, 131, 135, 141
   penalties and   96–97
Intention   96, 99, 115, 116, 121, 122,
   123
International Olympic Committee   183
International relations   147, 149, 152,
   183, 184; *see also* War
Interpersonal relationships and
   spectator sports   168

Justice, *see also* Perceived injustice
   morality and   53, 62
   sports violence and   83
   systems of   90–100

Karate   164
Knappan   132–133

Law and sports violence   2, 33–45,
   157

Masculinity and aggression   138, 139,
   142–145
Mass media   1, 2, 3, 93, 95, 148,
   168–171, 190, 195–211
   content analysis   204–205
   effects on sports   171–172
   exploitation of sports
      violence   204–209
   Olympic games and   190
   perceptual effects   201–202
Mayans   9
Methodology   57, 97, 147, 151–153,
   157, 162, 165–166, 169–170
Militarism   138, 139, 186, 191
Modeling, *see* Social learning theory
Moral development   50–55
   cognitive-developmental view   51
   Gilligan's stages of   58–60
   interactionist theories of   53–55
   moral reasoning vs.   68–69
   psychoanalytic view   51
   social learning view   51
   stages of   52–55
   vs. moral behavior   75–76
Morality
   sex differences   57–60
   sports and   60
   sports violence and   12–13, 50–77
   structure of   52

National Football League   39, 196, 205
National Hockey League   36–37, 205
Nationalism   7, 185, 186, 191
Nonviolence   57
Norm of reciprocity   121
Norms,   *see* Social norms

Officiating   87, 123; *see also* Penalties
   improving   92–95
   perceived injustice and   87, 91–99
   sports violence and   87, 90
   types of error in   91

Olympic games
aggression and   185–186
catharsis and   185–191
history of   7, 183–184
mass media and   190
politics and   183–185
success in   185
war and   185–191
Outcome of play   24, 91, 94, 103, 157, 171–177
importance of   134
spectators and   175–176

Penalties, *see also* Officiating
deterrent-based   95, 96–98
equity-based   95–98, 101, 103–105
instrumental aggression and   96–97
perceived fairness   97
rugby   134
sports violence and   141
Perceived injustice
definition   86–87
reducing   85, 92, 93, 94, 97, 98
riots and   90
types of   90–100
violence and   83–85, 87–88
Perceptual distortion   93, 94
Play   3, 66, 199
Player draft   105
Political values and sports   185
Politics
Olympic games and   183–185
sports fans and   16–18
Population density   187
Power and aggression   47, 55, 58
Prison   105
Prosocial behavior   191; *see also* Moral development
Psychoanalytic theory   51, 160
Punishment, *see* Penalties

Quasi-criminal violence   38–42

Rationalization   94
Reduction of violence   4, 83, 92, 93, 96–98, 117, 150
Referees, *see also* Officiating
violence toward   27

Reinforcement   190; *see also* Social learning theory
Relative deprivation   86, 99
Responsibility attribution   116
Restitution   102, 103, 104; *see also* Penalties
Retaliation   121
Riot   84, 87, 90; *see also* Crowd disorder
types of   23–24, 87–88
Ritual aggression   2, 3, 129, 130, 131, 139, 141, 143, 170–171
Rugby   131, 141, 204
civilizing of   134
origins of   132–133
Rugby Football Union   134
Rules, *see also* Officiating
changes in   94
fairness of   95–99
formalized   24–25, 134
perceived violations of   93–94, 111, 190

Segmental bonding   135, 136–138
affective violence and   138–139
soccer violence and   142–143
socialization and   139
Segregation as crowd control   25–26
countereffects of   26
Situational factors in aggression   111, 114, 115–118, 121, 123
Soccer   21–31, 33, 84, 90, 111–124, 131, 142, 148, 173
Soccer "hooliganism"   2, 8, 89, 142–145
segmental bonding and   143
Social bonding, *see* Bonding
Social class and bonding   137, 142–145
Social control   104, 138–140
Social convention vs. morality   61–66
Social interaction as unit of analysis   114
Socialization   139, 141; *see also* Moral development
Social learning theory   3, 51, 149, 184–185
aggression and   55, 57, 112, 170–171, 185, 190
moral development and   51

Social norms   3, 111, 114, 116
  sports violence and   85
  violence and   138, 143
Social structure and violence   89,
    100−105, 129−146
Sociobiology   143
Spectators, *see also* Fans
  acceptance of violence   37−38
  appeal of violence to   168,
    197−203
  athletes' perceptions of   38
  catharsis among   22, 184
  comparison with participants   15
  political involvements of   15
  reactions to sports violence   13
Spectator violence   8, 14−17, 23; *see
    also* Crowd disorder; Riot; Violence
  alcohol and   26−27
  as protest   16
  crowd density and   28
  crowds and   28
  gambling and   26−27
  politics and   23−24, 29
  responsibility for   153−154
  suffrage and   24
  types of   23−24, 87−88, 99
Sport(s), *see also specific sports*
  as drama   199−200
  communication   49
  contextual factors   153
  cooperation in   151
  definition   9, 158
  international relations and   147,
    183−191
  militarism and   185, 186, 191
  politics and   154, 183−185
  prosocial aspects of   151, 191
  society and   85, 100−105
  structure of   151−152
  symbolic aspects of   151, 153
  televised   168−169
  war and   185−191
Sportsmanship   104
Sports policy   153−154
Sports violence
  ancient sports   7−19, 150
  appeal of   195−209
  archival studies   163−164,
    183−193

  as entertainment   3, 202
  as evidence of competition   206
  attitudes toward   1, 35−36, 150, 190,
    191
  case studies of   16, 42−44, 119−123
  civil suits and   39
  coaches and   196
  criminal   33, 40, 42−44
  culture and   49, 149−150, 185, 186
  death, due to injury   1, 8−14, 33,
    35−44, 64−65, 112, 115−116, 117,
    122, 196, 207
  definition   2−3, 8
  dominance and   199
  escalation of   164, 208−209
  incidence of   1, 2, 22, 129, 132−133,
    139, 141, 142
  justification of   2, 34, 36−38, 48
  legitimate vs. illegitimate   8, 34−44,
    57, 63
  moral development and   60
  opposition to   12, 13
  origins of   2, 3, 12, 132−133
  perceived injustice and   83−106
  public reaction to   35
  reduction of   4, 83, 92, 93, 97, 98,
    150, 152−154, 191, 209
  religious aspects of   9, 13−14
  responsibility for   41−42
  situational factors and   111, 114, 115,
    117−118, 121, 123
  social psychological
    perspective   113−119
  social structure and   17, 89,
    100−105
  spectator acceptance of   37−38, 41
  temporal aspects of   4, 164, 190,
    208−209
  types of   34−44, 87−89
  victims of   102
  women and   12, 57
Stadium
  capital investment in   22
  paid admission to   26
  sports violence and   10, 89
Stigma   101
Stress, athletes and   66
  ego defense and   66
Swimming   166

Television   93, 148, 168; *see also* Mass
    media
  instant replay   93, 95
Temporal factors, *see* Aggression
Tennis   84–85, 148, 163, 202–203
Thanatos   55
Thematic Apperception Test   162

Values   3, 185; *see also* Moral
    development
  political   185
Verbal aggression   163
Victims, compensation of   102
Victory, *see* Outcome of play
Violence
  "affective" vs. "rational"   131, 133,
    134, 138–142
  aggression and   47

  appeal of   3, 197
  control of   150
  cultural factors and   49, 129–146
  definition   8, 47
  emotion and   28
  internalization of   132
  legitimate vs. illegitimate   8, 34–44
  social control of   138–140
  social structure and   129–146
  types of   130–131
  valuing of   49–50

War
  Olympic games and   186–191
  population density and   187
  sports and   131, 149–150, 183–191
Wrestling (professional)   166